CYBERCRIME AND SOCIETY

CYBERCRIME AND SOCIETY

Sue Strickland-Lord

SOCIETY Publishing

www.societypublishing.com

Cybercrime and Society

Sue Strickland-Lord

Society Publishing
4164 Lakeshore Road
Burlington, ON L7L 1A4
Canada
www.societypublishing.com
Email: orders@arclereducation.com

ISBN: 978-1-77956-396-5 (Hardcover)

ABOUT THE AUTHOR

Sue Strickland-Lord is a college lecturer in Social Sciences, lecturing for over twenty years in several UK colleges. She specialises in Criminology and has a 1st Class degree in Criminology from the University of Winchester and a MSc in Criminal Justice, with merit from the University of Portsmouth. Sue achieved particularly high grades in her dissertations with pass percentages at 85% and she has been able to pass on those skills to many of her students who have excelled in their educational achievement.

Sue works hard to introduce students to the world of Criminology and inspires students to research the subject thoroughly and understand it fully to support their own academic writing. Many of her students have gone on to gain their educational aspirations and go on to work in areas such as criminal justice, policing, law and prison services. Her own career as also included working with vulnerable victims and writing educational programmes within prison reform.

TABLE OF CONTENTS

LIST OF FIGURES

ABSTRACT

The advent of modern technology has transformed cybercrime into a pervasive global problem that impacts individuals, organizations, and nations alike. This book provides a thorough analysis of cybercrime and its extensive impact on society. The proliferation of technology has led to an increase in the severity of cyber-attacks, necessitating a comprehensive understanding of the risks and consequences of cybercrime by both individuals and organizations. This book elucidates the concept of cybercrime with the aim of assisting readers in safeguarding themselves and their possessions in the dynamic realm of digital technology. The book emphasizes the significance of educating individuals about the escalating issue of cybercrime. Annually, cyberattacks incur financial losses, damage reputations, and result in legal complications for both businesses and individuals. This book enlightens readers about cybercrime and offers guidance on mitigating and addressing cyberattacks. It provides readers with a secure and reliable experience on the internet. This book on cybercrime is distinct due to its interdisciplinary approach. It encompasses the fields of criminology, sociology, law, and technology. Readers acquire a comprehensive comprehension of the intricate social, legal, and ethical consequences of cybercrime in order to make informed decisions regarding cybersecurity and risk management.

PREFACE

In the modern era of technology, the rise of cybercrime has emerged as a pressing issue that affects people, organizations, and nations across the globe. Technology's rapid advancement has ushered in a host of new opportunities and challenges. Cybercriminals, always adapting their tactics, exploit vulnerabilities in the digital landscape. It is of utmost importance for us to grasp the significance of cybercrime on society and the steps that can be implemented to minimize its consequences.

This book is significant because it provides a timely and comprehensive analysis of cybercrime, which is a rapidly growing phenomenon that has far-reaching consequences for society. With the ever-growing dependence on technology, the looming danger of cyber-attacks becomes more apparent. It is of utmost importance for individuals and organizations to grasp the risks and consequences associated with cybercrime. This book offers a comprehensive understanding of cybercrime, empowering readers with the necessary knowledge and resources to safeguard themselves and their assets in our ever-evolving digital landscape.

This book is of utmost importance in light of the growing danger of cybercrime and the widespread lack of awareness and understanding about this critical issue. Every year, countless individuals and organizations suffer the devastating consequences of cyber-attacks. These attacks not only lead to significant financial losses, but also cause irreparable damage to their reputation and expose them to potential legal repercussions. This book aims to empower readers by shedding light on the complexities of cybercrime and providing practical advice on how to prevent and respond to cyber threats. It is designed to help readers navigate the digital landscape safely and securely.

This book stands out and is highly recommended due to its unique and valuable interdisciplinary approach to the study of cybercrime. It incorporates perspectives from various fields such as criminology, sociology, law, and technology. The book provides a comprehensive analysis of cybercrime, exploring its various aspects and shedding light on its social, legal, and ethical implications. By delving into the intricate world of cybercrime and its far-reaching consequences on society, readers will develop a holistic understanding that empowers them to make well-informed choices regarding cybersecurity and risk management.

This book is likely to attract a diverse audience, encompassing students, academics, professionals, policymakers, and individuals with an interest in the convergence of technology, crime, and society. This book is an invaluable resource for students studying criminology, cybersecurity, sociology, or law. It offers a solid foundation in the field of cybercrime, equipping them with essential knowledge for their studies. This book provides a comprehensive analysis of cybercrime and its societal implications, making it valuable for academics and researchers in related fields.

Through the act of reading this book, individuals will gain numerous advantages. First and foremost, individuals will develop a more profound comprehension of cybercrime and its repercussions on society. This will empower them to identify the indicators of cyber threats and adopt a proactive approach to safeguarding themselves and their organizations. In addition, readers will gain insights into the most current trends and advancements in cybercrime, enabling them to stay one step ahead of cyber criminals. Readers will be motivated to support enhanced cybersecurity measures and policies, thereby fostering a safer and more secure digital environment for everyone.

This book on Cybercrime and Society provides a comprehensive understanding of cybercrime and its implications for society. It is a valuable resource for anyone seeking to gain knowledge in this field. Through an in-depth analysis of the scope, importance, relevance, motivation, uniqueness, target audience, and potential benefits of this book, readers will gain a comprehensive understanding of the intricate realm of cybercrime and develop the necessary skills to safeguard themselves against cyber threats. For individuals from various backgrounds such as students, academics, professionals, or policymakers, this book provides valuable insights and practical advice on effectively tackling the challenges presented by cybercrime in our modern digital era.

CHAPTER 1

INTRODUCTION TO CYBERCRIME AND SOCIETY

Contents

Cybercrime refers to unlawful activities that occur in the digital realm. It is a pervasive online threat that has far-reaching consequences, affecting all aspects of society. In our interconnected society, privacy is a concept that has become increasingly elusive. Bank accounts, social media chats, and even geolocation can be vulnerable to security breaches. In today's digital age, a staggering majority of individuals worldwide, exceeding 60%, have embraced the internet, thereby providing an abundance of opportunities for hackers to exploit. Everyone is susceptible, regardless of age. However, it is often the case that young people, the elderly, and children bear the greatest impact. It is of utmost importance to remain vigilant and collaborate in this ever-changing landscape (Saulawa & Abubakar, 2014) (Figure 1.1).

Figure 1.1. *The complexity of cyber security threats.*

Source: Hagen (2023).

1.1. THE IMPACT OF CYBERCRIME ON SOCIETY

Cybercrime is a pervasive problem that has far-reaching consequences for individuals. It encompasses various forms such as virus attacks, cyberfraud, and exploitation or extortion, all of which inflict significant harm. Perpetrators of this activity can range from individuals to organizations involved in cybercrime. The execution of such acts is commonly attributed to hackers or cybercriminals. Cybercrime has extensive implications for businesses, society, and the economy, as highlighted by Das and Nayak (2013).

In the realm of cybercrime, nothing remains private - not our bank accounts, our social media conversations, or even our geolocation. Given the staggering statistic that over 60% of the global population is currently connected to the internet, it becomes alarmingly easy for malicious hackers to pinpoint and exploit individuals who may have vulnerabilities. It is important to note that cybercrime affects not only children and the elderly, but also other demographics.

Cybercrime, including cyberbullying and solicitation, has a significant impact on teenagers. Cybercrime has a significant impact on individuals' psychological well-being, leading to feelings of trauma, depression, and anxiety (Das & Nayak, 2013). Cybercrime encompasses a wide range of activities, ranging from grave matters such as terrorism to less significant internet scams aimed at small-scale theft. Regardless of the issue at hand, the potential consequences for society could be significant.

1.1.1. The Impact of Cybercrime on Businesses

When a consumer makes an online payment, the e-commerce company receives their credit card information. This enormous company has millions of clients. Consider a scenario where a significant majority of their clientele, approximately 70%, opt for digital wallets, debit cards, credit cards, UPIs, and similar payment methods for their transactions. It can be observed that the company has acquired a substantial number of customers online. It is crucial for businesses to prioritize the protection and encryption of sensitive financial information in order to prevent hackers from exploiting even the tiniest security flaws and gaining unauthorized access to internal systems. They have the capability to acquire the card information of their customers, trace it to their bank accounts, and embezzle funds. It is worth noting that the potential financial losses could have a significant impact on the community, leading to a considerable amount of commotion among its members (Das & Nayak, 2013).

1.1.2. The Impact of Cybercrime on Infrastructure

Cyberterrorism is indeed a significant threat that our society faces. It is crucial to recognize the potential dangers posed by cyberterrorists who have the ability to infiltrate critical systems, such as air traffic control, and put countless lives at risk. There is a direct correlation between the level of technological development in a nation and the potential risk of cyberterrorism. Healthcare websites are not immune to the attention of cybercriminals. Exposing patients' and hospital staff's sensitive data is a significant concern. Cyberattacks targeting the healthcare industry can have far-reaching consequences beyond mere financial losses. These attacks can potentially jeopardize the lives of patients, as highlighted by Das and Nayak in 2013.

1.1.3. The Impact of Cybercrime on Individuals

Cyberbullying involves the act of exploiting individuals online through the use of threats to expose their private information. Just like cyberattacks on medical facilities, cybercrime has far-reaching consequences that extend beyond mere financial harm. One possible cause of suicidal thoughts is the presence of mental health conditions like depression and anxiety.

It's fascinating to see how digitalization has made various objects smarter. Smart homes have become a reality, thanks to the advancements in artificial intelligence (AI) and the internet of things (IoT). With these technologies, it is now possible to control various gadgets simply by using voice commands. It is important to note that while your modern smart TV offers the convenience of signing up for multiple streaming services, it is crucial to consider the potential vulnerability of your credit card information to hackers. This issue was highlighted by Das and Nayak in 2013.

1.1.4. The Impact on Healthcare and Public Safety

Compromising private patient information, interfering with medical services, and disrupting emergency response protocols and transportation networks can have significant consequences for healthcare and public safety. Cybercrime has the potential to spread misleading information, leading to significant social and political consequences. Additionally, it can exacerbate cyberbullying and harassment, resulting in emotional and psychological distress. Social media platforms serve as a powerful instrument utilized by individuals with malicious intentions to achieve financial, political, or personal advantages. Additionally, they can be utilized to exercise control, deceive, or exert influence over individuals.

1.1.5. Prevention and Mitigation Strategies for Cybercrime

In the digital era, the landscape of cybersecurity risks has become increasingly intricate and widespread. In order to protect oneself from the detrimental consequences of cybercrime, individuals, organizations, and society at large can employ a range of preventive and mitigating measures.

First, it is crucial for individuals to prioritize their online security in today's digital age. By implementing a few key practices, individuals can greatly reduce their risk of falling victim to cyber threats.

Taking precautionary steps such as creating strong passwords, implementing two-factor authentication, regularly updating software and systems, and exercising caution with suspicious emails and texts can greatly enhance security. It is of utmost importance that individuals regularly back up their important data and familiarize themselves with the best practices and risks associated with cybersecurity (Das & Nayak, 2013).

When it comes to cybersecurity measures for businesses, there are several best practices that can help guard against cybercrime. These include conducting regular security risk assessments, implementing access control measures, and continuously monitoring for security breaches. It is also important to provide cybersecurity training for staff, encourage the use of strong passwords and two-factor authentication, and ensure that critical data is encrypted. Additionally, having an efficient backup and recovery plan in place, as well as keeping software and hardware systems up to date, are essential steps to maintaining a strong cybersecurity posture (Das & Nayak, 2013).

By obtaining creator insurance, content producers can ensure the safety of their intellectual property and mitigate the risk of financial losses resulting from lawsuits and other potential threats. Creator insurance provides a wide range of coverage that includes accidents, damage to property or equipment, protection for intellectual property, legal expenses, reimbursements, and other costs associated with legal claims. Content producers can fully concentrate on their work without any concerns about financial losses or legal consequences.

Furthermore, to effectively combat the rising threat of cybercrime, it is crucial to emphasize the importance of awareness and the implementation of preventive measures. Cybercrime poses significant risks to both financial security and reputation, making it a pressing issue that demands immediate attention. Some important aspects to consider in the realm of cybersecurity include implementing best practices, obtaining cyber insurance, prioritizing cybersecurity training, and establishing procedures to ensure accountability for offenders. It is essential for governments, corporations, and individuals to work together in order to mitigate the risks associated with cybercrime (Das & Nayak, 2013).

1.2. THE HISTORICAL BACKGROUND OF CYBERCRIME

Over the past decade, the world of cybercrime has experienced exponential growth, reaching a staggering $1.5 trillion industry. Within this realm, a complex network of illicit enterprises has emerged, functioning much like legitimate businesses. With ransomware-as-a-service (RaaS), certain providers go above and beyond by offering expert guidance, detailed instructions, and reliable customer support. Some of the most concerning threat actors have gone as far as eliminating pop-up advertisements that promote their products. The convergence of nation-state actors, individual hackers targeting specific companies, and widespread third-party hacks creates a complex threat landscape that poses significant challenges for IT and security teams to combat (Babanina et al., 2021). Although the cybercrime sector has experienced significant growth in the past decade, it is important to note that cybercrime is not a new threat.

In fact, the origins of this can be traced back centuries, rather than just a few decades. It is worth noting that the first recorded cyberattack occurred in France in 1834, a significant period of time prior to the development of the internet. The French telegraph system was unfortunately compromised by attackers who managed to obtain sensitive information regarding financial markets. However, it wasn't until the late 20th century that cybercrime really gained momentum. Propelled by the digital revolution, cybercriminals quickly harnessed technology and leveraged their advantage to devise clever schemes for pilfering money and data from both individuals and companies. Subsequently, there has been a significant surge in cybercrime, marked by the emergence of various strategies, methods, and procedures (TTPs) employed with malicious intentions (Babanina et al., 2021).

The history of cybercrime dates back to 1962 when Allen Scherr launched a cyberattack against the MIT computer networks, stealing passwords using punch cards. In 1971, Bob Thomas created the first computer virus, known as the "Creeper Virus," which warned of the potential harm viruses could cause to computer systems. Ian Murphy became the first person to be found guilty of a cybercrime in 1981 when he breached AT&T's internal networks and manipulated their computers.

In 1988, Robert Morris carried out the first significant cyberattack online with the "Morris Worm," compromising computer systems of organizations such as UC Berkeley, NASA, and Stanford. The same year, ransomware made its appearance with the AIDS Trojan ransomware strain, distributed through compromised floppy disks.

The late 1990s and early 2000s saw several notable cybercrimes, including Max Butler breaking into U.S. government websites, the outbreak of the Melissa Virus, and the DDoS attacks by "Mafiaboy" on major commercial websites. In 2000, the ILOVEYOU malware caused a significant phishing attack, infecting millions of endpoints worldwide.

The 2010s witnessed a boom in cybercrime, with the emergence of new dangerous programs and strategies. Ransomware became more prevalent, and cybercriminals had access to new attack vectors and resources. Notable cybercrimes during this period include the Stuxnet infection targeting Iranian nuclear sites, the Zeus Trojan virus stealing millions from American banks, and the Operation Aurora attack by Chinese military hackers.

In 2013, Edward Snowden's disclosures about the NSA's PRISM monitoring program brought attention to government surveillance and data privacy. Other significant cybercrimes in this decade include the Target data breach, the Ashley Madison leak, and the WannaCry and NotPetya ransomware attacks. In 2018,

GitHub experienced the largest DDoS attack in history, and Coinhive became a notable crypto jacking threat. The following years saw major data breaches at Capital One, Neiman Marcus, and the U.S. government through the SolarWinds attack. In 2021, the Colonial Pipeline ransomware attack caused disruptions to fuel supplies, and the REvil gang targeted Kaseya, affecting hundreds of businesses worldwide. The year 2021 also saw the discovery of a critical exploit in the Log4j Java logging library, leading to widespread efforts to mitigate the threat. In 2022, Costa Rica's Social Security administration was shut down by a ransomware attack, and Rockstar Games and Uber were targeted by hackers.

In 2023, cybercrimes included credential stuffing attacks on 23andMe, ransomware attacks on Sony's Insomniac Games and MCNA Dental, and the MGM Resorts hack caused by social engineering. These incidents highlight the evolving nature and increasing impact of cybercrime in recent years.

1.3. TYPES OF CYBERCRIME

There are various manifestations of cybercrime. Cybercriminals have developed a multitude of malicious software and social engineering techniques to carry out cybercrimes, targeting computers and networks. These methods can be used individually or in combination to cause significant harm.

Here is an overview of some of the most common cybercrimes (Figure 1.2).

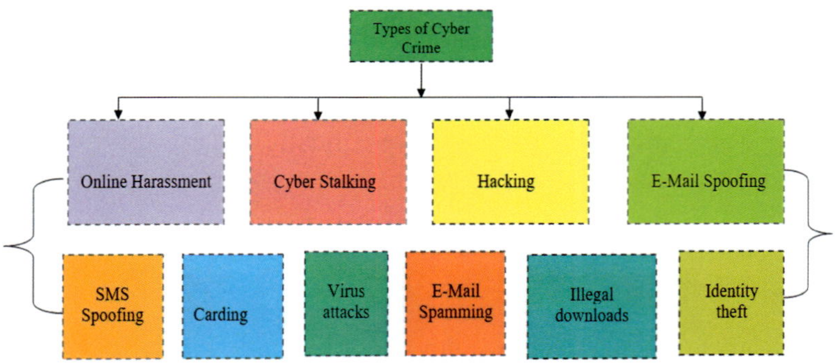

Figure 1.2. *Types of cybercrimes.*

Source: Tuli et al. (2022).

1.3.1. Hacking

Unauthorized access to data on a computer or network is commonly referred to as criminal hacking. One of the ways in which data is compromised is through the exploitation of vulnerabilities in various systems. Hackers are able to gain unauthorized access to a wide range of sensitive information, including government intelligence, corporate secrets, and personal data. In addition to compromising networks, hackers may also disrupt government and corporate operations. According to the FBI, computer and network attacks result in significant financial losses, amounting to billions of dollars annually (Stabek et al., 2010).

1.3.2. Malware

This is a type of malicious software that can cause significant harm to computer systems. It is important to be aware of the potential dangers associated with malware and take necessary precautions to protect your devices. Malware, also referred to as malicious software, encompasses any code designed to disrupt the normal functioning of a computer or engage in online criminal activities. Malware commonly manifests as various types of malicious software, such as adware, spyware, ransomware, worms, trojans, and other hybrid applications.

Based on the data provided by the FBI, it is evident that there has been a noticeable increase in the frequency and complexity of ransomware attacks. Ransomware attacks involve the encryption of critical digital assets and the demand for a fee in order to regain access.

These attacks are often executed by trojans, a type of malware that disguises its true intentions. Ransomware typically gains access to a system via email, where it deceives the recipient into either opening an attachment or visiting a website that harbors malicious malware. This, in turn, results in the victim's machine becoming infected. Ransomware attacks commonly target hospitals, schools, state and municipal governments, law enforcement organizations, and corporations. Ransomware is known to specifically target users who possess sensitive data, such as private files, images, or other valuable information (Stabek et al., 2010).

1.3.3. Identity Theft

This is a serious issue that can have devastating consequences for individuals. Identity theft involves the illegal acquisition of someone's personal information, which is then used for fraudulent purposes or theft, as stated by the FBI. Cyberattacks can lead to the unauthorized acquisition of personal data, often through the use of trojans and spyware. Phishing is a frequently used method in identity theft, where cybercriminals employ emails or messages to gather sensitive information. Perpetrators often pretend to be reputable entities such as banks or well-known corporations. Their main goal is to deceive victims into revealing personal data, such as social security numbers and account passwords. Phishing emails often employ storytelling techniques to entice recipients into clicking on links or opening attachments. One example of an interesting discovery is the sender's observation of unusual behavior with an account (Stabek et al., 2010).

1.3.4. Utilizing Social Engineering Techniques

Social engineering refers to the psychological manipulation of individuals in order to get them to carry out tasks or reveal confidential information. Social engineering is a technique employed by cyber criminals to deceive individuals online. Platforms such as online dating services provide opportunities to initiate conversations with potential victims. Once the perpetrator has established a connection and gained the trust of the target, they proceed to request money or sensitive information. Technology components are often combined with social engineering strategies. Phishing attempts often involve the use of malware and fake websites, accompanied by deceptive and manipulative language (Stabek et al., 2010).

1.3.5. Software Piracy

This is a serious issue that needs to be addressed. It involves the unauthorized copying, distribution, or use of software without the proper licenses or permissions. This not only violates copyright laws, but it also has negative consequences for the software industry and the economy as a whole. It is important for individuals and organizations to understand the ethical and legal. Illegally obtained software can be discovered in unauthorized downloads and reproductions, counterfeit commercial products, and licensing agreements that impose limitations on the number of users allowed for a particular program. BSA, the Software Alliance, reports that a significant portion of software installed on personal computers worldwide is not authorized, reaching up to 37%. In addition to being illegal, pirated software also facilitates the dissemination of malware. Cybercriminals can introduce malicious software into unauthorized copies of software.

1.4. CYBERCRIME LAWS AND REGULATIONS

The cybercrime law serves as a safeguard for individuals who utilize information and communication technology (ICT), ensuring the prevention or mitigation of any potential harm to people, data, systems, services, and infrastructure. The document also outlines the expected conduct for ICT users, sets penalties for cybercrime, ensures the protection of human rights, enables the investigation and prosecution of online offenses, and encourages global collaboration in addressing cybercrime (Siregar & Sinaga, 2021). The cybercrime law sets forth guidelines for individuals, organizations, and government entities to adhere to when utilizing computers, the Internet, and other digital technologies. It also encompasses criminal procedure, evidence, and various other facets of criminal justice in the realm of cyberspace. Additionally, it explores strategies to mitigate the risk of cybercrime and minimize the potential harm it can inflict on individuals, businesses, and infrastructure. Substantive, procedural, and preventive law are all encompassed within cybercrime law, as noted by Siregar and Sinaga (2021).

1.4.1. Substantive Law

Substantive cybercrime laws encompass statutes that prohibit specific types of cybercrime and impose penalties for violations of these laws. Various factors have contributed to the emergence of laws specifically designed to address the issue of cybercrime in numerous countries. China, Japan, and Germany have made modifications to the relevant sections of their criminal codes in order to address cybercrime.

It is worth noting that governments have utilized existing legislation designed for traditional, offline crimes to address specific instances of cybercrimes and individuals involved in cybercriminal activities (Siregar & Sinaga, 2021). In substantive law, the primary emphasis is placed on the specific details of crimes. This includes examining the various elements of a crime, including the mental state of the offender and the specific activities that are prohibited. States have the authority to determine what actions should be considered criminal, leading to the possibility of different definitions and laws across jurisdictions. In various jurisdictions, the prosecution of similar behavior can vary, as each jurisdiction has its own set of rules determining the level of accountability for a person's actions, specifically in terms of their state of mind and the degree of criminal culpability.

1.4.2. Procedural Law

Procedural law encompasses the regulations that govern the enforcement of substantive law and the necessary steps and protocols for its implementation. Criminal procedure is a crucial aspect of procedural law as it encompasses comprehensive regulations and guidelines that dictate how suspects, accused individuals, and those who have been convicted should be managed and processed by the criminal justice system and its agents. Procedural cybercrime laws encompass a wide range of legal aspects, such as jurisdiction, investigative powers, rules of evidence, criminal procedure, data gathering, wiretapping, search and seizure, data preservation, and data retention (Siregar & Sinaga, 2021).

1.4.3. Preventive Law

This is a crucial aspect of legal practice that focuses on anticipating and mitigating potential legal issues before they arise. It involves a proactive approach to identifying and addressing potential risks and legal pitfalls. By implementing preventive measures, individuals and organizations can minimize the likelihood of legal disputes and costly litigation. Cybersecurity laws, such as The Law of Ukraine on the Basic Principles of Ensuring the Cyber Security of Ukraine of 2017, and data protection laws, such as the EU General Data Protection Regulation of 2016 and the African Union Convention on Cyber Security and Personal Data Protection of 2014, aim to mitigate the financial consequences of criminal breaches of private data in the event of a cybercrime and to enhance individual resilience against cybercrime. Through the provision of necessary tools, protocols, and measures, additional legislation empowers law enforcement authorities to identify, investigate, and bring charges against cybercriminals (Siregar & Sinaga, 2021).

1.5. CYBERCRIME PREVENTION STRATEGIES

- ***Make Secure Passwords:*** It is important to use a separate user ID and password combination for each account and avoid writing them down. As suggested by Shah, Jones, & Choudrie (2019), it is recommended to enhance the strength of passwords by incorporating special characters, numbers, and a combination of letters. It is also advisable to ensure that the passwords are at least 10 characters long and to change them regularly.
- ***Protect Your System:*** A crucial measure in safeguarding against hackers and certain viruses is the implementation of a firewall. This essential security tool acts as a barrier, effectively blocking access to untrusted or fraudulent websites. It is also recommended to regularly installing and upgrading anti-virus software in preventing viruses from infiltrating your computer. To effectively prevent spyware from infiltrating your computer, it is crucial to install and regularly update anti-spyware software.
- ***Understand Social Media:*** It is important to ensure that your social media accounts, such as Facebook, Twitter, YouTube, MSN, and others, are set to private. Please ensure that your security configurations are properly verified. It is important to exercise caution when sharing information online. According to Shah, Jones, & Choudrie (2019), any content that is shared online has the potential to remain accessible for an indefinite period of time.

- ***Protect Your Mobile Devices:*** It is important to be aware of the fact that hackers and malware have the ability to target your mobile device. It is important to ensure that you only download and install programs from trusted and reliable websites.
- ***Update Your OS with the Most Recent Updates:*** It is important to regularly update your software and operating system (such as Windows, Mac, or Linux) in order to ensure that you have the latest system updates. Enabling automatic updates is crucial in order to protect your software from potential security risks. It is important to keep your software up to date to ensure that you are shielded from any potential threats that may arise (Shah, Jones, & Choudrie, 2019)
- ***Ensure the Protection of Your Personal Information*:** It is highly recommended to utilize encryption for your most sensitive files, such as tax returns or financial records. It is important to consistently back up your critical data and keep it stored in a separate location.
- ***Protect Your Wi-Fi Connection:*** It is important to ensure that household wireless networks are properly secured to prevent any potential compromises. Please carefully analyze and make any necessary modifications to the settings. Hotspots and public Wi-Fi can also be vulnerable to security risks. As mentioned by Shah, Jones, & Choudrie (2019), it is advised to avoid conducting business or financial transactions over these networks.
- ***Guard Your Online Identity:*** It is important to exercise caution when sharing personal information online, including your name, address, phone number, or financial details. It is important to ensure the security of websites, especially when conducting online transactions. Similarly, it is crucial to enable privacy settings when using social networking sites to protect your personal information.
- ***Steer Clear of Scams:*** It is important to carefully evaluate your choices before clicking on a link or a file from an unfamiliar source. It is important to resist the urge to feel obligated by any emails. Take a closer look at the original source of the message. It is advisable to refer to the source if you have any doubts. It is important to exercise caution when receiving emails that request you to verify your login credentials, user name, or password. Such requests may be attempts to gain unauthorized access to your personal information (Shah, Jones, & Choudrie, 2019)

1.6. CYBERCRIME INVESTIGATION TECHNIQUES

Cybercrime investigation involves the identification, assessment, and resolution of computer-based crimes and other forms of malicious activities occurring in the digital realm. One must delve into various forms of cybercrimes, such as hacking, phishing, malware, data breaches, and identity theft, employing specific tools and tactics. Cybercrime investigators play a crucial role in the investigative process. They collaborate closely with law enforcement organizations to ensure that cybercriminals are held accountable for their actions. Additionally, they are responsible for preserving evidence and conducting thorough and meticulous investigations. Cybercrime investigation plays a vital role in ensuring justice for victims and protecting individuals and organizations from the escalating threat of cybercrime (Oerlemans, 2017). Conducting cybercrime investigations is of utmost importance due to the increasing danger it poses to individuals, governments, and companies worldwide. The field of cybercrime investigation is a complex and constantly evolving area, driven by the rapid advancements in technology and the ever-present threats it brings. In order to effectively investigate and address cybercrimes, it is crucial for investigators to remain up-to-date on the latest methods and resources (Oerlemans, 2017).

1.6.1. Cybercrime Investigation Techniques

The investigation of cybercrimes involves a combination of technical and non-technical methods to gather information and pinpoint possible perpetrators. Digital forensics plays a crucial role in the investigation of cybercrime. Digital evidence gathering, preservation, and analysis are integral components of the field of digital forensics. Digital forensics involves a range of techniques, including recovering deleted files, analyzing metadata, and examining network traffic logs. Some commonly used tools in the field of digital forensics are Autopsy, FTK, and EnCase (Oerlemans, 2017).

Cybercrime investigators often utilize a range of supplementary techniques alongside digital forensics to gather information and pinpoint possible culprits. One way to approach this is by examining the flow of funds through careful analysis of financial records, reviewing surveillance footage, and conducting interviews with witnesses.

As part of their investigative methods, investigators may also utilize social engineering techniques. This can involve assuming the identity of potential victims or fabricating social media profiles. Collaboration plays a crucial role in the pursuit of understanding and combating cybercrime. Collaboration among investigators is of utmost importance in cybercrime investigations, as they involve multiple authorities and organizations. This allows for the efficient sharing of resources and information. Collaboration with governmental, business, or law enforcement organizations that specialize in cyber security may be necessary. When detectives collaborate, they have the opportunity to exchange ideas, analyze suspects, and identify recurring patterns (Oerlemans, 2017).

1.6.2. Cybercrime Investigation Tools

It is imperative to employ specialized equipment and software in order to effectively collect, safeguard, and examine digital evidence in the course of a cybercrime investigation. These instruments are capable of effectively locating suspects, closely monitoring their movements, and meticulously gathering information to build a strong case against them. Here are some of the commonly used tools that investigators rely on to investigate cybercrimes:

- **Software for Digital Forensics:** One of the main uses of this tool is to examine network traffic records, conduct data analysis, and retrieve deleted items. EnCase, FTK, and Autopsy are among the widely used software for digital forensics, as mentioned by Oerlemans in 2017.
- **Network Analysis Tools:** Their role involves tracing data flow, detecting suspicious activities, and monitoring network traffic. Some useful tools for network investigation are NetScout, tcpdump, and Wireshark.
- **Tools for Analyzing Malware:** Professionals in this field are responsible for analyzing malware and reverse engineering it in order to understand how it operates and trace its source. OllyDbg, Binary Ninja, and IDA Pro are commonly used in the field of malware analysis (Oerlemans, 2017).
- **Tools for Recovering Passwords:** Recovering passwords from encrypted files, databases, and other digital evidence sources is made possible through their utilization. Hashcat, John the Ripper, and Cain and Abel are just a few examples of password recovery tools.
- **Tools for Analyzing Social Media:** Their primary responsibility is to closely observe the activities and locations of individuals under suspicion, while also gathering evidence from various social media platforms. There are several tools available for social media analysis, such as Mention, Followerwonk, and Hootsuite (Oerlemans, 2017).

By skillfully utilizing these tools, they can effectively safeguard individuals and companies from the growing threat of cybercrime.

1.7. EXAMINING REAL-LIFE EXAMPLES OF CYBERCRIME

There are numerous instances of cybercrimes, such as online grooming, online scams, ransomware, malware, and intimate image abuse.

1.7.1. Online Scams

These are a prevalent issue in today's digital age. It is important for individuals to be aware of the various types of scams that exist and to take necessary precautions to protect themselves. Scammers often use deceptive tactics to trick unsuspecting victims into providing personal information or financial details.

Romance and dating scams revolve around individuals who masquerade as potential partners, preying on those seeking love and companionship. These fraudsters often exploit social media platforms, dating websites, or mobile applications. They exploit emotional triggers in order to obtain money, gifts, or personal information. According to Smith et al. (2011), individuals who fall victim to romance baiting are often enticed into pursuing a seemingly lucrative investment opportunity.

Let's examine the case of Amara, a retired widow. While serving in Afghanistan for peacekeeping, Hungarian soldier Ferenc sent Amara a friend request. Amara agreed. Ferenc and Amara developed a closer bond. Upon presenting her with a series of photographs, Ferenc proceeded to inform Amara of the tragic loss of his wife due to cancer. Amara's personal experience mirrored this situation. Specifically, her husband, who was elderly, passed away from cancer two years ago.

Ferenc mentioned that his military service was nearing its end, despite the fact that he would be deployed to Cyprus. Ferenc informed Amara that upon his retirement, he had plans to open a jewelry store. Ferenc notified Amara about his upcoming meeting with her, but mentioned that he was encountering difficulties with his bank card in Cyprus. Additionally, he expressed his concerns regarding the payment of the export tax on his jewels. Amara provided a loan of fifteen thousand dollars to Ferenc in order to settle the tax bill. Shortly thereafter, Ferenc informed Amara that during his journey to Australia, he had encountered an unfortunate situation where he was apprehended by local authorities in Malaysia. In order to cover his court costs and legal bills, he needed a sum of $20,000. Upon contacting the Malaysian police, Amara was informed that they had no knowledge of Ferenc. Upon learning that Amara was unable to provide the additional funds, Ferenc's frustration escalated, leading him to express his anger through text messages and ultimately severing all communication (Smith et al., 2011). Amara was deeply affected and left feeling confused. She experiences a sense of being misled and tricked. Despite being aware that this was a hoax, there is a lingering sense of guilt that she may have failed Ferenc and that he could still be alive. Amara had to resume her job to fulfill her financial obligations and repay the loan she had borrowed. By providing the con artist known as Ferenc with extensive personal information, she exposes herself to the potential danger of identity theft (Smith et al., 2011).

1.7.2. Ransomware

This is a form of extortion that utilizes malicious software, commonly referred to as malware, to restrict users' access to their system or personal files. The perpetrators then demand a ransom to be paid in order to regain access to the system.

Let's examine a case study: Jin and Bella, a family-run accounting company, provide outsourced bookkeeping and accounting services to small businesses in Victoria. Client organizations can conveniently access the business's online platform through a secure website portal. This platform efficiently handles a range of bookkeeping tasks for them, such as processing receipts, calculating deductions, and monitoring spending.

Shortly before tax season, an email of questionable origin resulted in the unfortunate ransomware infection of Jin and Bella's company computers. The malware caused a disruption in customer access to the company's platform by effectively locking it down. In order to restore the network's functionality, the criminals demanded a sum of $100,000 in Bitcoin, which is a form of digital currency. Bella and Jin refused to make the payment. The hackers have issued a serious threat to expose the confidential data of Jin and Bella's clients. Bella and Jin found themselves in a state of confusion, unsure of how to proceed. Insufficient funds were available to provide the necessary compensation for the ransomware. Jin and Bella contacted Victoria Police to report the incident. A significant number of Jin and Bella's clients faced challenges in submitting their tax returns within the designated timeframe. The level of customer dissatisfaction with the service was significant. According to the Australian Cyber Security Centre, it is advisable to refrain from paying ransoms. Understanding the implications of paying the ransom can potentially increase the vulnerability of an individual or organization to future ransomware attacks. In addition, it cannot be guaranteed that making a payment will effectively rectify the damage (Smith et al., 2011).

Jin and Bella's business experienced a significant decline in reputation, resulting in a loss of customers. Jin and Bella were deeply affected by the attack, experiencing a significant amount of tension and concern.

CHAPTER 2

CYBERCRIMINALS

Contents

Cybercriminals are individuals or organizations that employ technology to execute harmful activities on digital networks or systems, aiming to acquire confidential or sensitive corporate information and generate profits. Cybercriminals engage in the trading of illicit goods and services, such as hacking tools and stolen data, within the underground markets of the deep web (Bada & Nurse, 2021). Specialized goods or services are often found in cybercriminal underground markets, which are frequented by those in the cybercriminal community.

There are ongoing changes in cybercrime laws across various nations worldwide. One ongoing challenge for law enforcement is the task of finding, apprehending, prosecuting, and proving cybercrimes.

2.1. PROFILE OF CYBERCRIMINALS

In order to gain insight into the motivations, workings, and thought processes of cybercriminals, it is imperative to possess a comprehensive understanding of their profile. Due to the exceptional resourcefulness, competence, and knowledge of cybercriminals, it becomes quite difficult to anticipate or apprehend them. Criminological research on criminal personalities aims to identify and evaluate the distinct traits that play a role in the perpetration of criminal offenses (Bada & Nurse, 2021).

Criminals, including cybercriminals, possess a range of distinct personality traits. These traits include impulsivity, a high level of aggression, difficulty in foreseeing the consequences of their actions, inflexibility, a tendency to lie, selfishness, egocentricity, a preoccupation with wealth, unconventional beliefs and judgments, unpredictable behavior, detachment from social norms, and a lack of moral and legal conscience (Bada & Nurse, 2021).

Personality behavior is greatly impacted by the various qualities that make up an individual's personality. An individual possesses inherent characteristics that are commonly observed. A criminal's personality consists of various undesirable traits that are specific to the type of crime and the individual offender. A cybercriminal is more than just an individual with a specific status and set of responsibilities. They are a complex being composed of various elements: (i) needs, interests, and abilities; (ii) emotions, thoughts, and determination; and (iii) disposition, nature, and value orientation (Bada & Nurse, 2021).

Various factors, such as individual needs, temperament, values, and other influences, can all play a role in the commission of a criminal offense. The personality of a criminal is influenced by three key factors: heredity, socialization and self-actualization.

- *Heredity:* The transmission of an organism's genetically determined features across generations is referred to as heredity. There have been multiple studies conducted that have revealed the biological effects and genetic factors at play. For instance, one particular study delved into the intricacies of genetics by conducting a meta-analysis of individual traits and hereditary characteristics. Based on an extensive analysis of data from over 14 million twin pairs across 39 nations over a span of 50 years, it has been concluded that all traits are inherited and remain consistent in their significance.
- *Socialization:* This refers to the acquisition of accepted standards of conduct within a specific social setting, encompassing micro, macro, and overall social environments (Bada & Nurse, 2021). Examining multi-factor studies on the emergence of criminal behavior, it has been found that certain key elements play a crucial role in shaping the fully grownup existence of children between the ages of 8 and 10. These elements include mental health, family stability, and home circumstances.
- *Self-Actualization:* It encompasses aspects such as one's understanding of nature, intelligence, and life values. The dynamics of the various factors that contribute to the formation of personality revolve around the concept of self-actualization, which plays a crucial role in understanding the underlying motivations behind criminal behavior. These elements are intricately linked to the circumstances that give rise to a particular criminal offense through the criminogenic motivation milestone. This milestone serves as the underlying cause for the commission of the criminal offense (Bada & Nurse, 2021).

Most cybercriminals tend to display a range of characteristics. They could belong to a wide range of technical knowledge backgrounds, ranging from highly skilled IT professionals who acquire "malicious code on the dark web" to individuals with less technical expertise who are considered "hackers." Individuals who possess a strong inclination towards risk-taking often find themselves attracted to activities that offer a sense of excitement and thrill. They have a tendency to manipulate targets, cyber professionals, and even law enforcement because of their "controlling" nature. Some individuals tend to justify why certain laws are invalid or should not be applicable to them, while others simply choose to ignore the law altogether. One possible motivation for committing the crime could be financial gain, intense emotions, adherence to specific political or religious beliefs, sexual desires, or even sheer boredom. The three main components of most successful prosecutions are motive, means, and opportunity.

According to Bada and Nurse (2021), cybercriminals could potentially reduce the occurrence of their crimes if they abstained from using computers. However, it is worth noting that the more proficient cybercriminals strategically employ networks and computers to streamline their illicit activities, thereby enhancing their efficiency. A highly effective technique utilized by law enforcement is the implementation of a sting operation. This method involves officers assuming the role of a potential target, strategically designed to attract the attention of criminals with the intention of apprehending them. By strategically deploying a "honeypot" on a network, it is possible to attract malicious individuals and gather valuable insights.

2.2. MOTIVATIONS FOR CYBERCRIME

The multiple factors that drive hackers are discussed in the following subsections.

2.2.1. Monetary Profit

Money serves as the primary motivation for hackers, who employ various methods to acquire it. There are various methods that individuals with malicious intent can employ to gain unauthorized access to your financial accounts. These methods include directly breaking into a bank or investment account, obtaining passwords to financial websites and transferring assets, using sophisticated spear phishing techniques to deceive employees into initiating money transfers, or even launching ransomware attacks on your entire company. According to Neufeld (2010), hackers generally have a strong desire to make a profit, despite the numerous options available to them.

2.2.2. Recognizing Achievements and Accomplishments

For certain individuals, the thrill of infiltrating a major system is a powerful motivator. Although individuals or groups may work independently, they still desire a certain level of recognition. It is interesting to note that cybercriminals are driven by a sense of competition and derive satisfaction from the challenges posed by their actions (Neufeld, 2010). Indeed, it is common for them to inspire one another to complete more challenging hacks.

2.2.3. Dangers from Within

It is important for individuals who have access to critical data or systems to consider the potential consequences of misusing that access, as it could have a negative impact on their organization. Some of the most significant cyber security risks that companies face can stem from various sources such as partners, contractors, suppliers, or internal staff members. However, according to a report by Crowd Research Partners, it is worth noting that not all insider threats are intentional. Over half of these incidents stem from a lack of attention, disregard, or falsified qualifications. However, even in an unintended scenario, the consequences can still be significant.

2.2.4. The Political Objective of "Hacktivism"

Cybercrime groups often direct their hacking expertise towards major organizations. Typically, there is a purpose driving them, such as championing human rights or highlighting systemic issues within a prominent company. On the other hand, individuals may come across organizations whose beliefs clash with their own. These groups often employ DDoS attacks, which involve overwhelming a website with excessive bandwidth in order to force it to crash. According to Neufeld (2010), individuals have been known to take advantage of their right to free expression by unlawfully obtaining information.

2.2.5. State-Based Players

One important aspect to consider is the financial and logistical assistance that a nation-state offers to individuals or groups who have been sponsored by the state. They engage in cybercrime with the intention of furthering the interests of their nation. They often engage in the illicit acquisition of funds to support their covert activities and pursue exploitative agendas, including the theft of intellectual property, personally identifiable information, and monetary assets. However, it is important to note that there are actors who receive state sponsorship and engage in destructive cyberattacks. These actors claim that their cyberespionage activities are authorized by the state that sponsors them (Neufeld, 2010). In order to effectively safeguard your company's IT systems, it is crucial to gain a comprehensive understanding of the motivations that drive hackers. In order to enhance the safety and security of your company, a comprehensive cyber security plan with multiple layers can be highly effective. Ensuring the protection of your data and systems is of utmost importance. This involves taking measures to secure your networks, devices, apps, transmissions, privileges, and storage (Neufeld, 2010). It is important to regularly educate your employees about the latest trends in cyber threats, phishing attacks, and ransomware.

2.3. PSYCHOLOGICAL FACTORS OF CYBERCRIMINALS

Cybercriminals possess a high level of expertise in the art of manipulation, exploiting the vulnerabilities of individuals to advance their own motives. Some of the psychological strategies they employ includes:

- *Social Engineering Strategy:* This is a concept that involves manipulating individuals to gain unauthorized access to information or resources. It is a technique that requires careful planning and execution. Cybercriminals often employ phishing emails and fake social media profiles as tactics to exploit people's curiosity and reliance, with the intention of deceiving them into revealing personal information or clicking on malicious links (Jadhav et al., 2022).
- *Anxiety and Urgency*: Cybercriminals frequently employ this strategy to instill a sense of anxiety or urgency. As an illustration, ransomware attacks often instill fear in victims by threatening irreversible data loss or public exposure, thereby increasing the likelihood of them paying the ransom.
- *Cognitive Bias Manipulation*: Cybercriminals are quite cunning when it comes to manipulating cognitive biases. They exploit biases like confirmation bias and the halo effect to deceive individuals into revealing information they wouldn't normally share or making irrational judgments (Jadhav et al., 2022).
- *Impersonation*: This is a common tactic used by cybercriminals to deceive their victims. They pretend to be trustworthy individuals, reputable businesses, or even government institutions in order to manipulate their targets into following their instructions or unknowingly revealing sensitive information.
- *Exploitation of Cryptocurrencies*: With the increasing popularity of cryptocurrencies, cybercriminals now have a wider range of avenues to engage in money laundering. They exploit vulnerabilities in cryptocurrency wallets and exchanges, or they engage in crypto jacking techniques to exploit individuals' unsuspecting computing power.
- *Advanced Persistent Threats (APTs)*: These are a category of sophisticated cyber-attacks that are typically sponsored by nation-states. These attacks are known for their high level of skill, as well as their targeted and complex nature. Typically, these campaigns require a significant amount of time to complete and focus on establishing long-term access to specific targets. APTs utilize a range of techniques and strategies to evade detection and compromise sensitive information (Jadhav et al., 2022).

Cybercriminals run networks of compromised computers, commonly known as "zombies" and operating as "botnets." Botnets can be utilized to carry out various malicious activities, such as Distributed Denial of Service (DDoS) attacks and spam email campaigns. Botnets pose a significant threat as they continue to grow in size and sophistication.

- *Zero-Day Exploits*: Cybercriminals are particularly attracted to zero-day exploits due to their ability to exploit software vulnerabilities that have not yet been discovered by developers and vendors. One interesting point to consider is that individuals with certain skills may have an edge when it comes to infiltrating systems. This advantage stems from their ability to exploit vulnerabilities before security measures are strengthened or updated, as noted by Jadhav, and their colleagues.

To enhance security, it is highly recommended to implement strong passwords, regularly update programs, and utilize antivirus software. These measures are essential in safeguarding your digital environment. It is crucial for both individuals and businesses to fulfill their responsibility of protecting financial and personal information, remaining vigilant for any suspicious activity, and promptly reporting any instances of cybercrime. It is crucial for individuals to prioritize online safety and take proactive steps to strengthen their defenses against cybercriminals. It is important to remember that cybersecurity is a responsibility that we all share (Jadhav et al., 2022). Through collaboration, they have the ability to overcome the ever-evolving challenges in the digital realm.

Establishing a strong defense strategy preventing cybercrime requires a deep understanding of technological developments and the implementation of effective cybersecurity technologies. However, it is equally important to consider the impact of human factors in this complex equation. Some of the key strategies include:

- *Education and Awareness:* These are crucial when it comes to cybersecurity. Providing consistent and thorough training can help individuals in recognizing and effectively dealing with cyberthreats. Staying updated on the latest strategies used by cybercriminals is of utmost importance.
- *Psychological Profiling:* Understanding the psychological characteristics of cybercriminals can greatly assist in developing effective countermeasures. By carefully analyzing common characteristics and qualities, one can effectively identify potential dangers before they materialize.
- *Employing Ethical Hackers, also Known as "White-Hat" Hackers:* This can aid companies in detecting security vulnerabilities in their systems and ensuring they stay ahead of cybercriminals.
- *Putting in Place Multiple Layers of Defense:* It is crucial to avoid relying solely on a single line of defense. Implementing multiple

layers of security, including intrusion detection systems, firewalls, and antivirus software, can significantly reduce the risk of cyberattacks (Jadhav et al., 2022).

2.4. CYBERCRIME ORGANIZATIONS

Due to the prevalence and profitability of cybercrime, organized groups of cybercriminals collaborate to carry out large-scale internet heists. These groups of cybercriminals consist of programmers, hackers, and other tech criminals who collaborate and pool their skills and resources to execute large-scale crimes that would be unfeasible to accomplish on their own. Below are ten most prominent organized cybercrime syndicates in history.

2.4.1. The Cobalt

This cybercrime organization was responsible for the Carbanak and Cobalt malware assaults, which targeted 100 financial firms in over 40 countries worldwide. The sophisticated computer campaigns executed by these robbers enabled them to successfully steal over $11 million in each robbery. According to a study conducted by Broadhurst et al. (2013), the banking industry experienced losses exceeding $1 billion. Bank employees were targeted in a typical Cobalt assault through spear-phishing emails containing malware attachments, resulting in the compromise of financial organizations. Through the download of malware, the hackers were able to successfully breach the infected computer and infiltrate the internal network system. Over the course of several months, extensive research was conducted on the bank's procedures and internal workings within the compromised networks. It became increasingly alarming when they began tampering with the ATM control systems, as documented by Broadhurst et al. (2013).

During the previous robbery, the ATMs were programmed to dispense cash at specific intervals from a remote location. A money mule would patiently await the collection of payments at these designated locations, employing a technique commonly referred to as "jackpotting." It is now believed by authorities that the remaining members have carried on with their activities, observing similar attacks on various institutions soon after the ringleader's imprisonment in 2018.

2.4.2. The Lazarus Gang

The Lazarus group has been responsible for a multitude of devastating cyberattacks targeting various institutions and organizations. Some experts have suggested a potential connection between this group and North Korea. Two notable examples include the 2014 Sony Pictures hack and the infamous

WannaCry cyberattack, which inflicted significant harm on the National Health Service (NHS) in England. There has been a recent leak of Sony images. Upon discovering that their company's network had been compromised during the well-known Sony Pictures incident, staff members were quite surprised. A significant amount of private data was compromised by hackers, who went as far as deleting specific files and issuing threats to Sony in order to force compliance with their demands.

During periods of system unavailability, staff members were instructed to utilize whiteboards as a means of communication. After a few days, the hackers began granting the media access to the stolen classified information (Broadhurst et al., 2013).

The emergence of the WannaCry Ransomware has caused significant concern and disruption in the digital landscape. There is a strong belief that the Lazarus group was responsible for the 2017 WannaCry ransomware attack, which had a significant impact on more than 250,000 systems in 150 countries. Several companies and establishments, including the NHS in the UK, were severely impacted by this. The attack on the NHS was unprecedented in its history. The NHS experienced significant disruption due to the WannaCry cyberattack, resulting in the cancellation of over 6,000 appointments and incurring estimated costs of $100 million (Broadhurst et al., 2013).

2.4.3. The Syndicate Mage Cart

This e-commerce hacking ring, consisting of multiple gangs operating together, became infamous for their extensive collection of credit card and customer data. A software skimmer virus was utilized to accomplish this task, intercepting payment services on e-commerce websites and capturing credit card information. Throughout the years, there have been multiple instances of Mage Cart gangs targeting various e-commerce platforms and websites where users often provide their credit card information. As an example, in 2018, the data of British Airways was compromised by a MageCart group. The event had a significant impact on a staggering number of 380,000 individuals, putting at risk their valuable financial and personal information. However, the assault on the airline was merely the beginning.

Shortly after the British Airways breach, MageCart launched a significant credit card skimming operation targeting hardware merchant Newegg. It is believed that MageCart was also behind the Ticketmaster data breach, which resulted in the exposure of personal information for 40,000 consumers (Broadhurst et al., 2013).

2.4.4. Evil Corp

The organization's name suggests a potential inclination towards causing disruption. An international cybercrime group, operating out of Russia, employs a variety of viruses to strategically target various organizations, one of which being a school system in Pennsylvania. For several years now, this elusive group has managed to avoid detection, leaving a trail of victims in their wake, primarily targeting American and European institutions. The cybercriminal organization has gained significant attention due to their utilization of the advanced Dridex banking Trojan. This malicious software has enabled Evil Corp to successfully acquire login credentials from numerous banks and financial institutions across 40 countries. According studies, Evil Corp managed to acquire approximately $100 million during the peak of the Dridex operation. The videos showcasing the purported leaders' extravagant sports vehicles and lavish lifestyles have gained immense popularity due to their audacious nature. Despite the formal charges filed against them by U.S. officials in December 2019, there are concerns among many observers regarding the feasibility of bringing their leaders to trial in the United States. The accusations did not have any impact on the organization.

Several recent incidents targeting small and medium-sized enterprises in the US during 2020 have been attributed to Evil Corp. In June 2020, Symantec made a significant discovery regarding a scheme targeting numerous US companies. WastedLocker, a recently discovered strain of ransomware, has been employed in targeted attacks against a total of eight prominent Fortune 500 companies (Broadhurst et al., 2013).

2.4.5. The GozNym Gang

This global criminal network is responsible for the development and distribution of the GozNym malware, a sophisticated Trojan that is designed to avoid detection by security tools. GozNym is a unique and formidable creature, combining the powerful Gozi virus with the cunning Nymaim. Due to the nefarious collaboration, malicious email attachments or URLs have the potential to infiltrate a customer's computer. Subsequently, the malware remained undetected, patiently biding its time for an opportune moment when an individual would access their bank account. The funds were unlawfully taken and subsequently moved to various accounts in the United States and abroad, where individuals were employed to rectify the situation. Over 41,000 devices were targeted in a cyberattack, leading to the unfortunate loss of over $100 million from the accounts of unsuspecting individuals. Europol has reported that the individuals responsible for the GozNym malware have been apprehended (Broadhurst et al., 2013).

2.4.6. DarkSide

The May ransomware attack on the Colonial Pipeline, attributed to DarkSide, had significant consequences for the U.S. petroleum distribution system, causing disruptions in gasoline delivery. Large corporations are the primary focus of this strategy, as they possess the financial means to potentially pay a ransom in the event of service disruption. Furthermore, these organizations face significant repercussions if they fail to address such interruptions.

In these types of businesses, cyber insurance is quite common, indicating a potential opportunity for criminals to make quick profits. DarkSide's business model revolves around providing ransomware services. Essentially, it lessens the culpability of unknown wrongdoers by executing ransomware attacks on their behalf. The heist is then evenly divided between the mastermind and the executioner. Online forums are offered by cybercrime-as-a-service companies to individuals seeking to enhance their hacking abilities. One aspect of this could be instructing someone on the integration of ransomware and DDoS attacks to increase leverage during negotiations. It is important to note that a DDoS attack has the capability to halt the processing of new orders, whereas a ransomware attack can significantly impede a company's ability to fulfill orders from both the past and present (Broadhurst et al., 2013).

2.4.7. REvil

REvil, a ransomware-as-a-service company, has garnered significant attention due to its involvement in the ongoing Kaseya problem and a recent attack on the global meat processing business JBS. During the years 2020 and 2021, this particular group has exhibited a significant amount of aggression. In April, REvil obtained technical information on upcoming Apple products through a cyberattack on Quanta Computer, a company based in Taiwan that manufactures Apple computers. In order to prevent the stolen information from being disclosed, a sum of $50 million is being demanded. The uncertainty surrounding whether this payment was made has been discussed by Broadhurst et al., (2013).

2.4.8. Clop

In 2019, a notorious gang unleashed the Clop ransomware, proudly claiming responsibility for a staggering half a billion dollars in theft. Their sole motivation? Pure greed. The Clop group is known for their expertise in a technique called "double-extortion." This method involves demanding a ransom in return for a decryption key that allows businesses to regain access to their compromised data. In order to maintain the confidentiality of the material, victims will be required to make an additional payment as ransom. Based on historical data, it has been observed that businesses that have paid a ransom in the past tend to be more inclined to do so again in the future. As a result, it is not uncommon for hackers to repeatedly target the same companies, increasing their demands for money with each attack.

2.4.9. The Electronic Army of Syria

The Syrian Electronic Army has been utilizing online attacks to spread political propaganda since 2011, which sets them apart from other cybercrime groups. Their exceptional drive and dedication has led them to be recognized as a prominent hacktivist group. While the group is often linked to the regime of Bashar al-Assad, it appears to primarily consist of online activists who aim to act as the media arm of the Syrian army. Their strategy involves utilizing trustworthy channels to disseminate inaccurate information. In 2013, the Associated Press, a renowned news institution, sent out a single tweet that caused a significant drop in the stock market, resulting in billions of dollars lost (Broadhurst et al., 2013).

The Syrian Electronic Army capitalizes on the inherent trust that many internet users possess when it comes to interpreting and responding to information. Additionally, this serves as a compelling illustration of the challenges in differentiating between terrorist and criminal organizations on the internet compared to offline.

2.4.10. FIN7

One of the most notable cybercrime syndicates in history is FIN7, a highly successful group hailing from Russia. It has been operating since 2012. For years, the majority of its operations went unnoticed. Instances of cross-attack events, where cyberattacks are utilized to achieve multiple objectives, have been effectively utilized in various security breaches. As an illustration, ransomware extortion could be facilitated, enabling the attacker to generate profit by selling the victims' data to a third party (Broadhurst et al., 2013).

In 2017, FIN7 faced charges for allegedly orchestrating a cyberattack on US firms that had submitted documents to the Securities and Exchange Commission. The confidential information was exploited and subsequently used to extort a ransom, which was then utilized for the purpose of purchasing stocks. As a result, the organizations were able to generate significant profits from the exchange of sensitive information. It is challenging to determine the exact extent of the financial damage caused by the extensive insider trading scheme. However, the estimated cost amounts to billions of dollars.

2.5. CYBERCRIME NETWORKS

Cybercrime networks consist of individuals or groups that engage in illegal activities on the internet. These networks operate in a covert manner, exploiting vulnerabilities in networks, devices, or computer systems. Goals can vary greatly, encompassing everything from financial gain to personal, political, or other objectives. Cybercrime networks utilize advanced strategies such as phishing, extortion, and virus attacks (Broadhurst et al., 2013). Their impact extends far beyond individual victims, reaching governments, corporations, and society at large.

Cybercrime networks employ a range of strategies to attract fresh recruits, capitalizing on vulnerabilities in human behavior and technological expertise.

- *Social Engineering:* Cybercriminals employ various methods, such as social media, phone calls, or email, to establish contact with potential victims. Individuals exploit the trust or financial vulnerability of others through manipulation. Take workers in contact centers or retail establishments, for instance. They may find themselves singled out due to their comparatively lower pay scale. In challenging times, the idea of gaining extra income by collecting customer information can be quite tempting (Broadhurst et al., 2013).
- *Privileged Insiders*: Cybercriminals often focus their attention on individuals who have significant access or responsibilities in system management, as they are considered privileged insiders. These individuals have already been granted authorization to access specific organizations. Potential targets for cyber-attacks encompass a range of individuals, such as IT administrators, contract workers, attorneys, and senior executives. These targets may include both third-party contractors and former employees (Broadhurst et al., 2013).
- *Motivation-Oriented Insiders*: One demographic that cybercrime networks often target are individuals who are primarily motivated by financial gain. Even though retail or call center workers may earn lower wages, they might still willingly disclose private or sensitive information. Exchanging customer records for additional cash can have a significant impact on customers' loyalty. Financial incentives play a significant role in this context, as highlighted by Broadhurst et al. (2013).

2.6. CYBERCRIME TOOLS AND TECHNIQUES

There are various tools and techniques employed in the field of cyber security to protect networks, systems, and data from cyberattacks. Some of these are discussed in the following sections.

2.6.1. Firewalls

Firewalls are network security mechanisms that monitor the flow of data entering and exiting the network. The data that travels along their borders is carefully evaluated, and decisions are made regarding which information is allowed to pass through and which is not, all according to a set of predetermined rules (Al-Khater et al., 2020) (Figure 2.1).

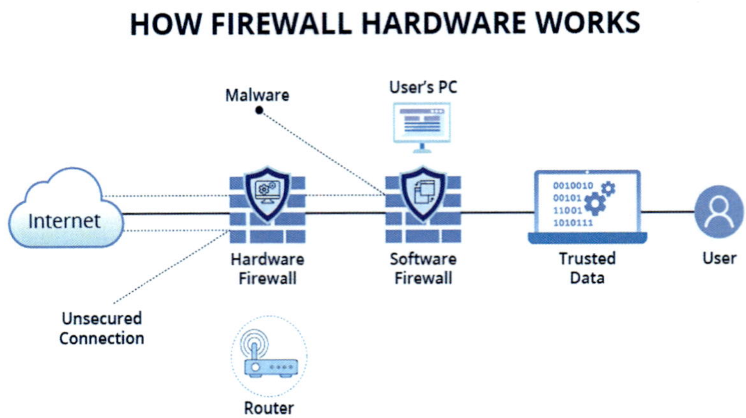

Figure 2.1. *Firewall functionality.*

Source: Howard (2023).

There are several different types of firewalls, but here are the three most commonly used ones:

- *The Packet Filter:* The packets sent between computers are carefully examined, and access is granted or refused based on a list of access controls. The list provides guidance to the firewall on which packets need to be analyzed further and which data should result in the rejection or destruction of a file. While it is true that these firewalls may be considered outdated and not capable of providing complete network security independently, they can still play a valuable role in preventing cyberattacks with minimal effort (Al-Khater et al., 2020).
- *Connection Tracking Firewalls:* It is also known as second generation firewalls, operate in a similar manner to first generation

packet filters. They perform a similar form of packet inspection, but they also record the port number associated with each IP address for data transmission and reception. It is possible to analyze both the data exchange and the packet content.

- *Application/Layer 7:* When it comes to application/layer 7, application firewalls have a significant advantage over connection tracking or packet filter firewalls. They are much more powerful in terms of their capabilities. One can understand a variety of applications, such as DNS, file transfer protocol (FTP), and hypertext transfer protocol (HTTP). This capability allows them to effectively identify non-standard ports and unwanted programs. Their ability to perform web filtering makes them valuable on the internet (Al-Khater et al., 2020).

2.6.2. Software to Prevent Malware

One of the software-based cyber security technologies is anti-malware. It has the ability to detect and eliminate malware from devices and systems, effectively preventing any infections on a computer. There are three well-known categories of anti-malware software, each employing a distinct approach to detect and remove malware:

- *Behavior-Based Detection:* This is a method used to identify and analyze patterns of behavior in order to detect and prevent potential threats or risks. It involves closely monitoring and analyzing the actions and activities of individuals or systems to identify any deviations or anomalies that may indicate malicious intent or suspicious behavior. This software is highly effective in its ability to utilize advanced technologies, such as machine learning algorithms, to actively detect and identify malware. In order to expedite the eradication of the infection, the focus is placed on understanding its behavior rather than its outward appearance (Al-Khater et al., 2020).
- *Sandboxing:* This is a crucial feature that effectively isolates applications that may pose a potential threat. It provides a secure environment to contain and prevent any potential harm that these applications may cause. Prior to causing any potential damage to the system, it has the capability to filter out files. Once the harmful software has been isolated, the anti-malware can effectively remove it. This method is highly effective in eliminating common viruses such as keyloggers and adware. One of the key features of this software is its ability to identify and remove common malware

through signature detection. Once a specific piece of malware is removed, the software will automatically eliminate any other malware that shares the same signature.

2.6.3. Antivirus Software

Antivirus software is a commonly known cyber security tool among computer users. In order to safeguard devices from the perils of malicious software, it is commonly recommended that users take the proactive step of installing an anti-virus software.

"Next-gen software" refers to the most powerful anti-virus software currently available in the market. This approach is characterized by a shift towards signature-less detection and has been in active use since 2014. The programming of antivirus software of this nature often incorporates advanced techniques such as machine learning for behavioral detection, artificial intelligence, and cloud-based file detonation (Al-Khater et al., 2020).

Cyber security specialists must remain up-to-date on the latest advancements in anti-virus software to effectively protect the businesses they serve. It is crucial for companies to constantly stay informed about the latest advancements in anti-virus technology in order to effectively combat ever-evolving infections. It is important for them to promptly update their software whenever new versions are released.

2.6.4. Packet Sniffers and Auditing Passwords Cyber Security Experts

These are responsible for evaluating passwords and monitoring networks with the help of specialized equipment. It is crucial to understand that the use of weak passwords poses a significant threat to the security of an entire network and the critical data it manages. Password auditing tools are valuable resources for system administrators and analysts to monitor and evaluate the strength of passwords in order to protect against potential hacking attempts. John the Ripper is a powerful tool that allows for the rapid and efficient assessment of password strength. Its purpose is to minimize the risk of network vulnerability caused by weak passwords (Al-Khater et al., 2020).

Hashcat is a widely utilized password-cracking program that finds great utility among system administrators and penetration testers. Through the process of transforming passwords into a hash, which consists of a collection of randomly generated characters, password hashing serves as a protective measure for passwords. It is important to note that password hashing is different from encryption, as encryption is specifically designed to conceal data. In simple terms, the program utilizes a hashing technique to generate a potential password, which is then compared to the target password it is attempting to crack. This process is then repeated iteratively (Al-Khater et al., 2020).

2.7. CYBERCRIME TRENDS

2.7.1. Overview of Cybercrime

When we look at the numbers, it becomes evident that there has been a significant rise in cyberattacks globally in 2021, with a staggering 125% increase compared to the previous year. Furthermore, the impact of these attacks on individuals and organizations continued to escalate in 2022, as highlighted by Broadhurst and Chantler (2006).

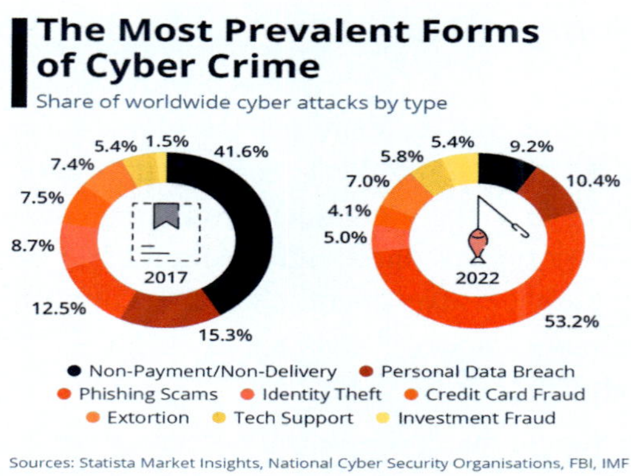

Figure 2.2. *The most prevalent forms of cyber-crime.*

Source: Zandt (2023).

Phishing remains the most prevalent type of cybercrime. In 2021, a staggering number of 323,972 internet users fell victim to phishing attempts. It is evident from the data that a significant number of users fell victim to phishing attacks after experiencing a data leak. During the height of the pandemic, there was a significant surge in phishing attacks, with an alarming increase of 220%. In the year 2021, a staggering number of approximately 1 billion emails were compromised, significantly affecting a substantial portion of internet users, specifically 1 in 5 individuals. It is worth noting that phishing assaults continue to be prevalent, as evidenced by the research conducted by Broadhurst and Chantler in 2006 (Figure 2.2). Despite its prevalence, phishing actually results in relatively low victim loss. On average, individuals lose $136 due to phishing attacks. The cost of a data breach is significantly higher than the amount mentioned here (Broadhurst & Chantler, 2006). A look at the threat of ransomware, it is evident that it continue to pose a significant danger to individuals and organizations alike. The perpetrators are employing ever more advanced tactics, putting immense pressure on their victims to comply with their demands. In the first half of 2022, a staggering number of 236.1 million ransomware attacks were recorded globally (Broadhurst & Chantler, 2006).

2.7.2. The Cost of Cybercrime

There is a clear increase in both the frequency and cost of data breaches. Since 2001, there has been a significant increase in the number of victims, rising from 6 per hour to 97. This represents a staggering 1517% increase over a span of 20 years. On a global scale, there has been an increase in the average hourly cost of data breaches. In 2001, the average hourly rate for individuals was $2054. According to Broadhurst and Chantler (2006), the hourly loss rate has increased over time and has reached $787,671 in 2021.

It is becoming increasingly evident that the global threat posed by cyber security is prompting more individuals and organizations to prioritize its importance. According to a study conducted by Broadhurst and Chantler in 2006, a significant majority of small and medium-sized businesses (SMBs) are planning to increase their investment in cyber security in the coming year. Additionally, a large percentage of SMBs acknowledge the urgent need to take action in order to mitigate security risks.

It is concerning to note that a significant percentage of small and medium-sized businesses feel ill-equipped to handle data breaches. However, it is worth noting that there has been a decrease in this problem. In fact, a significant number of small and medium-sized businesses, specifically 89% in 2022 compared to 74% in 2020, have started collaborating with Managed Service Providers to address their cyber security concerns (Broadhurst & Chantler, 2006).

The epidemic had a significant impact on cybersecurity as companies were forced to rapidly transition to remote work environments. As these changes unfolded, cybercriminals took advantage of network misalignments and security vulnerabilities. According studies, there was a significant increase of 358% in malware attacks in 2020 compared to the previous year.

It is undeniable that the impact of Covid-19 on the victims has been significant. Based on the latest cybercrime statistics from 2019, it was found that there were 53 reported victims every hour. In 2020, the number of casualties per hour saw a significant increase, reaching 90. This marked a 69% rise compared to previous years, reflecting the impact of the pandemic (Figure 2.3).

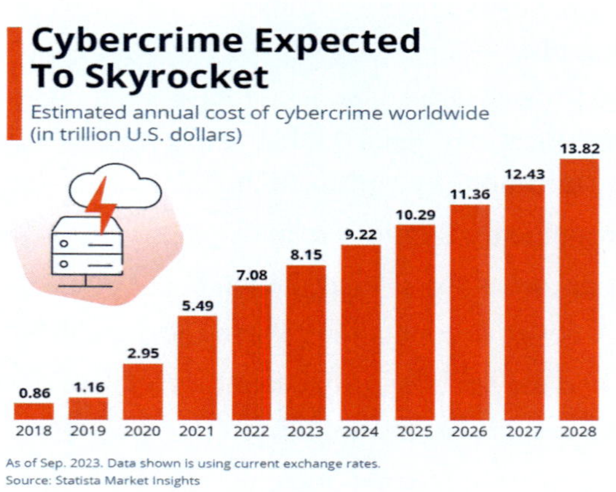

Figure 2.3. *The global cost of cybercrime.*

Source: Fleck (2024).

2.7.3. Statistics Surrounding Cybercrime on a Global Scale

When considering the strength of cyber defenses among nations, it is important to analyze various factors that contribute to their effectiveness. Factors such as investment in cybersecurity infrastructure, government policies, and the level of collaboration between public and private sectors all play a crucial role. By examining these aspects, we can gain a better understanding of which nation may have the most robust cyber defenses.

According to the National Cyber Security Index, it has been found that Poland is leading the way in terms of cyber security (Broadhurst & Chantler, 2006). The NCSI assesses a country's ability to effectively mitigate cyber threats and manage cyber incidents. As of December 2023, the top five nations with the highest NCSI scores are:

- Poland: 90.83
- Estonia: 85.83
- Ukraine: 80.83
- Latvia: 79.17
- United Kingdom: 75.00

Identifying the organizations that are particularly susceptible to cybercrime is a crucial endeavor. It is essential to understand the factors that contribute to their vulnerability. By examining various aspects such as their security measures, data protection protocols, and technological infrastructure, we can gain insights into the organizations that are at higher risk. This knowledge can then be utilized to develop targeted strategies and interventions to mitigate cyber threats effectively.

In the year 2021, there was a significant increase in the number of attacks targeting Asian organizations on a global scale. Below is a breakdown of assaults against organizations by continent in 2021:

- Asia accounts for 26% of the total.
- Europe accounts for 24% of the total.
- North America accounts for 23% of the total.
- Africa and the Middle East account for 14% of the total.
- Latin America accounts for 13% of the Americas.

The UK has seen a significant increase in cybercrime victims, with a staggering 40% rise from 2020. In 2022, there were 4783 victims per million internet users, solidifying the UK's position as a global leader in this unfortunate statistic. In 2022, the United States of America secured the second spot in terms of victims per million internet users. The number stood at 1494, reflecting a 13% decrease compared to 2020. According to Broadhurst and Chantler (2006), it was found that in 2021, a significant number of internet users in North America experienced a breach of their accounts. This highlights the alarming rate at which online security is being compromised.

When we examine the cybercrime statistics of various nations, it becomes evident that the UK and the USA stand out with a significantly higher number of victims per million internet users. In the year 2021, the USA witnessed a staggering 759% increase in victims compared to Canada, which held the second-highest position.

The Netherlands has experienced the largest surge in victims, with a staggering 50% increase compared to the previous year. Greece has seen a significant decrease in the number of victims, with a staggering 75% decline compared to the previous year.

In 2021, data breaches occurred at an alarming rate, with an average of 97 victims every hour worldwide. Between May 2020 and May 2021, there was a significant increase of 168% in cybercrime in the Asia-Pacific region. During the month of May 2021, Japan experienced a significant increase in cyberattacks compared to other months of the same year, with a rise of 40% (Broadhurst & Chantler, 2006). During the period between Q2 and Q3 of 2022, there was notable increases in data breaches across several nations.

- China has seen a significant number of compromised accounts, with a staggering 14,157,775 accounts affected, accounting for a whopping 4852% of the total.

- Japan had a staggering increase of compromised accounts, reaching a whopping 1,246,373, which represents a significant surge of 1423%.
- South Korea has experienced a significant number of compromised accounts, totaling 1,669,124. This accounts for a staggering 1007% of the total compromised accounts.

2.8. THE CHALLENGES OF CYBERCRIME

Cybercrime investigation and surveillance encounter significant issues and challenges.

2.8.1. Technical Challenges

Every computer that has access to the Internet has the ability to communicate with any other device that is also connected to the Internet. When a computer establishes a connection with our system, it is possible for us to access the public IP address associated with that computer. The IP address, being a universally unique number, allows us to identify the country and internet service provider from which the device is connected. One concern arises when an attacker is able to conceal their IP address or employ a counterfeit one, giving the impression that they are connecting from a different IP address. In addition, it is worth noting that criminals have the ability to hide and obscure their access to darknet sites through various methods in order to evade detection by law enforcement (Baharudin, 2022).

Another technical problem revolves around software. Software is the essential component that enables the operation of computers. Software encompasses not only the programs you use, but also the online services you interact with, such as websites. It is a well-known fact that software vulnerabilities are quite prevalent. A vulnerability refers to a potential problem in a software or a misconfiguration that can grant unauthorized access to sensitive information, such as downloading credit card details of customers.

Identifying vulnerabilities can pose a significant challenge for software businesses, especially when dealing with extensive and constantly evolving software projects. At times, attackers are able to discover a zero-day vulnerability before the program manufacturer does. When it comes to the impacted software, it's unfortunate that patching is not an option. Additionally, it's worth noting that even anti-virus programs with signature-based scanning capabilities are unable to detect the attack in question due to the unknown vulnerability. When hackers exploit vulnerabilities to compromise the availability, confidentiality, or integrity of software and its users, the company becomes aware of it (Baharudin, 2022).

2.8.2. Legal Obstacles

Cybercrime is a pervasive issue that knows no boundaries. It has the potential to impact anyone, regardless of their location or online presence. Access to and cross-border data sharing are often essential for cybercrime investigators due to the nature of their work.

According to Baharudin (2022), achieving the goal of retaining desired data and establishing mechanisms for law enforcement agencies to access it is possible. One of the main challenges in investigating and prosecuting cybercrime lies in the differences between national cybercrime laws, legal systems, and criminal procedure and evidence rules across different nations. These disparities can create obstacles for law enforcement agencies when it comes to obtaining digital evidence. For example, whether or not a court order is obtained, the application and scope of regional and multilateral cybercrime treaties can vary.

2.8.3. Ethical Challenges

Law enforcement organizations are responsible for the management, evaluation, and interpretation of evidence during the course of their legal and moral investigations into various crimes, including cybercrimes. Information and communication technology (ICT) raises ethical concerns for various stakeholders, including individuals, groups, businesses, organizations, and governments. When it comes to using ICT ethically, it is crucial to avoid causing harm to individuals, systems, or data, and to always uphold the law and respect human rights (Baharudin, 2022).

2.8.4. Operational Challenges

Collaborating with international partners to address cybercrime investigations poses a considerable operational challenge. It is imperative to establish harmonized rules among cooperating nations in order to facilitate international collaboration on cybercrime investigations. Requests for aid from one nation to another can be made through instruments such as mutual legal assistance treaties. These treaties are agreements between countries to collaborate in the investigation and prosecution of offenses that are illegal under their respective national laws. Foreign assistance requests, unfortunately, often fail to yield the desired outcomes such as crime prevention or the production of court-admissible evidence. Moreover, these requests can be time-consuming (Baharudin, 2022).

CHAPTER 3

CYBERSECURITY

Contents

Cybersecurity refers to the practice of protecting internet-connected systems, such as data, software, and hardware, from cyberthreats (Craigen et al., 2014). Both individuals and businesses utilize it to protect against unauthorized access to data centers and other digital systems.

Cyber security is of utmost importance as it safeguards individuals and organizations against cyberattacks and the potential compromise or theft of valuable information. Cybersecurity is responsible for monitoring systems that protect confidential government data, trade secrets, intellectual property, and personal data such as personally identifiable information (PII), protected health information (PHI), and financial information (Craigen et al., 2014).

The following are the primary benefits of implementing cyber security measures for businesses:

1. *Ensures the Protection of Personal Information*: Personal data is an invaluable asset, whether for businesses or individual users. Malware possesses the capability to collect personal data and put at risk the privacy of organizations, employees, or consumers. Cybersecurity protects information from various types of risks, including both intentional and unintentional threats, allowing employees to freely use the internet without worrying about cyberattacks (Craigen et al., 2014).
2. *Assists in Preserving Reputation*. Establishing customer retention and brand loyalty for a company requires a significant amount of time and effort. Data breaches have a significant negative impact on the reputation of a business. Companies can mitigate unforeseen disruptions by implementing a robust cyber security system. Cloud and network security technologies, such as authentication and access controls, can enhance security measures. This may facilitate the emergence of proposals, initiatives, and advancements in the future (Craigen et al., 2014).
3. *Enhances Productivity*: With the progression of technology, criminals are employing increasingly sophisticated methods to infiltrate and manipulate data. Viruses negatively impact networks, workflows, and overall functioning, resulting in decreased productivity. The company's service disruption could lead to a state of stagnation within the organization. A key advantage of cybersecurity is its potential to enhance business productivity by leveraging tools such as automated data backups and advanced firewalls.
4. *Assists in Managing the Remote Office*: Thanks to the remote working model, employees can now access a diverse range of remote models

for their workflows from different locations. The dissemination of sensitive data across the globe, where cybercrimes may occur through IoT, Wi-Fi, and personal devices, can be unsettling for businesses. Ensuring the security of sensitive data is crucial for companies, as the rise in remote work has led to a significant increase in the average financial impact of data breaches, amounting to $137,000. Strategies, analytics, and sensitive data are consistently vulnerable to hacking and unauthorized disclosure. However, cyber security measures can effectively prevent the tracking of users' data through home Wi-Fi networks and provide a secure environment for data storage (Craigen et al., 2014).

5. *Compliance with Regulations:* Regulations such as GDPR, SOC, PCI DSS, HIPAA, and SOC play a crucial role in protecting the interests of both individuals and businesses. Breaking these rules leads to significant repercussions.
6. *Improves One's Online Presence and Security:* Cybersecurity provides comprehensive digital security for businesses, enabling employees to freely, flexibly, and safely access the internet. By simply clicking on a unified dashboard, advanced cyber security technology monitors each machine in real-time. Implementing this strategy enhances cybersecurity protocols to mitigate threats and empowers organizations to automate their responses, ensuring smoother operations in the event of a cyberattack (Craigen et al., 2014).
7. *Enhanced Data Management Capabilities:* Data forms the fundamental basis for both product development and marketing strategy. If data is compromised and falls into the hands of competitors or hackers, it could potentially enable other businesses to begin anew and obtain a competitive edge. Therefore, it is imperative for companies to consistently verify their data to ensure the accurate implementation of data security protocols.
8. *Facilitates the Training and Education of Workers:* By educating employees about potential risks such as ransomware, data breaches, malware, and other security threats, you can enhance the level of protection implemented in your company's daily activities. The staff members will exhibit increased resilience against phishing attacks and possess the necessary knowledge to respond appropriately in the event of any mishap (Craigen et al., 2014).
9. *Enhances the Preservation of Credibility and Confidence:* When there is a robust cyber security system in place, customers and investors can have increased confidence and trust. Violations of

conditions have a detrimental impact on an organization's reputation, resulting in a significant decrease in its audience. Conversely, when a company demonstrates a consistent history of safeguarding client and business data, it experiences an expansion in its customer base.

10. *Streamline the Authorization Procedure*: Organizations gain a sense of control over every activity by effectively managing both internal and external processes. Businesses can establish accountability for strategic management by prioritizing other crucial responsibilities. The expedited access to systems, computers, and resources reduces the risk of cybercrime (Craigen et al., 2014).
11. *Assists the IT Department*: Cyberattacks have a detrimental effect on sales and revenue, leading to significant disruptions in critical areas. Additionally, they can incur penalties from regulatory bodies and give rise to customer lawsuits. Cybercrimes have the ability to disrupt daily activities. With the advancement of technology, there has been an emergence of increasingly sophisticated hacking techniques. The IT staff must stay updated on the rapidly evolving internet environment. An IT team with extensive knowledge, tools, assistance, and strategies can effectively handle even the most sophisticated cybercrime.

3.1. CYBERSECURITY THREATS

Cybersecurity threats refer to deliberate actions carried out by malicious individuals with the aim of illicitly acquiring data, causing harm to computer systems, or disrupting normal operations. Common cyber threats include malware, social engineering, man-in-the-middle (MitM) attacks, denial of service (DoS), and injection assaults. Cyber threats can originate from various entities, including adversarial nations and terrorist groups, individual hackers, and trusted individuals who abuse their power to engage in malicious activities, such as contractors or employees (Liu et al., 2022).

3.1.1. Common Sources of Cyber Threats

1. *Nation States*: Nation states have the capacity to launch cyberattacks against local businesses and institutions in order to disrupt communication, create disorder, and inflict damage.
2. *Terrorist Organizations*: These engage in cyberattacks with the purpose of sabotaging or exploiting critical infrastructure, endangering national security, disrupting economies, and harming individuals.

3. *Cybercriminal Organizations and Illicit Syndicate:* They attempt to infiltrate computer systems with the intention of gaining financial benefits. These groups engage in online fraudulent activities, including scams, extortion, and the unauthorized acquisition of private information through methods such as phishing, spam, spyware, and malware (Liu al., 2022).
4. *Hackers*: Individual hackers employ various attack techniques to target businesses. Common motivations for their actions include political activism, financial gain, revenge, or personal benefit. Hackers often create new risks to enhance their criminal capabilities and gain recognition within the hacker community.
5. *Malicious Insiders*: This include individuals who have authorized access to corporate resources but exploit their position to unlawfully obtain data or undermine computer systems for personal or financial gain. Insiders refer to individuals who may include the target organization's partners, suppliers, contractors, or employees. They could potentially be individuals from outside the organization pretending to be the owner of a privileged account that has been compromised (Liu et al., 2022).
6. *Cybersecurity Threat by Malware:* They encompass various types of attacks perpetrated by malicious software, commonly known as malware. Malware, short for "malicious software," is the most widespread form of cyberattack and includes viruses, worms, trojans, spyware, and ransomware. Malware commonly infiltrates a system through an unauthorized software download, a hyperlink on an untrustworthy website, or an email. The software is installed on the intended system, where it collects confidential data, alters and blocks access to network components, and has the capability to erase data or completely disable the machine. Some of prevalent categories of malware attacks include:

- Viruses which are software applications that inject harmful code into other software applications. The malicious code executes upon the application's initiation.
- Worms which are malevolent software that exploit backdoors and vulnerabilities in operating systems to gain unauthorized access. Once the worm is introduced into the network, it has the capability to initiate distributed denial of service (DDoS) attacks
- Trojans which are malevolent programs or code that disguise themselves as reliable ones and can be encountered in email

attachments, games, and applications. Once the trojan is downloaded, an unsuspecting victim unwittingly grants it authorization to seize control of their device.

- Ransomware which is a type of malicious software that uses encryption to prevent individuals or organizations from accessing their own systems or data. There is no guarantee that paying the ransom will genuinely restore complete access or functionality. Usually, the assailant seeks compensation in return for a cryptographic key.
- Crypto jacking which is to surreptitiously install software on a target's device and exploit its processing power for the purpose of generating cryptocurrency, all without the victim's knowledge. Crypto jacking kits can have a detrimental effect on the stability of computer systems and result in a decrease in their performance.
- Spyware which enables a malicious individual to gain unauthorized access to the sensitive information of an unsuspecting user, such as passwords and credit card numbers. Mobile devices, desktop programs, and desktop browsers can all be affected by spyware.
- Adware which is a type of software that monitors a user's online activities in order to identify and analyze patterns of behavior and interests. Advertisers utilize this data to specifically tailor advertisements to the user. Adware, like spyware, does not require the user to install software on their device and may not always be used with malicious intent. However, it can still be employed without the user's consent, posing a threat to their privacy.
- Fileless malware which is a type of malicious software that does not leave any traces in the operating system's installed applications. Malicious functions can be activated by modifying core files, such as PowerShell and WMI. Antivirus programs are incapable of detecting this nuanced form of attack due to the fact that the compromised files have the appearance of being genuine.
- Rootkits which are a type of software that can be inserted into operating system kernels, firmware, applications, or hypervisors in order to provide remote administrative access to a computer. The assailant has the ability to gain complete authority over the computer, install additional malicious software, and initiate the operating system in a compromised setting.

3.2. MEASURES TO ENSURE THE SECURITY OF COMPUTER SYSTEMS AND NETWORKS

Cybersecurity measures encompass a range of proactive actions taken to safeguard networks, computers, and data from the threats posed by cybercriminals and other online hazards. The measures encompassed in this approach consist of implementing preventive actions such as limiting access to sensitive data and providing training to staff members to recognize potential risks. Additionally, technical solutions such as firewalls and antivirus programs are employed. Common measures encompass the following:

- Firewalls utilizing encryption
- Controls regulating access to antivirus software
- Security patches for intrusion detection systems
- Education for workers

3.2.1. Essential Measures for Cybersecurity

Below are the top cybersecurity practices that all businesses should implement.

1. **Zero Trust Architecture (ZTA):** This is a fundamental concept that businesses should prioritize in cybersecurity. ZTA aims to prevent unauthorized access to sensitive information and systems, even if an attacker manages to breach the network perimeter, although this is highly unlikely. ZTA, or Zero Trust Architecture, is a security framework that mandates authentication prior to granting access to any resources, as it assumes that all network traffic is untrustworthy. Consequently, comprehensive authentication and permission protocols are enforced for all users, devices, and network traffic, considering them all as potential vulnerabilities (Hubbard & Seiersen, 2023).

   The adaptability and flexibility of ZTA enable enterprises to establish customized security controls that align with their specific needs. Enhanced security can be attained by integrating it with supplementary security measures, such as Identity and Access Management (IAM) systems. When granting Zero Trust Access (ZTA), it is essential to bear in mind the following crucial principles:

- Least privilege: this refers to the practice of granting users and devices access only to the specific resources that are necessary for them to successfully carry out their assigned tasks.
- Micro-segmentation: this refers to the strict regulation of access and the division of network traffic into small, separate units.

- Continuous validation: irrespective of its origin within the network, all traffic is monitored and authenticated.
- Multiple levels of security: various security measures are implemented, including intrusion detection and prevention systems, firewalls, and unified endpoint security.

The crucial aspect of this guidance lies in recognizing that ZTA is an ongoing procedure rather than a singular occurrence. According to Hubbard and Seiersen (2023), by 2024, the use of AI-powered real-time authentication and activity monitoring will allow the zero trust security model to evolve from a technical network approach to a more flexible and all-encompassing one.

2. **Multi-factor Authentication (MFA):** Many individuals employ multifactor authentication (MFA) as a means of safeguarding their bank, email, and other online accounts. Another application for it is the management of physical access to buildings and other restricted areas. Implementing multiple authentication stages enhances the level of security by raising the barriers for hackers attempting to gain unauthorized access to a system or account (Hubbard & Seiersen, 2023). In the coming year, organizations that are implementing MFA should be aware of the three main categories of authentication factors:

- An item of knowledge-this could be a security query, a personal identification number (PIN), or a secret code used for authentication.
- An item that you possess- a smart card, security token, or smartphone can be considered as such.
- An attribute that you personify-this could potentially be a biometric scan using facial recognition or fingerprint technology.

By 2024, it is imperative for organizations to implement MFA universally, as there are minimal, if any, justifications for operating without it. Due to advancements in artificial intelligence, the integration of MFA (Multi-Factor Authentication) will become more widespread in the coming year and beyond. Artificial intelligence (AI) will enhance the ability to protect against evolving cyberthreats and enhance the speed and adaptability of authentication systems (Hubbard & Seiersen, 2023).

2. **System User Audits:** As part of a system user audit, an organization's IT environment evaluates and examines system users, also known as "accounts." The objective is to ensure that each user of the system is properly authenticated and that their access is appropriate and

secure. In the coming year, organizations can expect an increase in the demand for comprehensive system user audits that make use of the capabilities of artificial intelligence such as:

- *Enumeration of System Users:* This list serves the purpose of ensuring the absence of unauthorized accounts and the accurate approval of all accounts.
- *User roles and Permissions:* Every user is assigned a specific set of roles and permissions to ensure that they are appropriate and in line with their job responsibilities.
- *User Activity:* Monitoring and ensuring that each system user is utilizing authorized resources and fulfilling their assigned responsibilities.
- *Password Administration:* Policies and procedures regarding password administration ensure the avoidance of weak, easily guessed passwords.

Any security flaws or vulnerabilities will be identified and resolved through a combination of system user audit results and AI insights. It is recommended that organizations conduct system user audits on a quarterly basis as a standard procedure (Hubbard & Seiersen, 2023).

3.3. CYBERSECURITY TECHNOLOGIES

Presented below are several highly sought-after cybersecurity technologies.

3.3.1. Behavioral Analytics

Behavioral analytics is a method used to gather and analyze data in order to understand how users behave on websites, mobile applications, systems, and networks. Cybersecurity experts can utilize behavioral analytics platforms to detect potential risks and vulnerabilities. Analyzing patterns of activity can help identify odd occurrences and behaviors that may indicate cybersecurity risks (Kemmerer, 2003).

Behavioral analytics can identify a specific device that is generating unusually large amounts of data. This suggests that a cyberattack is likely to happen soon or may have already started. Unforeseen event timing and unanticipated action sequencing are additional indicators of malicious activity. Utilizing behavioral analytics offers two benefits: the ability to detect potential assaults at an early stage and the capability to predict future attacks. Organizations can utilize behavioral analytics to automate the process of detecting and responding to events (Kemmerer, 2003).

3.3.2. The Cube for Blockchain Symbol

Data blocks are securely stored within a database known as a blockchain. Cryptography is employed to establish a connection between the blocks. Blockchain technology enables the gathering of data while preventing any modifications or deletions. Cybersecurity experts can utilize blockchain technology to safeguard devices or systems, establish security procedures that adhere to industry standards, and effectively eradicate hacker infiltration into databases. Blockchain technology offers several advantages, including enhanced user privacy, reduced human error, improved transparency, and cost savings resulting from the elimination of third-party verification.

Furthermore, blockchain effectively addresses the security concern associated with centralized data storage. Instead, data is dispersed across networks, establishing a decentralized system that is more resistant to cyberattacks. The cost and lack of effectiveness of blockchain technology pose difficulties (Kemmerer, 2003).

3.3.3. The Cloud Encryption

Cloud services offer cost reduction, enhanced productivity, and improved capability for businesses to deliver superior remote services. Data vulnerabilities may increase if data is stored remotely in the cloud. Before being stored in the cloud, data undergoes encryption using cloud encryption technology (Figure 3.1), which converts it from a readable format into an unreadable code.

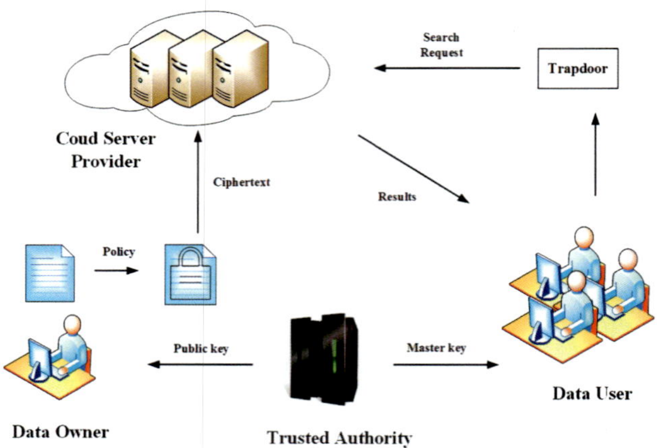

Figure 3.1. *Cloud computing cryptography.*

Source: Crasto (2021).

Cybersecurity experts employ a mathematical technique to complete cloud encryption. Data is rendered legible again when authorized users, who possess an encryption key, unlock the code. The restricted access minimizes the likelihood of unauthorized individuals compromising data. According to experts, cloud encryption is considered one of the most effective cybersecurity technologies for safeguarding data. Cloud encryption ensures that valuable data remains inaccessible to unauthorized individuals. Moreover, the implementation of cloud encryption can assist businesses in achieving better adherence to legal obligations and enhancing customer confidence in cloud services (Kemmerer, 2003).

3.3.4. The Clock Indicator

Context-aware security is a type of cybersecurity technology that helps companies make more informed security decisions in real-time. Traditional cybersecurity approaches employ binary inquiries to ascertain whether or not an individual should be granted authorization to access a system or data. The denial of some valid users may impede productivity due to a straightforward process (Kemmerer, 2003). Context-aware security reduces the probability of denying access to a valid user. Context-aware security verifies a user's authenticity by considering various corroborating factors, including time, location, and URL reputation, instead of relying solely on answers to yes-or-no questions. Context-aware security enhances the efficiency of data-accessing procedures for authorized users. However, there is a concern regarding the privacy of end-users.

3.4.5. The Shield-Check Symbol

Cybersecurity professionals can utilize defensive artificial intelligence (AI) to detect and prevent cyberattacks. Due to the increased complexity of technologies such as adversarial machine learning and hostile artificial intelligence, conventional cybersecurity methods struggle to identify them, allowing cunning hackers to exploit their capabilities.

Offensive artificial intelligence encompasses deepfakes, which are fabricated personas, images, and videos that convincingly depict individuals or events that are either non-existent or never occurred. Malicious actors can exploit adversarial machine learning to manipulate machines into malfunctioning by feeding them with false data. Cybersecurity experts can employ defensive artificial intelligence (AI) to detect and prevent offensive AI from attempting to assess, test, and integrate into the operations of the system or network. Defensive AI can enhance algorithms, rendering them more resistant to being deciphered. According to Kemmerer (2003), researchers in the field of cybersecurity have the ability to subject machine learning models to more thorough vulnerability testing

3.3.6. Extended Detection and Response (XDR)

Extended detection and response (XDR) is an advanced cybersecurity technology that identifies and resolves security threats and incidents. XDR responds to networks, cloud, and endpoints. It evolved from the traditional endpoint detection and response. XDR establishes connections between data from multiple sources in order to present a more comprehensive and holistic representation. This technology enables cybersecurity experts to identify and assess threats at a more sophisticated and automated level. This can mitigate or reduce the risk of data breaches in both the current and future contexts across the entire asset ecosystem of a business. XDR is a valuable tool for cybersecurity professionals to effectively address and detect targeted attacks, automatically verify and link alerts, and generate comprehensive analytics. XDR offers several benefits, including robust automatic detection, streamlined automation of repetitive tasks, and a reduction in the number of incidents that require investigation.

3.3.7. The Manufacturer Usage Description (MUD)

The manufacturer usage description (MUD) standard was created by the internet engineering task force with the aim of enhancing security for internet of things (IoT) devices in household and small business networks. Internet of things devices can be targeted by network-based attacks. These intrusions possess the capacity to obliterate confidential information or incapacitate a machine. IoT devices should possess safety features while maintaining affordability and simplicity. Utilizing MUD offers various benefits, including enhanced and more cost-effective security for IoT devices. Cybersecurity experts can utilize MUD to enhance device defenses against distributed denial-of-service attacks. In the event of a successful attack, MUD can help mitigate the damage and prevent data loss.

3.3.8. The Zero Trust Concept

The principle of conventional network security was “trust but verify,” assuming that users within the network perimeter of an organization did not pose any threat to the enterprise. On the other hand, zero trust follows the principle of “never trust, always verify.” Zero trust is a network security paradigm that mandates user authentication as a prerequisite for accessing any data or applications within an organization. The fundamental concept of zero trust is that network users cannot be assumed to be more trustworthy than external entities (Kemmerer, 2003). The organization’s overall information security may enhance as a consequence of this more rigorous scrutiny of all users (Figure 3.2).

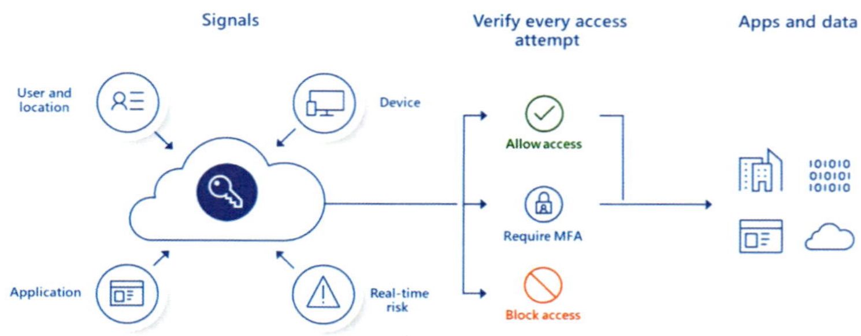

Figure 3.2. *Zero trust security model.*

Source: GlobalDots (2022).

3.4. CYBERSECURITY BEST PRACTICES

Undoubtedly, cybercrime is one of the fastest-growing crimes worldwide, continuing to impact companies in all industries. To prevent your business or organization's name from being publicized as a result of a security breach, it is crucial to stay updated on the latest cybersecurity best practices and advice. Nevertheless, ensuring your security against cyberattacks poses a challenging task. Staying ahead of fraudsters who are continuously seeking new ways to expose security weaknesses is a difficult task (Mughal, 2019). Nevertheless, there are several cybersecurity guidelines that can help prevent online threats.

- *Please Ensure That You Update Your Software:* Software updates are typically issued by software companies with the primary objectives of improving security, resolving known software glitches, and introducing new features. It is essential to regularly update your software to the latest version in order to protect yourself from any new or existing security vulnerabilities.
- *Avoid Clicking on Suspicious Emails:* Refrain from accessing emails that appear suspicious, as they could potentially be fraudulent attempts to obtain personal information through phishing. There is a possibility that an individual is utilizing a fraudulent identity in order to gain unauthorized access to your confidential information. Emails may sometimes include hyperlinks or attachments that have the potential to damage your electronic devices (Mughal, 2019).
- *Upgrade Your Hardware:* Obsolete computer hardware may not be compatible with the most recent software security updates. Moreover, antiquated equipment hinders the speed of response

during a cyberattack. Make sure you are utilizing contemporary computer hardware.

- *Use a Robust File-Sharing Program to Encrypt Data*: If you regularly exchange sensitive information, it is imperative that you promptly adopt a secure file-sharing platform. It is not advisable to send sensitive documents through regular email because doing so raises the likelihood of unauthorized individuals intercepting one's messages and gaining access to valuable information.
- *Using a Secure File-Sharing Service:* Using a secure file-sharing service like TitanFile ensures protection against data breaches by automatically encrypting sensitive information. The security of files is contingent upon the selection of tools used for sharing them (Mughal, 2019).
- *Employ Malware and Antivirus Software:* Attaining absolute security against malware is unattainable as long as one maintains an internet connection. However, by ensuring that your personal computers are equipped with both an antivirus program and at least one anti-malware program, you can significantly reduce your vulnerability.
- *Use a Virtual Private Network (VPN) to Ensure the Privacy of Your Connections:* Employ a virtual private network (VPN) to establish a network that is both more confidential and secure. Your connection will undergo encryption, ensuring that your personal data remains concealed from unauthorized individuals, including your internet service provider (Mughal, 2019).
- *Prioritize Inspecting Hyperlinks Before Selecting Them:* It is prudent to thoroughly verify before clicking on a hyperlink as they can be easily misrepresented. On the majority of web browsers, when you hover over a link, the target URL will be displayed. Prior to clicking on any links, it is advisable to verify their authenticity.
- *Exercising Diligence While Generating Passwords:* Exert more diligence when devising passwords. To assess the security level of your passwords, employ a tool like howsecureismypassword.net.
- *Disable Bluetooth When Not in Use:* Through the use of Bluetooth, devices can be vulnerable to compromise, resulting in the potential theft of your personal data. Disable your Bluetooth if it is not necessary.
- *Enable Two-Factor Authentication:* In order to enhance the security of your accounts, it is now possible to establish 2-factor authentication on numerous platforms. This supplementary security measure helps

to verify that you are the legitimate user accessing your account, rather than an unauthorized individual. At your earliest convenience, activate this security feature.

- *Remove Any Adware from Your Computers:* Adware collects personal data to display more targeted advertisements. To safeguard your privacy, it is advisable to eliminate all adware from your computer. AdwCleaner can effectively eliminate adware and unwanted programs from your computer.
- *Double-Check Websites for HTTPS Verification:* There is no guarantee of the security of information exchanged between you and the server of a website that does not use the HTTPS protocol. Prior to disclosing sensitive or private information, it is advisable to confirm a website's utilization of HTTPS on two separate occasions (Mughal, 2019).
- *Refrain from Storing Confidential Information in Insecure Locations:* It is advisable to securely store online information in a location that is inaccessible to unauthorized individuals.
- *Scan External Storage Devices for Malware:* Malware has the ability to infect both internal and external storage devices with equal effectiveness. Connecting an infected external device to your PC could lead to the rapid spread of the infection. Before utilizing an external device, it is imperative to ensure that it is devoid of any malicious software.
- *Avoid Using Public Networks:* When you connect to a public network, you are essentially sharing the network with all other users who are also connected. Any data that you send or receive on the network is vulnerable to being accessed or intercepted. It is advisable to refrain from using unsecured networks. In the event that you do connect to one, it is recommended to utilize a Virtual Private Network (VPN) for added security (Mughal, 2019).

3.5. TRAINING IN THE FIELD OF CYBERSECURITY

Cybersecurity serves as our protective shield in a society where our lives are becoming more and more intertwined with the digital realm.

As technology advances, various threats such as malware, data breaches, phishing attempts, and others continue to arise. Cybersecurity education acts as our safeguard against these imperceptible adversaries.

3.5.1 The Importance of Cybersecurity Training Awareness

Cybersecurity education enhances our understanding of the potential risks. It should be utilized by all individuals, not exclusively those with expertise in information technology. This encompasses chief executive officers, staff members, grandparents, and students.

- *Skills Acquisition*: We acquire the capacity to identify phishing emails, generate robust passwords, and protect sensitive information. Practicing cyber hygiene becomes second nature.
- *Capacity for Adaptation:* Cybersecurity training equips us with the necessary knowledge and skills to anticipate and defend against new methods of attack, enabling us to maintain a competitive advantage (Nagarajan et al., 2012).

3.5.2. Target Audience Corporate World

Employees regularly undergo training to recognize suspicious connections, safeguard corporate assets, and understand regulatory compliance. Students in educational institutions are instructed in digital citizenship, ethical hacking, and responsible online behavior. Government organizations, comprised of cybersecurity experts, protect the national interests. They undergo continuous and rigorous training (Nagarajan et al., 2012).

3.5.3. Important Cybersecurity Threat Environment Components for Training

- *Writing secure code*: Acquiring the skill to write robust and secure code is essential for developers.
- *Incident response*: The set of procedures to be followed in the event of a breach, which include containing the breach, eradicating the threat, and recovering from the incident.
- *Ethical hacking*: Cultivating a hacker mindset to enhance defensive strategies.

3.5.4. Challenges and Advancements Human Vulnerability

Individuals remain the most susceptible. Training should focus on addressing human vulnerabilities. This include:

- *Continuous Education*: Cyberthreats are constantly evolving. Ongoing training is more favorable than single-session instruction.
- *Gamification*: This involves engaging learners through interactive instruction that is based on scenarios. Conducting cyberattack

simulations enhances the ability to withstand and recover from cyber threats.

Staying abreast of the latest cybersecurity threats is crucial in our dynamic and constantly evolving digital landscape. Here are several effective strategies for individuals to remain up-to-date:

a. *Stay Informed:* Achieve this by following trustworthy blogs and news outlets that specialize in cybersecurity.

b. *Engage with Experts in the Field of Cybersecurity:* Utilize social media platforms to track the activities and updates of researchers, professionals, and organizations within the specific field of interest. You can remain informed about the most recent progress by accessing their shared information and insights.

c. *Enroll in Notifications and Newsletters:* Subscribe to receive notifications and newsletters from reputable cybersecurity companies, government organizations, and industry leaders. These typically comprise analysis, threat intelligence, and useful guidance.

d. *Participate in Live Events and Webinars:* Engage in workshops, conferences, and webinars. These events serve as a platform for experts to engage in discussions about the latest trends, potential risks, and strategies to reduce or prevent them.

d. *Validate Risk and Vulnerability Advisory Feeds*: Websites like the National Institute of Standards and Technologies (NIST) monitor and keep records of common vulnerabilities. To remain informed, regularly monitor their updates.

e. *Access Podcasts Focused on the Topic of Cybersecurity*: Podcasts address topics related to cybersecurity and offer interviews, discussions, and valuable perspectives. They provide a convenient method for learning while mobile.

3.6. CYBERSECURITY POLICIES

Businesses' data and systems are susceptible to a multitude of risks. A multitude of cyberattacks specifically focus on company employees, exploiting their negligence or employing social engineering and phishing tactics to manipulate them into taking action.

The rise of remote work has raised new concerns due to the widespread adoption of BYOD policies and the potential connection of hacked devices to corporate networks (Harknett & Stever, 2011). Cybersecurity guidelines help protect the company against online attacks and ensure compliance with applicable laws. These rules mitigate an organization's risk by instructing staff members to abstain from certain behaviors. Additionally, they can enhance the effectiveness of incident response by providing guidelines for the identification, cessation, and resolution of issues (Harknett & Stever, 2011).

3.6.1. Types of Cybersecurity Policies

An organization has the option to utilize a range of cyber security protocols. Some of the most popular options include:

- *IT Security Policy*: The IT security policy of an organization establishes the guidelines and practices to protect the company from online attacks. An IT security policy encompasses various components such as the proper utilization of company resources, incident response plans, business continuity plans, and the organization's approach to achieving and maintaining regulatory compliance (Harknett & Stever, 2011).
- *The Email Security Policy*: This is designed to protect the company from ransomware, phishing scams, and spam by establishing guidelines for the appropriate use of corporate email systems. Additionally, it aids in the prevention of misuse of corporate email. This type of policy not only includes specific instructions on how to deal with suspicious links and email attachments, but also encompasses general guidelines for the proper and acceptable use of corporate email (Harknett & Stever, 2011).
- *BYOD Policy*: The act of bringing your personal device to the workplace is subject to specific guidelines outlined in a BYOD policy. When accessing corporate networks and IT assets through an untrusted network, these policies usually define security requirements for these devices, including the use of an endpoint security solution, robust passwords, and virtual private networks (VPNs).

3.6.2. Who is Responsible for Formulating Cybersecurity Policy?

A cyber security policy can have a significant impact on multiple departments within the company and carries wide-ranging consequences. For example, the IT personnel may be responsible for implementing the policy, while the legal or HR departments may be responsible for enforcing it (Harknett & Stever, 2011).

Therefore, a team consisting of individuals from various fields such as IT, legal, HR, and management should be formed to develop and supervise IT policy. This ensures that the policy can be effectively implemented through technical measures or disciplinary measures, and that it aligns with the company's strategic objectives and relevant regulations (Harknett & Stever, 2011).

3.6.3. Guide to Creating a Cybersecurity Policy

The subsequent steps outline the primary stages involved in the multi-stage process of formulating a cyber security policy:

- *Analyze the Potential Areas of Vulnerability*: Different policies are designed to address specific risks and threats that could impact the organization. The initial step in formulating a policy is to acquire a comprehensive understanding of the systems and procedures that require regulation, such as the utilization of personal devices for work purposes.
- *Identify Applicable Requirements:* Company security objectives and legal obligations, such as HIPAA and PCI DSS, are examples of external and internal factors that can impact a company's cybersecurity policy. The subsequent stage in the development of a cyber security policy involves establishing the specific criteria that the policy must adhere to.
- *Formulate the Policy*: The policy should be formulated once the requirements have been established. This task should be completed by a committee comprising individuals from the IT, legal, HR, and management departments.
- *User Input*: A cyber security policy is most successful when it is comprehensible and easily comprehended by staff members. Soliciting input from staff members who are not affiliated with the policy group can help in averting miscommunications and associated issues (Harknett & Stever, 2011).
- *Provide Training to Employees*: After the policy is created, it needs to be disseminated throughout the entire company. To ensure staff members' compliance with these policies, it is imperative that they also undergo training on them.
- *Revise the Policy Often*: Regulations can become outdated and their specifications can change. In order to maintain their relevance, it is necessary to regularly inspect and revise them.

3.7. COMPLIANCE WITH CYBERSECURITY MEASURES

In the realm of cyber security, compliance entails adhering to regulations and guidelines pertaining to safeguarding data and ensuring information security, thereby mitigating the potential financial and legal liabilities associated with non-compliance. In order to safeguard valuable information resources, it is required that organizations implement relevant technical measures and strictly follow established security guidelines (Mohammed, 2015).

Although compliance requirements vary across industries and sectors, they often necessitate the adoption of specific organizational protocols and technologies to protect data. Various cybersecurity compliance standards, such as ISO 27001, the NIST Cybersecurity Framework, and CIS, offer controls (Mohammed, 2015).

Ensuring cybersecurity compliance is imperative. Cybersecurity compliance standards provide a systematic approach to protecting confidential client information, thereby increasing credibility and trust in the market. It decreases the probability of data breaches and conveys the organization's dedication to upholding secure business protocols. Given that cyber security is not the highest priority at that particular moment, small and medium-sized businesses (SMBs) are typically the ones that are targeted. This facilitates the exploitation of vulnerabilities by hackers, enabling them to carry out expensive and destructive cyberattacks. Small businesses derive the greatest advantage from cyber compliance as it is simpler to adhere to pre-established guidelines rather than establishing a large security team to fulfill their requirements (Mohammed, 2015).

3.7.1. Key Factors That Emphasize the Importance of Adhering to Cyber Security Regulations for Businesses

Safeguards Their Reputation: A cyberattack can result in sensitive data theft, disruption of company operations, unwanted media attention, reduced customer confidence, and legal consequences. Rectifying the damage may necessitate a substantial investment of labor and time.

Ensures the Preservation of Trust from Consumers or Clients: A company can ensure the safe handling of client data by maintaining a robust security posture and adhering to compliance regulations. It simplifies the process of signing corporate contracts and serves as an indication of well-planned and executed internal procedures.

Assists in the Identification, Assessment, and Preparation for Potential Data breaches: Organizations must proactively prepare for possible data breaches and other cybersecurity vulnerabilities while following a structured framework. Furthermore, the development of these plans also enhances their future security.

Enhances the Security Posture of a Business: Becoming compliant necessitates a substantial amount of effort and meticulousness towards security.

The overall security posture of a company improves once it achieves compliance. Several advantages have a direct impact on the financial stability of a company. It is widely recognized that establishing a solid reputation, earning the trust and confidence of clients, and sustaining these relationships are essential factors for achieving success.

3.7.2. Regulations Regarding Different Categories of Cyber Security Compliance

While numerous cyber security compliances exist, corporations typically only engage with a limited number of them. Here are some essential cyber compliances (Figure 3.3):

1. SOC 2, also known as Service Organization Control 2, is an audit report that assesses the policies and practices implemented by service companies to safeguard customer information. The SOC 2 framework is built upon the Trust Services Criteria established by the American Institute of Certified Public Accountants (AICPA). SOC 2 compliance necessitates adherence to security, accessibility, processing integrity, confidentiality, and privacy standards (Mohammed, 2015).
2. HIPAA stands for the Health Insurance Portability and Accountability Act. The United States enacted the Health Insurance Portability and Accountability Act (HIPAA) as a federal law in 1996 to safeguard the confidentiality and security of personal health information. Healthcare providers, health plans, and other covered organizations are required to implement specific security measures under HIPAA in order to protect the confidentiality and integrity of patient protected health information (PHI). This encompasses various security measures, such as password security, encryption, access controls, and periodic evaluations of security risks, which include physical, technical, and administrative aspects. HIPAA is applicable to all health plans, clearinghouses, and healthcare providers that engage in the electronic transmission of protected health information (PHI). This also applies to any business associates who may acquire Protected Health Information (PHI) on their behalf. Violations of HIPAA standards can result in significant financial penalties and legal consequences (Mohammed, 2015).
3. The Payment Card Industry Data Security Standard (PCI DSS) ensures that credit card data is securely protected in all businesses. Yearly verification is necessary to ensure organizational compliance.

Failure to comply with PCI DSS can lead to significant financial penalties, higher transaction expenses, decreased revenue, and harm to a company's reputation. Companies handling credit card information must take necessary measures to ensure compliance with the standard (Mohammed, 2015).

4. The ISO 27001 standard is a set of guidelines and requirements for implementing an information security management system. Organizations can utilize the ISO 27001 framework, which consists of best practices and procedures, to effectively handle information security risks and protect sensitive data. Businesses are required to establish and implement a systematic approach to identify, evaluate, and manage information security risks in compliance with the standard. Furthermore, it requires enterprises to implement various security protocols to mitigate these risks.

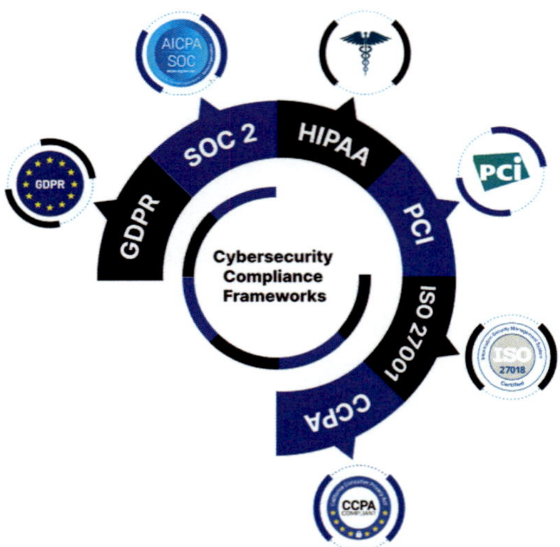

Figure 3.3. *Key cybersecurity compliance frameworks.*

Source: Arora (2023).

3.8. RESPONSE IN CASE OF CYBERSECURITY INCIDENTS

Organizations employ a systematic approach known as incident response to identify and resolve cybersecurity incidents. The National Institute of Standards and Technology (NIST) framework for incident response consists of four lifecycle stages: containment, eradication, and recovery; detection and analysis; preparation and prevention; and post-incident activities (Thompson, 2018) (Figure 3.4).

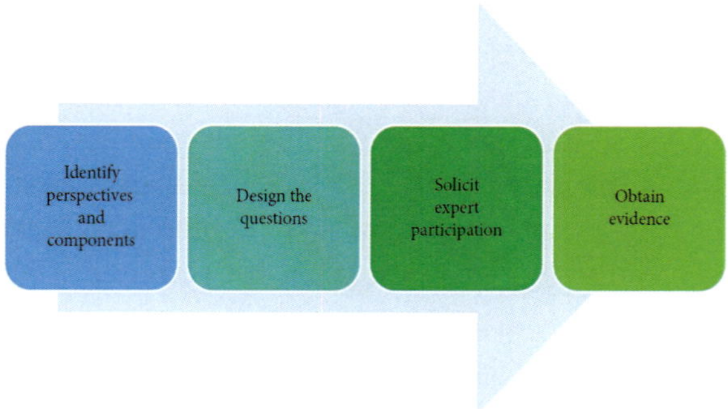

Figure 3.4. *Four steps to an effective security incident response according to NIST 800–61.*

Source: Faham (2023).

1. **The Incident Response Lifecycle:** This refers to the systematic process followed by organizations to handle and manage security incidents effectively. Organizations employ a systematic approach known as the incident response lifecycle to manage and resolve cybersecurity incidents. The lifecycle encompasses all essential measures to protect an organization's assets, mitigate damage, and ensure a swift recovery after security breaches occur (Thompson, 2018).

The incident response lifecycle is crucial for several reasons.

- *Mitigating Harm:* Swiftly confining threats reduces the extent of damage to systems and data. This is accomplished through a methodical response.
- *Enhancing Recovery Time:* Organizations can mitigate downtime and operational harm by expediting the recovery process through the implementation of a well-defined plan and established procedures.
- *Enhancing Security Posture*: Organizations can bolster their defenses and enhance their readiness for future incidents by regularly assessing and enhancing their incident response protocol.
- *Ensuring Compliance:* Organizations must possess incident response plans in order to adhere to various regulatory frameworks. Adhering to a designated duration of existence helps in meeting these responsibilities and preventing penalties.

2. **The NIST Incident Response Four Stages:** These are a framework that outlines the steps involved in responding to a security incident.

- *Create an Inventory of Your IT Assets:* This encompasses servers, networks, and endpoints. Indicate the significance of each asset, distinguishing between those that are important, crucial, and contain sensitive data. This will aid in devising contingency plans for potential emergencies. Implement surveillance measures to establish a standard reference point for normal behavior. Determine the security event categories that require additional investigation and create thorough response plans for common types of incidents.
- *Analysis and Assessment*: The detection process involves collecting data from individuals within and outside the organization, security tools, IT systems, and publicly accessible information. Precursors are early indications that an incident may happen in the future, while indicators are data that show that an attack has already occurred or is currently happening. Analyzing the impacted systems involves establishing a baseline or standard activity, identifying similar instances, and assessing any deviations from typical behavior.
- *Elimination, Restoration, and Control:* The objective of containment is to halt the advancing force before it exhausts resources or inflicts damage. The magnitude of the potential harm, the imperative to uphold critical services for personnel and customers, and the duration of the resolution—whether it is a temporary remedy lasting a few hours, days, or weeks, or a permanent solution—will all impact your strategy for containment. It is crucial to identify the host that is carrying out the attack and verify its IP address in order to effectively control and limit the impact of the attack. Furthermore, by identifying the threat actor and obstructing their communication, you can also proactively search for and terminate any additional means of communication that the attacker may be employing (Thompson, 2018).

After effectively containing the incident, it is imperative to take measures to completely remove any remnants of it from the surroundings during the eradication and recovery phase. This may involve identifying all compromised hosts, eradicating malware, and revoking or altering passwords for compromised user accounts. Once the threat has been eradicated, promptly reinstate systems and resume normal operations while implementing measures to prevent future attacks on the same assets (Thompson, 2018).

- *After the Occurrence:* Utilizing past events to improve the process is a crucial element of the NIST incident response methodology (Thompson, 2018). You should formulate the following inquiries, investigate them, and document the answers:

i. Please provide specific details about the time and nature of the event.
ii. How effectively did the incident response team handle the situation?
iii. Were the procedures followed and were they effective?
iv. Which information was urgently required?
v. Were any ill-advised decisions made that impeded the process of healing or resulted in harm?
vi. If faced with a similar scenario in the future, what measures could the staff undertake to avert its recurrence?
vii. Could employees have enhanced their communication with other departments or groups in a more efficient manner?
viii. Have we devised effective measures to prevent the recurrence of such incidents?
ix. Have we discovered any novel indications or cautionary signals of comparable circumstances that we should be vigilant for in the future?
x. What additional resources or tools are necessary to effectively prevent or reduce similar incidents?

CHAPTER 4

CYBERCRIME AND LAW ENFORCEMENT

Contents

Internet service providers must work together effectively in order for law enforcement to investigate cybercrime, as this is frequently not possible without their assistance (Broadhurst, 2006). Law enforcement is responsible for enforcing the law, whereas service providers are in charge of giving users the means of communication. Many nations are faced with the dilemma of how to best collaborate in order to increase Internet safety while simultaneously honoring their respective roles and users' fundamental rights (Broadhurst, 2006). Clear legislation that outlines roles, authorities, and limitations is an essential component of the solution and, in many respects, a prerequisite for cooperation. In this regard, it is imperative that the Convention on Cybercrime be fully implemented, paying particular attention to its procedural law provisions. Conversations in numerous nations across the globe have demonstrated the want for workable rules that can assist law enforcement and service providers in planning and arranging their collaboration (Broadhurst, 2006).

4.1. ROLE OF LAW ENFORCEMENT IN CYBERCRIME

Protecting our digital world and fighting cybercrime are major tasks for law enforcement. Below are what their duties are:

1. **Investigation and Arrest:** Law enforcement organizations look into a variety of cybercrimes, including as fraud, theft, and the exploitation of minors. They put forth endless effort to locate and detain people accountable for online crimes.
2. **Encouraging Safer Online Conduct:** Attorneys and judges remind the public that actions taken online have serious repercussions, just like they do offline. They aggressively urge safe online behavior and raise awareness of cybersecurity.
3. **Partnerships and Cooperation:** Universities, private companies, and internet service providers all work together with law enforcement. These collaborations improve intelligence gathering, information exchange, and teamwork in the fight against cyberattacks.
4. **Personnel Development:** It's critical to find and develop skilled employees. Officers who receive ongoing cybercrime training are more prepared to handle the changing digital landscape. Officers can track and apprehend cybercriminals using the resources they already possess if they adopt the appropriate strategy.

Thankfully, many of the tools required are already available to agencies and local police departments. To reduce the danger of cybercrime, facial recognition, video monitoring, and search technology can all be used. However, in order to employ these tools properly and effectively, departments must create cyber defense plans that enable them to deploy cutting-edge technologies for data analysis, cybercrime detection, deterrence, and capture (Thomas & Loader, 2000). Below are three tactics that law enforcement organizations need to use to combat cybercrime.

1. **Create a Plan for Cyber Defense:** Assessing areas of acute need should be the first step for agencies. There appears to be an increase in criminal behavior in the following areas: cryptocurrency, account hijacking, data theft, and cyberterrorism. Setting priorities can assist agencies in creating a plan and identifying the resources they require to address those issues (Thomas & Loader, 2000). Next, agencies ought to make a list of all the technologies they already employ and consider how best to utilize them. Among the inquiries that ought to be made are:

- Are our surveillance and recognition tools providing us with accurate, useful information?
- In what way are we utilizing that data?
- Are the instruments at our disposal strong enough to fulfill our requirements?
- Are they simple to operate? Is a more user-friendly solution required so that our officers may devote more time to finding suspects and less time to utilizing the software?

As usual, the expense will have to be assessed, but it should be weighed against the total expenses that law enforcement agencies incur while looking into cybercrimes, both in terms of monetary value and lost productivity hours. When thinking about introducing new technology, especially ones that could ultimately result in major efficiencies, agencies should take these costs into account. The funds they usually use for investigations may be used to acquire innovative solutions that would reduce the amount of time and resources needed for those investigations (Thomas & Loader, 2000).

2. Although malicious actors have long found refuge on the darknet, the issue became more serious during the COVID-19 outbreak. As more systems and users shifted to online services, more data became vulnerable. As a result, there was a substantial increase in the number of hackers pulling out cryptocurrency frauds. According to research published in the spring of 2020, in the first few months of the year, criminals may have made $1.4 billion from these crimes (Thomas & Loader, 2000). Agencies need to be able to track

bitcoin on the darknet and locate instances where data may have been compromised fast in order to counter these scams. This entails indexing and continuously monitoring darknet intelligence data to identify possibly illegal conduct, such as fraud.

The anomalies should then be able to be tracked by the police back to the start of the incident. It is crucial for officers to have access to information that enables them to pinpoint the initiator of a certain transaction, the destination of the funds, their intended purpose, and more. Officers can then utilize the information to look into the occurrence and lessen the harm (Thomas & Loader, 2000).

3. **Use AI to Gain Deeper Understanding and Expedite Resolutions:** Numerous law enforcement agencies have been early adopters of AI. It is difficult to locate a police force that does not now use image-enhancement or facial recognition technology. That's encouraging because it indicates that many of the instruments needed to combat cybercrime have already been purchased by agencies. It might not be necessary to make many more significant investments (Thomas & Loader, 2000).

   Nevertheless, law enforcement organizations need to be able to leverage the various data sources at their disposal. Information is abundant on cell phones, tablets, wireless networks, GPS, and other access points. These connections' data can be gathered, examined, and transformed into useful information that can profoundly impact investigations. Police officers can use digital evidence more quickly than ever before by first gathering the data and then analyzing it using forensic software powered by artificial intelligence. The program can find patterns in extremely complicated data sets and offer suggestions for future research directions (Thomas & Loader, 2000).

4.2. CHALLENGES FACED BY LAW ENFORCEMENT IN CYBERCRIME

4.2.1. Lack of Data Accessibility

Law enforcement may not be able to access data at all or may only be able to access extremely restricted data as part of a criminal investigation due to legislative changes like the General Data Protection Regulation (GDPR). Law enforcement faces a hurdle as a result of growing internet usage and technical advancement since it can be challenging to identify individual users from the vast volumes of data that are generated. While using cryptocurrencies like Bitcoin allows criminals to deal in the proceeds of crime with a certain level of secrecy, encryption is another weapon used by criminals to prevent incriminating data from falling into the hands of law authorities. Law enforcement suffers greatly, when necessary, data is not available, which frequently leads to investigations being put on hold or even abandoned (Ajayi, 2016).

4.2.2. Location Loss

Law enforcement faces tremendous obstacles when attempting to locate criminal infrastructure, electronic evidence, or perpetrators physically due to the use of encryption, cryptocurrencies, and other technologies like the dark web or cloud storage. Determining who is in charge of conducting investigations becomes challenging as a result of these complicated jurisdictional issues (Ajayi, 2016).

4.2.3. The Difficulties Posed by Country Legal Systems

Different European countries have different legal frameworks, which makes it very difficult to effectively investigate and prosecute cybercrime across borders. The primary distinctions have to do with what behaviors are illegal and how inquiries may be carried out. The latter greatly affects the gathering of electronic evidence and the surveillance of illicit activity on the internet, both of which are vital to any investigation into cybercrime (Ajayi, 2016).

4.2.4. Barriers to Global Collaboration

While national legal framework variations provide difficulties for collaboration amongst European member states, the absence of a global legal framework poses serious obstacles for global cooperation in general. This is especially troublesome when there are widespread cyberattacks that affect several continents. Mutual Legal Assistance is thought to be sluggish and inefficient, and evidence is frequently not obtained in a timely manner to guarantee the success of a criminal case (Ajayi, 2016).

4.2.5. Public-Private Partnership Challenges

The private sector can be essential in aiding in the dismantling of criminal infrastructures and frequently possesses the keys that enable law enforcement to obtain vital data to support investigations. Although cooperation between public and private sectors is important, there is currently no clear legal framework that specifies how the private sector can collaborate with law enforcement while guaranteeing that they are not violating the rights or privacy of their clients. Emerging technologies like artificial intelligence and quantum computing present further difficulties. Although it offers chances for detection and mitigation for the business sector and law enforcement, there is also a chance that unlawful exploitation will encourage cybercrime (Ajayi, 2016).

4.3. CYBERCRIME INVESTIGATIONS

To put it simply, it entails the following procedures:

- Locating, evaluating, and monitoring digital evidence in order to identify the offenders and their intentions.
- Studying the case and evaluating the circumstances.
- Carrying out the preliminary inquiry.
- Finding possible proof.
- Protective gadgets.
- Acquiring judicial directives.
- Reviewing the findings with the prosecutor.

Traditional investigative methods, careful planning, information collection, analysis of the evidence, and appropriate management of digital evidence are all used in this investigation. Data and information of investigative value saved on or sent by an electronic device is known as electronic evidence. These investigations have a clear objective. They try to find out who committed the crime, collect evidence, and present it in a way that will help the prosecution bring the offender to justice. Specialized methods and instruments are required for gathering and analyzing evidence because of the complexity of cybercrimes, including their sheer volume and cross-border jurisdictions. In order to successfully combine resources and experience to combat cybercrime, law enforcement agencies and business sector companies collaborate through electronic crimes task teams, which are critical to attaining these aims (Oerlemans, 2017).

4.3.1. The Process of Investigation

The initial steps entail:

- Assessing the circumstances
- Conducting a preliminary investigation
- Finding possible proof
- Protective gadgets
- Acquiring the necessary judicial orders
- Analyzing the data collected in detail

- It requires painstaking attention to detail and analytical skill, much like putting together a challenging puzzle.

  The procedure also calls for the application of particular instruments and methods. In cybercrime investigations, digital forensics is essential for gathering, safeguarding, and evaluating digital evidence. Malware detection techniques, including as intrusion detection systems, antivirus software, and sandbox settings for dynamic malware analysis, are utilized in methods of identifying dangerous software (Oerlemans, 2017).

4.3.2. Challenges in Cyber Investigations

Cyber investigations present a variety of difficulties. For example, jurisdictional concerns greatly influence cybercrime investigations since they establish who has the jurisdiction to look into and prosecute the crime depending on where the victims, offenders, and effects of the cybercrime are located. Furthermore, the worldwide scope of cybercrimes necessitates international collaboration, which presents challenges in identifying suspects, obtaining extradition, and selecting a suitable jurisdiction (Oerlemans, 2017).

The speed at which technology is developing is another problem. Cybercriminals' strategies and equipment change along with technology. Because of this, investigators must keep up with the latest advancements in technology and modify their methods of investigation accordingly. Dealing with multinational cybercriminals that operate in several nations makes these issues more complicated (Oerlemans, 2017).

4.3.3. Key Players in Cybercrime Investigations

Fighting cybercrime requires a team effort. Law enforcement authorities, trade associations, industrial bodies, and security companies are just a few of the entities involved. The FBI, Europol, Interpol, and national law enforcement agencies are the main law enforcement organizations taking part in these investigations. These organizations put out endless effort to protect our digital environment by using their knowledge to identify and bring cybercriminals to justice (Oerlemans, 2017).

To combat cybercrime, however, law enforcement is not sufficient on its own. Working together is essential. Collaborations between the public and private sectors guarantee information and resource sharing, improve institutional responses to cyber risks, and facilitate the creation of laws. Furthermore, formal structures including bilateral, regional, and multilateral cybercrime treaties are being used by international bodies to work together in the fight against cybercrime. In order to combat the growing and international nature of cybercrime, international cooperation is essential (Oerlemans, 2017).

1. **Law Enforcement Agencies:** Numerous law enforcement organizations are working on cybercrime investigations all across the world. Among them are:

- Europol
- Interpol
- The FBI, a federal agency in the United States
- The National Crime Agency (NCA) in the UK
- Federal Police of Australia (AFP)
- The RCMP, or Royal Canadian Mounted Police
- Federal Police of Germany (BKA)
- Police Nationale Française (PNF)
- The Italian Postal and Communication Police
- Agency for National Police in Japan (NPA)

For instance, in the US, the Secret Service focuses on financial crimes involving cyberspace, while the FBI concentrates on cyberattacks and intrusions. The main law enforcement organizations in Europe entrusted with cybercrime investigations are Europol and Interpol. To improve their ability to handle cybercrime cases, prosecutors, investigators, and judges in Asia can receive specialized training from organizations such as ICHIP Kuala Lumpur and the UNODC (Oerlemans, 2017).

2. **Public-Private Collaboration:** Collaborations between the public and business sectors play a major role in combating cybercrime. These collaborations enable:

- Professionals in law enforcement and commercial enterprise exchanging cyber-information and resources
- Combining knowledge
- Data exchange
- Cooperating on research projects

Every stakeholder contributes different abilities and viewpoints to the joint effort. The Cyber Fraud Task Forces, which emerged from cooperation between the Secret Service, other law enforcement agencies, and the commercial sector, are effective instances of this kind of cooperation. These collaborations aid in the creation of laws that adhere to global norms, such as those established by the Budapest Convention on Cybercrime. These partnerships have shown to be a successful tactic in the fight against cybercrime, despite possible sectoral tensions and the limited resources of law enforcement organizations (Oerlemans, 2017).

3. **International Cooperation:** International cooperation is necessary due to the global nature of cybercrime. Countries work together through bilateral, regional, and multinational cybercrime treaties, as well as official and informal agreements, to:

- Look into and bring charges against online offenders.
- Exchange data and insights.
- Create standardized procedures and best practices.
- Bolster cybersecurity competencies.

In order to combat crimes that cross national borders and legal jurisdictions, international collaboration is essential. Organizations taking part in this global partnership include: Council of Europe, CCIPS, EC3, UNODC, INTERPOL.

There are difficulties, undoubtedly. It can be difficult to comply with international regulations and to develop formal systems like treaties. Nonetheless, the benefits of global collaboration in the fight against cybercrime greatly surpass these difficulties (Oerlemans, 2017).

4.3.4. Investigative Tools and Techniques

Investigating cybercrime necessitates using a variety of instruments and methods. These consist of:

- Digital forensics-this is the study, gathering, and examination of digital evidence.
- Locating harmful software.
- Examining monetary exchanges.

Every tool and method is essential to identifying the digital links connecting cybercrimes.

Certain instruments frequently employed in digital forensics consist of:

- Axiom of Cellebrite Magnet
- Velociraptor
- Wireshark
- 4X-Ways Forensics· The Sleuth Kit
- Autopsy
- Digital Forensics Framework
- Open Computer Forensics Architecture (OCFA)

These resources support investigators in locating, examining, and retrieving forensic data that may be used as electronic proof of a crime (Oerlemans, 2017).

4.4. CYBERCRIME PROSECUTIONS

The primary piece of UK law pertaining to offenses or attacks on computer systems, like denial-of-service attacks or hacking, is the Computer Misuse Act 1990.

Violations of the CMA 1990:

- Causing a computer to carry out a task with the intention of securing unauthorized access to computer material is covered by Section 1 CMA 1990. This offense, which involves "access without right," frequently serves as a springboard for more serious offenses. Merely being careless is insufficient; the perpetrator must have knowledge that the access is illegal. Additionally, access to a computer's stored program or data must have been intended. Take note that the crime is committed whether or not access is granted (Arnell & Faturoti, 2023).
- Unauthorized access with the aim to commit or assist in the commission of additional offenses is covered by Section 2 of the CMA 1990.
- Unauthorized acts with the purpose to hinder computer operation are covered under Section 3 of the CMA 1990. If someone acts carelessly with the knowledge that their actions could damage, block access to, or interfere with a computer's ability to function, they are guilty of an offense. When dealing with DDoS, Section 3 should be taken into account (Arnell & Faturoti, 2023).
- Unauthorized acts that cause or pose a risk of substantial harm to the environment, the economy, human welfare, or national security are included under Section 3ZA. The people who want to attack the vital national infrastructure are the target of this section.
- Manufacturing, supplying, or getting articles for use in offenses against sections 1, 3, or 3ZA CMA 1990 is covered by Section 3A CMA 1990. The CMA 1990's Section 3A addresses people who produce or distribute malware (Arnell & Faturoti, 2023).
- Cyber dependent crimes may coexist with violations of sections 170 to 173 of the Data Protection Act of 2018. Among them are: Willfully or negligently acquiring or revealing personal information without authorization; securing the revelation of any personal information to a third party without authorization or after keeping personal

information without that person's consent; selling personally identifiable information that has been revealed or kept without authorization (Arnell & Faturoti, 2023).

4.4.1. Cyber-Enabled Crimes

These are crimes that have been altered in scope or form by the use of the internet and communications technology, but they are not dependent on computers or networks (Arnell & Faturoti, 2023). They fit into the subsequent groups:

1. **Financially Motivated Cybercrime:** Such as:

- Phoniness
- Intellectual property crimes, including forgeries, counterfeits, and piracy
- Online stores selling illicit goods
- Aggressive and malicious communications, such as: text messages transmitted via email or other social media platforms
- Cyberbullying and trolling
- Mobbing virtually

2. **Crimes Directed Exclusively at Individuals:** Such as cyber-enabled violence against:

- Women and girls (also known as "VAWG"):
- Revealing personal intimate photos without permission
- Cyberstalking and intimidation
- Control and coercion
- Indecent pictures of children and child sexual offenses including:
    a. Sexual assault of children
    b. Internet styling
    c. Forbidden and offensive pictures of kids
    d. Graphic pornography, lewd publications, and forbidden photos

4.4.2. Cybercrime with an Economic Affair

Cybercrimes related to the economy encompass unauthorized access, sabotage, or utilization of computer systems with the aim of generating financial advantage for the offender or financial detriment to the victim. It could include computer fraud or forgeries, virus propagation, or hacking to steal valuable or personal data for financial gain. For example, victims may choose not to report these crimes if they believe the incident is unimportant or do not realize that what has happened to them is indeed illegal. Furthermore, in cases when people's bank account information has been compromised or accessed, if the victim receives reimbursement from their bank, neither the bank nor the individual or both may choose to report the crime.

In a similar vein, certain companies might not file for the identical motives, out of concern for reputational harm, or they can decide to handle such matters internally (Arnell & Faturoti, 2023).

4.5. CYBERCRIME FORENSICS

Digital or cyber forensics is another name for computer forensics. A subfield of digital forensic science is involved. Computer forensics assists in identifying, gathering, and preserving evidence from an electronic device through the use of technology and investigative tactics.

Businesses, individuals, and law enforcement organizations can all employ computer forensics to recover lost or corrupted data in court (Holt et al., 2022).

4.5.1. What Makes Computer Forensics Crucial?

With every passing day, the importance of computer forensics grows along with the global digital connectivity. For the purpose of investigating cybercrimes and retrieving significant, compromised data, digital evidence management is essential. It is the responsibility of a computer forensics investigator to gather, review, and preserve this evidence (Holt et al., 2022).

1. **Computer Forensics Types:** In computer forensics, digital evidence must always be gathered and examined. Typical varieties include some of the following:

- Database forensics: Extraction and examination of information or metadata from databases.
- Email forensics is the process of recovering and examining emails, contacts, calendars, and other data from an email platform.
- Mobile forensics: Data extraction and analysis from mobile devices, including contacts, messages, images, videos, and audio files.
- Memory forensics is the process of recovering and examining data from a computer's cache and/or random-access memory (RAM).
- Network forensics: Using intrusion detection systems and firewalls, among other techniques, to keep an eye on network traffic.
- Malware forensics is the study of code to find dangerous programs such as Trojan horses, ransomware, and viruses.

2. **Typical Methods Used in Computer Forensics:** Computer forensics experts employ a variety of methods while investigating and analyzing evidence; here are a few examples:

- Recovering deleted files-using this method, files or pieces that have been erased by malware or a virus, or by an individual, can be recovered and restored.
- Steganography in reverse-steganography is the process of trying to conceal data inside a digital communication or file. Computer forensic experts can do reverse steganography by examining a message's hash or a file's contents. A hashing is a string of characters that is altered when somebody tampers with the message or file.
- Cross-drive evaluation-using this method, data from several computer drives is analyzed. Computers compare events from one computer to another using techniques like correlation and cross-referencing to look for anomalies.
- Instantaneous evaluation-this method entails examining volatile data that is, data kept in cache memory or random-access memory on a computer that is currently operating. This aids in identifying the source of unusual computer traffic.

4.6. CYBERCRIME INTELLIGENCE

Data that is gathered, processed, and examined in order to comprehend the goals, objectives, and attack patterns of a threat actor is known as threat intelligence. Threat intelligence helps us to shift from reactive to proactive behavior in the battle against threat actors and makes security decisions faster, better informed, and supported by facts. Threat intelligence is information regarding threats or dangers to assets that is supported by evidence and includes context, mechanisms, indications, implications, and recommendations for taking immediate action (Cascavilla et al., 2021).

4.6.1. Why is Threat Intelligence Important?

Advanced persistent threats (APTs) and defenses are always attempting to outwit one another in the field of cybersecurity. Knowing a threat actor's next step is essential to proactively adjusting your defenses and averting assaults in the future (Cascavilla et al., 2021).

Threat information is becoming more and more valuable to organizations. Receiving value and recognizing value are two different things. Without fully utilizing the insights that intelligence may provide, the majority of enterprises these days are concentrating their efforts on the most basic use cases, such as combining threat data feeds with already-existing network, IPS, firewalls, and SIEMs.

Businesses which only use this rudimentary level of threat intelligence are losing out on important opportunities to improve their security postures. The following justifies the importance of threat intelligence:

- Clarifies the unclear and helps security teams make more informed judgments
- Gives stakeholders in cyber security more leverage by disclosing the goals of the opposition and their methods, strategies, and practices (TTPs).
- Aids in the comprehension of the decision-making process of threat actors by security professionals and empowers business stakeholders, including executive boards, CISOs, CIOs, and CTOs, to make more informed decisions, invest wisely, reduce risk, and act more quickly.

4.6.2. With Threat Intelligence, Who Wins?

Organizations of all sizes gain from threat intelligence by processing threat data to comprehend attackers more fully, react to incidents more quickly, and anticipate the next move of threat actors. This data gives SMBs access to a level of protection that would not otherwise be possible. However, by utilizing external threat intelligence, businesses with sizable security teams can lower expenses and skill requirements while increasing the efficacy of their analysts. Every member of a security team can benefit from threat intelligence in a different way, from top to bottom, including: Sec/IT Analyst, SOC, CSIRT, Intel Analyst, Executive Management (Cascavilla et al., 2021).

The following are the advantages for each role and the particular use cases that relate to each:

- Sec/IT Analyst-Boost detection and prevention skills and fortify fortifications.
- SOC -Set incident priorities according to their risk and organizational impact.
- CSIRT- Quicken the process of managing, prioritizing, and investigating incidents.
- Intelligence Analyst-Find and follow anybody posing a threat to the company.
- Top Level Administration-Recognize the dangers that the company is exposed to and the ways in which you may mitigate their effects.

1. **Threat Intelligence Lifecycle:** The process of converting unprocessed data into final intelligence for use in decision-making and action is known as the intelligence lifecycle. In your research, you will come across numerous slightly different iterations of the intelligence cycle, but the ultimate objective remains the same: to lead a cybersecurity team in the creation and implementation of a successful threat intelligence program (Cascavilla et al., 2021). Threat intelligence is difficult because threats are ever-changing, necessitating swift adaptation and firm response on the part of enterprises. The intelligence cycle offers a structure that helps groups make the most use of their resources and react to the current threat environment.

Six steps make up this cycle, which creates a feedback loop to promote ongoing improvement:

a. *Conditions:* Because it establishes the guidelines for a particular threat intelligence operation, the requirements stage is critical to the threat intelligence lifecycle. Based on the requirements of the relevant stakeholders, the team will decide on the objectives and methodology of their intelligence program during this planning phase. The group may aim to ascertain:
   - The identities and motivations of the assailants
   - What is the attack surface and what particular steps need to be made to bolster their defenses in the event of another attack.

b. *Gathering:* The team then starts gathering the data needed to meet those goals after defining the requirements. The team would often look for traffic logs, openly accessible data sources, pertinent forums, social media, industry or subject matter experts.

c. *Handling:* The raw data must be transformed into a format that can be analyzed once it has been gathered. This usually means putting data into spreadsheets, decrypting files, translating data from other sources, and assessing the data for accuracy and relevancy.

d. *Evaluation:* The team has to perform a comprehensive analysis after processing the dataset in order to address the queries raised during the requirements phase. The team also strives to translate the dataset into useful recommendations and action items for the stakeholders throughout the analysis phase.

e. *Communication:* The threat intelligence team must deliver the findings to the stakeholders during the dissemination phase by condensing their analysis into an understandable style. The target audience will determine how the analysis is presented. The recommendations should typically be conveyed succinctly, without the use of bewildering technical jargon, in the form of a brief slide deck or one-page report.

f. *Remarks:* Receiving input on the submitted report is the last step in the threat intelligence lifecycle, which helps identify any changes that should be made for upcoming threat intelligence activities. It's possible that stakeholders will alter their priorities, the frequency with which they receive intelligence reports, or the manner in which information is shared or displayed.

4.7. CYBERCRIME COLLABORATION

Cybercrime is still a significant and widespread worldwide problem. Addressing the root causes of cybercrime is necessary for effective mitigation, and this can only be done with improved operational cooperation between the public and commercial sectors (Boes & Leukfeldt, 2017). In 2020, the Partnership against Cybercrime (PAC) was established to encourage public-private collaboration in the fight against cybercrime. It provides a forum for the exchange of ideas and ongoing investigation of strategies to promote effective cooperation in the fight against cybercrime. The PAC unites a committed group of multinational corporations, top law enforcement authorities on a national and international level, and top non-profit organizations. As a result of the PAC's efforts, the Cybercrime Atlas initiative was established in January 2023 with the goal of mapping and comprehending the ecosystem of cybercriminals (Boes & Leukfeldt, 2017).

1. **The Goal:** Through encouraging public-private cooperation and enlisting the help of the private sector, the PAC hopes to tip the scales in favor of cybercriminals against defenders.
2. **Final Results and Deliverables:** The PAC will oversee three topical workstreams throughout 2024:
   - Together with the cybercrime atlas, develop an operational coordination framework to combat cybercrime.
   - Enhance systemic defense by outlining possible upstream and systemic measures to stop cybercrime on a large scale, as well as by creating an implementation plan and policy suggestions.
   - Use AI to combat cybercrime by learning how cybercriminals use Gen-AI and how it may be used to fight cybercrime.
3. **Significance of Collaboration:** The term "cybercrime" refers to a broad category of malevolent actions, such as ransomware

attacks, phishing, identity theft, online fraud, and cyberbullying. These crimes harm people, groups, and governments all around the world, regardless of where they occur. Consequently, combating cyberthreats necessitates teamwork.

- *Cybercrime is Transnational:* Cybercriminals from one nation may target targets in another. Tracking down cybercriminals who operate across borders requires international cooperation. Information sharing-to exchange threat intelligence, corporations, governments, and law enforcement organizations must work together. Early information sharing aids in the detection and defense against cyberattacks. Harmonization of laws-extradition and prosecution are made easier when cybercrime laws are unified across national borders. The legal frameworks for cross-border inquiries are improved by treaties and accords.
- *An Integrated Method Governmental Organizations:* Law enforcement organizations are essential to the investigation of cybercrimes. But they can't take action by themselves. Working together with private organizations is essential. Private sector-real-time threat analysis, resources, and experience are provided by cybersecurity firms, financial institutions, and technology corporations. Their preemptive actions improve overall security. Education and awareness-working together also includes informing the public about the dangers of cyberspace. Awareness-raising efforts provide people the power to defend themselves and report questionable activity.
- 3.*Hackers with Ethics, Filling the Gap:* White hat hackers-also referred to as ethical hackers, white hat hackers assist companies in locating weaknesses in their systems. They aid in strengthening defenses by imitating cyberattacks (Boes & Leukfeldt, 2017). Red teaming-red team drills are staged assaults on the infrastructure of a company. These cooperative efforts identify gaps and direct security improvements.

4.8. CYBERCRIME LEGISLATION

Crimes done online fall under the broad category of cybercrime. These crimes affect people's lives, businesses, and governments. They range from identity theft and hacking to online fraud and data breaches (Khan et al., 2022). In order to define these offenses and provide a framework for enforcement, legislation is essential.

4.8.1. The Development of Cybercrime Laws

- *Initial Attempts to Combat Cybercrimes:* the criminal laws that were already in place were first modified. However, specific regulation was required due to the distinct nature of digital crimes.
- *Particular Laws*: Many nations have passed cybercrime legislation that is specific to their needs. Cyberterrorism, data manipulation, and unlawful access are all covered under these rules (Khan et al., 2022).
- *International Cooperation*: Working across borders is essential. Treaties and conventions make information exchange and cybercriminals' extradition easier.

4.8.2. Essential Components of Successful Law

- *Clear Definitions:* It's critical to provide accurate definitions of cybercrimes. Lawmakers need to be up to date on technology developments in order to address new risks.
- *Procedures:* Laws should specify how investigations, gathering of evidence, and prosecutions are to be carried out. Enforcing the law while respecting private rights is crucial.
- *Penalties and Dissuasion:* Tougher sanctions serve as disincentives. Cybercriminals face deterrents such as asset confiscation, fines, and imprisonment (Khan et al., 2022).
- *Public Awareness:* Cybersecurity education should be encouraged by law. Providing people with information on safe online conduct encourages a watchful community.

4.8.3. Challenges and Continual Adjustment

- *Complexities in Jurisdiction:* Cybercrimes are international in nature. Global legal harmonization is still difficult to achieve.
- *Emerging Threats:* Deepfakes, crypto jacking, and AI-driven attacks require evolving legislation.
- *Partnerships:* Partnerships between the public and commercial sectors improve enforcement. Cooperation among industries helps to reduce threats.

4.9. CYBERCRIME POLICY

Individuals, businesses, and public administration are worried about various risks that result from violations of the ethics, trust, and confidence that are deeply rooted in the information society. This Policy and Internet Special Issue centers on the policy implications of cybercrimes arising from the misuse of networked technologies. The article by Moitra (2005) presents a range of disciplinary perspectives that are highly sought after by policymaking communities. These perspectives have a significant influence on international efforts to combat transnational crime, promote public-private partnerships, and shape state and international legislation.

The Internet has profoundly impacted most aspects of international social and economic interactions. The development of technology provides opportunities for novel means of communication, exchange of information, and distribution. However, it also gives rise to significant and challenging ethical and public policy concerns. Trust, confidence, and security are essential concerns in the era of digital technology. Noncompliance with these fundamental principles results in a wide array of associated risks for individuals, businesses, the government, and electronic governance (Moitra, 2005).

The term "cybercrime" does not have a specific legal definition and can be interpreted differently depending on the context. However, it includes a broad range of inappropriate actions that are facilitated, either partially or entirely, by interconnected technologies. Cybercrime encompasses various types of attacks on information systems, such as compromising the confidentiality, integrity, and authenticity of data. It also encompasses conventional crimes like fraud, as well as content-related offenses that exploit technology, such as hate speech and the dissemination of pornographic or racist content. Cybercrime has a significant impact on both national and international laws, requiring cooperation between law enforcement agencies and coordination on a global scale to combat transnational crime. It also necessitates collaboration between the public and private sectors (Moitra, 2005).

Policymaking groups are actively soliciting diverse perspectives from multiple disciplines regarding the public policy implications of cybercrime. The special issue on cybercrime in Policy & Internet comprises seven articles that address the various issues that arise when networked technologies are misused and have a detrimental impact on Internet society as a whole (Moitra, 2005). The topics covered include the organized online release of "warez," the legal, regulatory, educational, and societal implications of "sexting," the economics of Internet security in countering cybercrime and protecting privacy, the use of technology to police child exploitation networks, and the adoption of public-private partnerships to respond to cyber-attacks on national critical infrastructure.

Nation states' criminal codes include precise definitions for conventional crimes such as murder and theft. However, according to the criminal code, a significant number of the reported cybercrimes that have caused public concern are not legally considered as criminal offenses. Thus, any behavior or results that do not neatly align with the specifications of the criminal code can be classified as cybercrime (Moitra, 2005). Thus, certain cybercrimes, such as cyber-rape and virtual property damage, may not always be supported by legal grounds. The current proposed solutions for addressing cybercrimes include legislation, education, industry accountability, and technological advancements. This analysis focuses on the financial implications of security seals, which indicate a website's level of protection and therefore enhance security against data breaches. It demonstrates that certain types of agreements enable websites to increase the prices of the products they provide (Moitra, 2005). Subsequently, it examines the extent to which market forces effectively oversee security and privacy. The analysis concludes that implementing regulations without mutual agreement could adversely affect consumers who may not prioritize protection but will still bear the financial burden of compliance through increased prices.

Markets are progressively being incorporated into the range of policy measures, alongside law, technology, and education. These factors encompass the "code," market or economic forces, societal norms, and legal regulations. The modalities mentioned are intrinsically interconnected and can be utilized in both the broader realm of cyberspace and the governance of cybercrime. Therefore, one can conceptualize this range of policy responses as existing on a spectrum, with private functions representing one extreme and state agencies or bodies representing the other (Moitra, 2005). State institutions endorse and enforce "top-down" regulation. Self-imposed private institutions serve as the origin of grassroots regulation.

The government's call for extensive cybersecurity regulations has grown in parallel with the escalating threat of civilian cyberattacks in recent years. After the 2021 Colonial Pipeline and SolarWinds cyberattacks, which had a significant impact on the country's economy and national security because the US government did not have access to crucial cybersecurity data in important businesses, these demands reached their highest point.

After these attacks, legislators and the general public displayed a revived interest in enacting laws that would mandate private companies to disclose cyberattacks, furthering an ongoing regulatory pattern. In 2020, 40 US states and territories introduced over 280 bills and resolutions related to cybersecurity (Moitra, 2005). A similar pattern has emerged in both Israel and Europe.

The public's willingness to accept laws and policies that limit individual civil liberties and privacy depends on finding a delicate equilibrium between security and privacy.

Privacy is often considered an acceptable trade-off for enhanced social and personal security in the face of emerging threats. However, the general public has developed a greater awareness of the importance of safeguarding online privacy and is knowledgeable about the ethical, legal, and political dilemmas associated with government monitoring of communications and online activities (Moitra, 2005). When civilians are subjected to political violence, they often undergo trauma, fear, and a feeling of helplessness in the face of threatening external forces. Political attitudes can be influenced by emotional reactions, regardless of whether they are triggered by conventional or extremely violent activities. Research has shown that conventional acts of terrorism have an impact on individuals' inclination towards peace and willingness to compromise with others, their political conservatism, exclusionary attitudes, and relationships within their own group (Moitra, 2005). Traditional terrorism focuses on deliberately attacking civilians and disrupting their everyday activities.

CHAPTER 5

CYBERCRIME AND PRIVACY

Contents

As globalization increases and information flows freely across national boundaries, cybercrime has emerged as a significant and alarming menace. This umbrella term encompasses a wide range of criminal activities related to digital technology, including online fraud, virus attacks, hacking, and identity theft. The progress of technology is accompanied by the evolution of fraudsters' tactics. Collaboration is crucial for effectively countering this menace. Law enforcement organizations play a crucial role in investigating cybercrimes, apprehending perpetrators, and promoting responsible online behavior. In order to enhance collective security and share information about potential threats, they engage in collaboration with businesses, technology companies, and cybersecurity organizations (Aziz et al., 2021). White hat hackers, also known as ethical hackers, identify vulnerabilities and strengthen security measures. However, the battle against cybercrime extends beyond the jurisdiction of law enforcement.

Privacy is also at risk. Our digital footprints, consisting of browsing histories, social media posts, and transaction data, make us vulnerable to exposure. Ensuring a harmonious equilibrium between user-friendliness and safeguarding personal data is of utmost importance. The General Data Protection Regulation (GDPR) is a comprehensive legislation that safeguards individuals' privacy rights while maintaining public safety. Understanding privacy and cybercrime is crucial as we navigate the digital landscape (Aziz et al., 2021). It is imperative to strive for a society where technology empowers us without impeding our personal freedoms.

5.1. PRIVACY ISSUES IN CYBERCRIME

Data is perceived as a valuable asset by both legal and illegal entities, whether it is in the digital realm or in physical form (Gillespie, 2019). Hence, data holds utmost importance for cybercriminals. Because of its insufficient security measures and vulnerability to unauthorized access and acquisition, data plays a critical role in the commission of numerous cybercrimes. Data breaches have been caused by various factors, including the theft or loss of encrypted flash drives and other storage devices, such as laptops and smartphones. Insufficient system and data security, unauthorized access to databases, exceeding permitted access limits, and unintentional disclosure, release, or publication of data have also contributed to these breaches (Gillespie, 2019).

Here are a few notable examples of data breaches:

- The biometric and identity data of 1.2 billion Indians, which includes their thumbprints and iris scans, is stored in Aadhaar, the national centralized government ID database of India. This database is utilized to authenticate the identities of individuals for a range of services, such as banking, government, and utility verification. In 2018, there was a database breach that impacted Aadhaar, resulting in the exposure of identity information such as phone numbers, email addresses, postal codes, and access names. However, it is important to note that biometric data was not compromised.

- In 2017, a prominent real estate organization in the country suffered a data breach, resulting in the exposure of personal information belonging to nearly 30 million South Africans. This information included their names, genders, income, job history, identity numbers, phone numbers, and home addresses, which were subsequently made available to the public online.
- In 2013, the personal data of more than three billion Yahoo users, which included names, email addresses, passwords with weak encryption, and dates of birth, was exposed.
- Around 350 client identities and passwords were compromised when an unsecured account at the multinational consulting firm Deloitte was breached.
- In 2016, personal information of almost 49 million Turkish residents, such as their name, gender, national identification number, parents' names, home address, date of birth, and city of birth, was made available through an internet searchable database.
- In 2016, cybercriminals employing unethical methods successfully infiltrated the database containing the biometric and personal data of over 55 million voters in the Philippines.

In addition to the compromised accounts, the theft of passwords can be detrimental because users often engage in password reuse, using the same passwords or parts of them, such as specific numbers, across multiple websites, email accounts, applications, and online platforms.

In addition to security breaches, the Deep Web hosts darknet sites and specialized online carding forums where medical, financial, and other personal information can be found (Gillespie, 2019). Compromised data can be revealed for the purpose of obtaining financial benefits, as well as to uncover individuals' actual or perceived unethical actions and behaviors, with the intention of humiliating them. An instance of this is the disclosure of the personal information (including names and email addresses) of nearly 37 million users of Ashley Madison, a platform that facilitated connections between individuals seeking extramarital relationships (Gillespie, 2019).

5.2. DATA PRIVACY

Data privacy, also referred to as information privacy, encompasses the proper management, unchangeability, safeguarding, and retention of confidential data. Data privacy is typically associated with the proper management of personally identifiable information (PII), which includes details like names, addresses, Social Security numbers, and credit card numbers. The concept, however, is also applicable to other types of private or sensitive data, including financial, intellectual, and health-related data. Vertical industry standards often regulate the requirements set by various governing bodies and territories, as well as activities pertaining to data privacy and protection (De Capitani et al., 2012).

Data privacy does not have a single concept or approach. Instead, it is an academic discipline that encompasses policies, procedures, standards, and tools to aid companies in establishing and maintaining the required levels of privacy compliance. Data privacy typically encompasses six key components:

1. *Legal Framework:* Data privacy laws are a type of existing legislation that has been established and enforced to address matters related to data.
2. *Regulations:* Created comprehensive company policies and protocols to ensure the protection of employees' privacy and the confidentiality of user data.
3. *Procedures:* These refer to the established best practices that govern data privacy, security, and infrastructure in the field of information technology.
4. *Collaborations with External Entities:* This includes any third parties, such as cloud service providers that handle data.
5. *Data Management:* Standards and procedures for accessing, storing, and securing data.
6. *Global Standards:* Differences in data privacy and compliance laws exist between international legal jurisdictions, such as the United States and the European Union (EU).

Data privacy is a component of the broader concept of data protection. It encompasses both the safeguarding of data and traditional methods of data preservation, such as data backups and planning for disaster recovery. The objective of data protection is to guarantee the confidentiality and safety of vital corporate information, while also maintaining its accessibility, uniformity, and unchangeability (De Capitani et al., 2012).

The significance of data privacy lies in its crucial role in safeguarding sensitive information. The monetary worth of data is directly linked to the importance of data privacy. Due to the growing data economy, businesses of all sizes are increasingly collecting and storing a larger amount of data from a wider range of sources. Data has various business applications, including the following:

- Identifying customers, understanding their needs, and providing them with products and services.
- Extracting insights from databases and other data sources to train machine learning and artificial intelligence (AI) systems.
- Understanding the business structure, infrastructure, and human behavior by analyzing data from networks and devices.

Data privacy aims to protect data from unauthorized access, theft, or loss. To ensure data privacy and security, it is crucial to implement effective data management practices and restrict unauthorized access, which can potentially result in data loss, manipulation, or theft. Personal data exposure can lead to identity theft, unauthorized account charges, or invasion of privacy for individuals. Illegitimate access to confidential information can have detrimental effects on the outcomes of data analytics and can potentially reveal proprietary information, intellectual property, and private communications for businesses (De Capitani et al., 2012) (Figure 5.1).

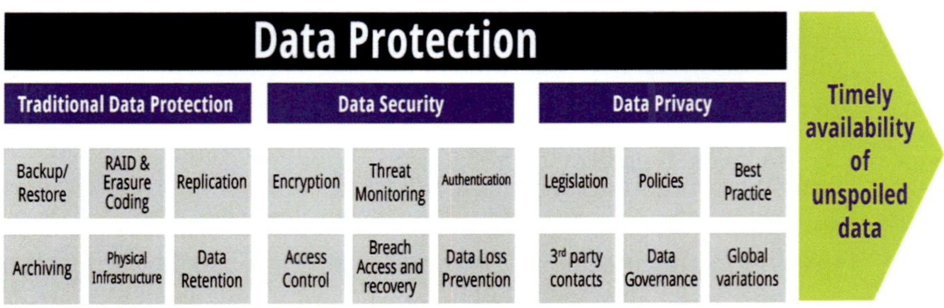

Figure 5.1. *The three categories of data protection.*

Source: What Is Data Privacy? | SNIA (2024).

5.2.1. Obstacles Faced in Maintaining the Confidentiality and Security of Data

Data privacy is a complex and intricate matter, posing challenges for companies to adhere to regulations and protect against security breaches in an ever-changing environment of regulations and threats. Some of the major barriers to data privacy include:

1. *Privacy is of Lesser Importance:* Business and technology executives frequently encounter challenges related to data privacy even after

they have set up their IT infrastructure and business strategy, which can make it challenging for them to understand and manage the complex requirements. Data privacy should be regarded as a fundamental business goal, and the development of IT infrastructure, tools, regulations, and training should all prioritize the requirements of privacy.

2. *Insufficient Clarity of Data:* The adage "You cannot effectively oversee what you cannot perceive" is relevant to the realm of data privacy. It is imperative for companies to possess a comprehensive understanding of the various categories of data they possess, the level of sensitivity associated with each category, and the specific locations where this data is stored. Subsequently, a company can determine the appropriate security and data protection measures to implement.
3. *An Overabundance of Information:* A corporation may require the management of petabytes of data, consisting of various files, databases, and stores, which are distributed across storage devices and cloud repositories. Data can be readily misplaced, allowing sensitive information to bypass security, privacy, and retention protocols. In order to manage large and growing amounts of data, an organization requires the suitable tools and protocols.
4. *Better is Not Always the Case:* Businesses are increasingly recognizing the importance of contextualizing and valuing data. The practice of retaining all data indefinitely incurs expenses related to storage, security, vulnerability to cyber-attacks, and potential legal risks during the process of discovery in court. When developing data retention policies for modern enterprises, it is important to consider factors such as the amount of data collected, its value to the company, and the criteria for reasonable retention requirements.
5. *An Abundance of Electronic Devices:* In the contemporary era, it is imperative for businesses to embrace technologies such as wireless connectivity, Bring Your Own Device (BYOD), Internet of Things (IoT), smart devices, and remote access. Managing data storage and access becomes increasingly challenging when dealing with devices that have multiple components. To ensure data privacy in this complex situation, it is necessary to effectively manage the infrastructure, implement strong access controls, provide comprehensive oversight, and establish well-designed data governance regulations.
6. A Surplus of Regulations: Data privacy regulations may be applicable to a firm at the federal, state, provincial, or industry level. These

existing limitations also extend to a company operating in a different state, province, or country. New controls are often introduced and may undergo changes. This leads to a wide-ranging, intricate, and ever-changing regulatory landscape.

5.2.2. Benefits of Complying with Data Privacy Regulations

Complying with data privacy regulations can offer a company four primary benefits, which are:

- *Decreased Costs Associated with Storage:* Preserving all data indefinitely can incur high costs and pose potential risks. Businesses that make logical decisions about which data to collect, store, and retain can reduce costs associated with primary and backup data storage.
- *Increased Utilization of Data:* Time is crucial for data. Accurate and prompt data can assist a company in making improved choices regarding the gathering and preservation of data. This can result in more precise and relevant analytical results.
- *Enhanced Brand and Reputation for the Business*: The reputation of a company holds equal importance to the quality of its products or services. Businesses that effectively implement and maintain data privacy policies demonstrate their commitment to protecting consumer information and data privacy. This not only improves their reputation but also strengthens their brand. Conversely, a significant data breach can cause lasting damage to a company's reputation and brand.
- *Compliance with Regulations*: By adhering to proper data privacy compliance, a company can prevent lawsuits and penalties related to data privacy violations.

5.3. ONLINE PRIVACY

The concept of privacy encompasses two essential elements: "the condition of being in solitude and free from observation or disturbance by others."

An individual experiences physical solitude when they are alone and engaged in browsing their preferred social networking application. However, in addition, they are "observed or disrupted by other individuals." Despite not being physically present in the same room, they remain mere numerical representations on someone's display. Furthermore, the incessant annoyance of advertisements that interrupt your movies, articles, and browsing persists.

Although it may not give the impression of being a private matter, it actually is. The concept of online privacy encompasses the reasonable and inherent expectation that personal information will be protected and that one's online activities will not be subject to surveillance when connected to the internet (Baruh, Secinti, & Cemalcilar, 2017).

5.3.1. Personal Data

According to the General Data Protection Regulation (GDPR), any information related to an individual who is alive and breathing is classified as personal data. Personal data encompasses additional data points that, when combined, can be utilized to uniquely identify a particular individual.

The fundamental requirement for safeguarding is the bedrock of digital confidentiality. Safeguarding your residence and tangible belongings comes instinctively to you, therefore it is imperative to extend the same level of protection to your digital existence. Irrespective of the technology employed or not employed, privacy empowers individuals to retain authority over their identity and all its constituent elements (Baruh, Secinti, & Cemalcilar, 2017).

However, the majority of individuals do not give precedence to internet privacy due to its intangible and less apparent nature. Moreover, attaining online privacy is a complex endeavor, owing to the intricate amalgamation of technological, legal, commercial, and social factors. However, it does necessitate it. Our interaction with the Internet is not limited to communication; it also serves as a means for the external world to communicate with us. For instance, we might be engaged in shopping either at a local convenience store or at a large shopping center, where surveillance cameras actively record our speech and facial features. Furthermore, this information is processed and stored in a manner that we are unable to object to, exacerbating the situation ((Baruh, Secinti, & Cemalcilar, 2017).

5.3.2. The Importance of Online Privacy

Prior to taking any action, it is essential for individuals to make a deliberate determination that safeguarding their internet privacy holds value. Online privacy encompasses everything from the advancement of technology to its impact on personal security and safety. Inadequate online privacy can result in tangible "offline" dangers such as doxing, harassment, extortion, and swatting, among others. Internet privacy is essential due to its ability to enable individuals to retain authority over their identity and personal information. Lack of proper control exposes individuals to the risk of having their identity exploited by individuals with the necessary motivation and resources, who may use it to advance their own interests. This could involve activities such as stealing one's savings or persuading them to purchase a more expensive vacation (Baruh, Secinti, & Cemalcilar, 2017).

5.3.3. Examples of Threats to Online Privacy

Reusing or Weak Passwords: At some stage, we have all employed weak passwords. It is possible that you still do. It is common. However, it remains one of the most significant threats to your privacy. The reuse of weak passwords is a key factor contributing to the notable data breaches frequently reported in the news. This is because it allows cybercriminals to gain access to multiple accounts at once and engage in financial fraud or identity theft, often both (Baruh, Secinti, & Cemalcilar, 2017).

- *Excessive Exposure to Sharing:* Thanks to social media and other technological advancements, it has become increasingly convenient to enhance our social connections by sharing various aspects of our lives with others. Oversharing is a common outcome of this behavior, often overlooked due to its widespread occurrence.

  Excessive disclosure can provide malicious individuals with a wealth of information about you that exceeds your desired level of sharing. By uploading footage of your house, you enable others to access a comprehensive map of your belongings and receive precise directions to locate them. Boarding permit photos display the destination and duration of your absence. Each post contributes to a more comprehensive depiction of your life, daily habits, significant connections, and possessions (Baruh, Secinti, & Cemalcilar, 2017).
- *Devices That are Part of the Internet of Things:* The proliferation of Internet-connected devices that constantly monitor, record, and gather personal information poses a significant risk to your online privacy.

  We have been generating this personal data for an extended period, yet there has been no previous interest in it. Instances of this data encompass our lists of items to purchase, our bodily temperatures, and the contents of our refrigerators. In the present day, various devices such as toasters, TVs, and toothbrushes are interconnected and designed to be easy for users to operate. However, this also increases the risks to your online privacy.
- *Unprotected Internet Browsing:* Undoubtedly, your browser is the application that you probably utilize the most on your devices,

whether you are aware of it or not. Your primary means of accessing the Internet is through your default web browser, which you utilize whenever you click on a link or perform an online search. It is conceivable that you granted permission for it to retain your passwords.

Cybercriminals possess a comprehension of this as well. Their focus encompasses all facets of it, encompassing links that direct to deceitful websites, extensions containing malicious software, compromised advertisements, and numerous other elements. Privacy and security risks often go hand in hand. Not only scammers and cybercriminals, but businesses can also construct an accurate profile of individuals by examining their browsing history (Baruh, Secinti, & Cemalcilar, 2017).

5.4. SOCIAL MEDIA PRIVACY

The prevalence of individuals utilizing social media platforms for the purpose of connecting, sharing content, engaging with others, and exchanging visual media is consistently increasing. However, it is imperative to comprehend the potential privacy risks and the methods to protect consumers' confidential information. There is a growing apprehension among individuals regarding privacy, specifically regarding their social media posts and how social media platforms handle user data. Strict privacy regulations may not fully guarantee the safety of sensitive user information (Smith et al., 2012).

Figure 5.2. *Privacy is something you will always have to think about when using the internet.*

Source: Sierra (2021).

Data privacy (Figure 5.2) on social media platforms must be overseen by social media managers, content producers, and company owners. Acknowledging privacy concerns on social media is the initial stage in addressing and resolving them. It is necessary to implement suitable measures to safeguard privacy on social media platforms (Smith et al., 2012).

5.4.1. Why is Privacy on Social Media Important?

Individuals often share sensitive and even personal details on social media platforms. In addition, a user's online behavior, such as the websites they visit, their social media interactions, and their previous purchases, can be monitored using tracking cookies, cross-site tracking pixels, or similar monitoring technologies.

Data owners collect, classify, and trade all of this information for marketing objectives (Smith et al., 2012). However, scammers and fraudsters may also gain access to this data and exploit it for malicious purposes. In the last five years, there has been a significant surge in reports of fraud originating from social media platforms. In 2020, a total of 46,000 individuals reported financial losses due to fraudulent activities. In 2021, the number of people who became victims of social media fraud exceeded 95,000 (Smith et al., 2012).

5.4.2. Typical Privacy Issues on Social Media Platforms

To comply with privacy regulations, it is necessary to understand the most common privacy concerns that exist on social media platforms. Ensuring compliance with regulations, protecting client data, preserving customer trust in your organization, and avoiding penalties for breaches of data security are all of equal significance.

The primary privacy concerns on social media are as follows:

- *Extraction of Data:* Scammers employ data mining techniques to perpetrate identity theft. Only a small amount of data is necessary for that. Indeed, they can more efficiently focus on potential victims by utilizing publicly available information on social media platforms. Scammers can readily acquire email addresses, usernames, phone numbers, and physical addresses. They can utilize this information to perpetrate phishing scams or acquire additional data, such as credit card numbers or password breaches.
- *Unauthorized Disclosure of Data:* When a business is hacked, one of the first things that is targeted is the social media information of consumers. People frequently share a significant amount of personal information on social media platforms, which has the potential to be exploited. Just like data mining, fraudsters may seek to acquire more information to carry out more severe online crimes or exploit this information for phishing scams.

Immediately inform your clients if you have experienced a data breach. It is imperative for individuals to exercise caution regarding phishing scams and regularly update their passwords on social media platforms. Practicing transparency and sincerity with your clients can contribute to retaining their patronage and safeguarding their public image (Smith et al., 2012).

- *Data Sharing by Third Parties:* Many social networking sites engage in data sharing with third-party services through partnerships. While it enables the integration of numerous services, there are significant privacy risks associated with it. Unbeknownst to users, they often inadvertently grant these third parties consent to share or trade their data. Prior to accepting cookies or agreeing to the Terms of Services agreement, it is important to thoroughly review the terms and conditions.
- *Privacy Settings Vulnerabilities:* Users often have a misconception about the level of privacy that their social media profiles provide. If you disclose any information to a friend and they provide feedback on it, such as commenting on it, the friends of your friend will also have the ability to access the shared information. Furthermore, the content you shared on social media has the potential to be shared by your friend, thereby making it available to completely different groups of people. Posts can be searched and members of a group have the ability to repost your content, even in closed groups, which are not completely private.
- *Establishing the Geographical Position:* When a user's location is combined with personal data, it can result in a user profile that contains comprehensive information. Scammers could potentially utilize this vast amount of data to pinpoint and focus on customers' physical locations or to collect additional digital information. Scammers possess the ability to track a device's location even if social media users deactivate their location settings by employing alternative methods such as public Wi-Fi, cellular towers, and other techniques. If you have concerns about your location being recorded, it is advisable to always deactivate GPS location services and utilize a VPN while browsing (Smith et al., 2012).
- *Cyberstalking and Digital Harassment:* Even in the absence of access to users' social media accounts, scammers can engage in harassment, threats, or emotional manipulation through text messages. One form of harassment involves the dissemination of offensive content on publicly accessible social media platforms. Cyberbullying refers to the act of disseminating harmful or offensive information about an individual through social media platforms. Doxing is a form of cyberbullying where an individual deliberately discloses derogatory details about another person, such as their phone number, address, or

private images, with the explicit aim of causing harm, embarrassment, or humiliation to the target. In addition, they promote the act of online harassment towards the individual by others.

- *False Information:* Dissemination of propaganda and deceptive information can spread rapidly through social media platforms. Trolls and bots often incite emotional responses from social media users. They have the ability to create a fraudulent account or assume a false identity in order to provide support. Furthermore, it has been utilized in the context of cyberbullying and harassment. Posts are systematically marked or removed over time, although most social networking sites employ content moderators or provide mechanisms for users to report inaccurate material. Always ensure the accuracy of information before sharing it or making conclusions based on it on social media.

5.5. LEGISLATION REGARDING THE PROTECTION OF PERSONAL INFORMATION AND THE RIGHT TO PRIVACY

Many countries have implemented comprehensive privacy and data protection laws that apply to both the identification system and any other public or private sector activity that involves handling personal data. Typically, these laws include detailed regulations and principles that are specifically related to the collection, storage, and utilization of personal information, in accordance with global standards for safeguarding privacy and data security (Liddle, 2014). These principles and provisions might encompass:

1. *Restriction of Purpose*: Personal data should only be collected and utilized for two specific purposes:

- Those that are legally mandated and can be known by the individual at the time of data collection, at least in theory
- Those for which the individual has given their consent.

2. *Reduction and Correlation*: In order to avoid unnecessary collection of data and the expansion of system functions beyond their original purpose, it is crucial that the data obtained is suitable for the intended use of the identification system, thus mitigating privacy risks. This concept is often articulated as the idea that only the essential data, including transaction metadata, should be collected in order to achieve the desired objective (Liddle, 2014).

3. *Legal Compliance:* The collection and use of personal data should adhere to legal principles, such as obtaining consent, fulfilling contractual obligations, complying with legal duties, protecting vital interests, serving the public interest, or pursuing legitimate interests.
4. *Objectivity and Transparency:* It is imperative to adhere to equitable and transparent procedures when gathering and utilizing personal data.
5. *Accuracy*: Personal information must be up-to-date and precise, and any mistakes must be promptly rectified.
6. *Storage Limitations:* It is imperative to refrain from keeping personal data, such as transaction metadata, beyond the necessary duration for the purposes of collection and processing. Individuals may be given the option to choose how long transaction metadata is kept.
7. *Privacy-Enhancing Technologies (PETs):* The prerequisites for utilizing privacy-preserving technology, such as tokenization of unique identity numbers, are to minimize or eliminate the collection of personal data, cease processing of personal data that is not required or desired, and facilitate compliance with data protection legislation (Liddle, 2014).
8. *Accountability*: Both the individuals whose data is being processed and a designated, impartial oversight organization should monitor the processing of personal data to ensure compliance with the mentioned guidelines.

Generally, personal information should be acquired in a lawful manner, typically with the individual's consent, for a specific purpose. It should not be used for unrelated purposes or for unauthorized government or third-party surveillance or profiling, unless legally mandated. Finally, it is essential for users to possess explicit entitlements regarding their personal data, including the ability to access and rectify any inaccurate information pertaining to them, as well as having accessible avenues for seeking redress to safeguard these rights (Liddle, 2014).

5.6. DATA PROTECTION REGULATIONS

To guarantee adherence to privacy and data protection regulations, which encompass the safeguarding of individuals' rights, the oversight of an autonomous supervisory or regulatory body is commonly applied to ID systems and overall data protection and privacy. The supervisory authority can be comprised of an ombudsman, a solitary government official, or a collective of individuals. An essential aspect of any such governing body is its authentic autonomy, which is influenced by structural factors such as the composition of the body, the method of member selection, the authority's power and duration in executing oversight responsibilities, the allocation of sufficient resources, and the body's ability to make significant decisions without external interference (Solove & Schwartz, 2020). While individuals whose data is collected have the right to pursue legal action through the courts, the supervisory body has the authority to address public complaints based on legal grounds. Possible actions to address the issue could involve the authority's power to compel the identification system to rectify, eliminate, or obliterate inaccurate or unlawfully acquired data (Solove & Schwartz, 2020). The duties and mandates of such an authority may encompass the following, as outlined in the Council of Europe's (CoE) Convention for the Protection of Individuals with regard to Automatic Processing of Personal Data, which has recently been updated as Convention 108+:

- Responsibilities to monitor, investigate, and ensure compliance with individuals' rights to privacy and data protection.
- Responsibilities to monitor alterations and their impact on individuals' rights to privacy and data security.
- The power to examine potential infringements on an individual's privacy and data protection rights, as well as to accept grievances regarding such infringements.
- The power to determine if these rights have been breached and to enforce significant penalties or corrective actions.
- Duties to enhance public comprehension of individuals' rights and organizations' responsibilities in relation to the collection and utilization of personal data.

The functions of data protection authorities include expressing views prior to implementing data processing procedures, providing guidance on governmental or administrative actions, suggesting moral guidelines or referring situations to national legislatures or other government agencies, and regularly issuing opinions, reports, and public statements to inform the public about their rights, responsibilities, and general data privacy concerns (Solove & Schwartz, 2020). Personal data must be securely handled and stored to prevent any loss, theft, unauthorized or illegal processing, destruction, or damage. The significance of this principle becomes more pronounced for digital identification systems in view of the menace posed by cyberattacks. Common measures to ensure data security that may be mandated by legislation include the following.

- Securing personal information through encryption.
- The process of anonymizing personal information.

- Pseudonymization of personal data.
- Ensuring the privacy and security of data and systems when handling or generating personal information.
- Ensuring the accuracy and reliability of data and systems that handle or generate personal information.
- The ability to restore data and systems that generate or use personal data after a technical or physical incident.
- Ongoing testing, evaluation, and assessment of the security of systems that utilize.

Furthermore, several global standards mandate that data controllers must notify data subjects about significant data breaches that involve their personal information. In addition, countries may have legal systems in place to acknowledge and mitigate cyber threats, as well as laws that punish unauthorized access, use, or alteration of data (refer to the section on cybersecurity below). Legislative frameworks should incorporate appropriate sanctions for data administrators and other third parties who illegally access, use, or modify personal data (Solove & Schwartz, 2020). The sanctions should encompass the following:

- Illegitimate entry into databases that store personal information, such as identification systems.
- Illegitimate utilization of personal information or the monitoring/ surveillance of identification systems or other databases that store personal data.
- Unauthorized alteration of data collected and stored in databases that contain personal information, such as identity systems.

Interconnecting databases can worsen privacy and data protection concerns. To mitigate these risks, regulatory frameworks should specify the permissible grounds for government and non-government organizations to share personal data within an identification system (Solove & Schwartz, 2020). In addition, in accordance with the "need-to-know" principle, public institutions may only have access to specific information that is essential for them to carry out their responsibilities.

Here are several benefits of sharing information:

- Enhanced ease and efficiency for both citizens and the government
- Enhanced delivery of government services
- Seamless transfer of services in the event that a person's data is relocated
- Improved risk management

- Cost savings resulting from the removal of redundant work
- Enhanced productivity by employing data in a more intelligent manner

5.7. PRIVACY POLICIES

A privacy policy provides a comprehensive explanation of how you plan to use any personal information that you collect through your website or mobile application. These guidelines are occasionally referred to as privacy notices or privacy statements. They function as legally binding contracts created to protect both the business and the customers. Cookie policies and data protection agreements differ from privacy policies. A data protection agreement, also referred to as an internal contract, outlines the collaborative efforts between your business, yourself, and any external vendors to ensure the secure management of consumer privacy. It is improbable that your clients will have a need to evaluate your data security policy (Earp et al., 2005).

A cookie policy notifies visitors to your website or application that you monitor and retain a portion of their activity through cookies, which are tiny snippets of code stored on their devices. These policies are usually displayed to visitors when they first visit a website, as opposed to privacy policies, which are typically shown only after visitors have provided personal information, such as when registering for an account (Earp et al., 2005).

5.7.1. The Purpose of a Privacy Policy

Privacy policies protect customers from unethical data acquisition methods. An effective policy will also protect your business by clearly defining the categories of client data you acquire, the reasons for collecting it, and the intended methods of utilization in the future. Suppose your business collects customer birthdates to calculate sales data for a specific group and enhance customer loyalty through the provision of birthday discounts. The privacy policy states that personal information will be used for internal sales tracking and marketing purposes.

The GDPR (General Data Protection Regulation) introduced regulations for data collection and processing in the European Union, starting in 2016. It applies to individuals and businesses operating within the EU. The California Consumer Privacy Act (CCPA) of 2018 provides protection to Californians against manipulative methods of collecting personal data.

Currently, there is no comprehensive federal legislation that governs the disclosure and collection of data by businesses. Nevertheless, it is probable that a portion of your internet clientele originates from California or the European

Union, where this legislation is currently in force. Furthermore, it is mandatory for you to safeguard any customer data that you collect in accordance with legal requirements. The Federal Trade Commission (FTC) governs and oversees customer complaints related to data acquisition and breaches. If you have a privacy policy in place, you can be confident that you won't have to be concerned about a situation where a client alleges that they were not informed about the collection of their data, which could potentially lead to a security breach (Earp et al., 2005).

5.7.2. The Elements of a Privacy Policy

Due to its legal nature, a privacy policy necessitates the inclusion of several highly specific provisions. The information used to develop the policy itself lacks flexibility. Privacy policies must be created in a clear and uncomplicated manner, as required by regulations such as the CCPA and GDPR. Robust privacy protocols encompass:

1. *An overview of the types of data collected by your organization and the methodologies employed for data collection:* Some websites only retain data that users explicitly provide to them, such as through an online form. With consent, other websites have the ability to request permission to collect and retain data regarding the location of your web browser or mobile device. To acquire more client data, your business could form partnerships with social media platforms. In such a scenario, it is crucial to have a privacy policy that is highly detailed and clear (Earp et al., 2005).
2. *The justification for your company's data collection:* Does your product marketing rely on data? Is it utilized to improve the customer experience? Is the main purpose of this to determine the identity of your target audience? It could be a combination of these and other variables. You must clearly articulate the rationale behind your business's collection and retention of client data. Complying with the GDPR regulations, you will also be required to provide evidence justifying the necessity of this data for conducting business.
3. *The entirety of your business's intentions regarding the use or non-use of client information:* The privacy policy of your company should clearly state whether it plans to engage in any partnerships with third parties for the utilization of customer data. It is important to consider whether law enforcement authorities will have the capacity to request the data for any reason. The privacy policy must explicitly state the data storage location and the security measures implemented to safeguard it against potential security threats. It is

necessary to clearly state the length of time for which data will be kept, as well as the method that will be used to securely erase the data either upon a customer's request or after a set period of time (Earp et al., 2005).

4. *The practice of choosing not to participate:* The California Consumer Privacy Act (CCPA) mandates that customers possess the capacity to delete collected data pertaining to them and to decline the sale of their personal information. Include instructions on how to do that in your privacy policy to inform your customers.

5.7.3. Limitations on Privacy Policies

A well-crafted privacy policy enables you to establish clear guidelines for how you manage your customers' data. It also imposes limitations on clients' expectations. If your privacy policy specifies that a third-party vendor is responsible for supervising and securing the data through measures like end-to-end encryption, your customers will not have the right to take legal action against you if the vendor fails to fulfill its obligations or experiences a data breach.

5.8. PRIVACY RIGHTS

The right to privacy is closely interconnected with various other human rights, such as the freedom of expression, the capacity to obtain, receive, and disseminate information, and the freedom of organization and assembly.

The significance of privacy rights lies in their fundamental importance. The reasons for this can be explained as follows:

- *Privacy Rights Prohibit Government Surveillance of Citizens (Without Justification):* While it is the responsibility of the government to protect its citizens, it often exceeds its authority when it comes to surveillance. Following Edward Snowden's disclosure of the NSA's surveillance program in 2013, privacy emerged as a prominent subject of discussion. Striking a balance between privacy rights, freedom of speech, surveillance, and national security poses a challenging task. The majority of individuals concur that the government should refrain from engaging in surveillance of an individual unless there is a legitimate justification for doing so. No individual aspires to live in a state governed by an authoritarian regime (Bernal, 2014).
- *Privacy Rights Prohibit Groups from Using Personal Data for Their Own Purposes:* Personal information can be a valuable asset when it falls into the wrong hands. An exemplary instance of this is the

Cambridge Analytica controversy. This group utilized Facebook data (acquired without users' consent) to influence voting behavior through political advertisements. Privacy rights prohibit groups from accessing and utilizing your data for their own purposes without your knowledge or consent. Privacy rights that prevent tech corporations like Facebook, Amazon, and Google from using personal data collected and stored by them are essential in today's age (Bernal, 2014).

- *Privacy Rights Establish Accountability for Individuals who Unlawfully Appropriate or Pilfer Data:* When the importance of privacy is recognized as a fundamental human right, individuals who violate it will experience consequences. While there are numerous instances where personal data is used for purposes like targeted advertising, it is important to note that there are limits defined by well-established privacy rights. If these limitations are not in place, governments and businesses are more prone to engage in data theft and misuse without facing any consequences. In order to safeguard the rights to privacy, it is crucial to have privacy laws in place (Bernal, 2014).
- *The Concept of Privacy Maintains Societal Limits:* Each individual possesses confidential knowledge that they would rather keep hidden from certain individuals. Establishing boundaries is crucial for maintaining healthy relationships and successful careers. Previously, the act of setting limits solely referred to the decision of avoiding discussions on specific topics. The proliferation of personal data stored online in recent times adds complexity to the process. Social media platforms often contain a wealth of sensitive information that we prefer to keep hidden from specific individuals or unknown individuals. Media platforms are obligated to incorporate security measures (Bernal, 2014). We can be reassured that we have control over who has knowledge of what.
- *The Preservation of Privacy Cultivates a Sense of Confidence and Reliance:* Trust is essential in any form of connection. Individuals must have confidence in the security of their personal information when sharing it with banks or healthcare providers. Respecting individuals' entitlement to privacy enhances their assurance. An individual who possesses privacy rights also experiences a greater sense of assurance that there will be consequences if the other party violates their trust (Bernal, 2014).

- *Privacy Rights Grant us Control Over our Data:* If the data belongs to you, you should take responsibility for it. Privacy rights ensure that your data can only be utilized with your explicit consent, and you possess the entitlement to retrieve any personal information concerning yourself. If you were without this control, you would experience a sense of powerlessness. Moreover, it would render you highly vulnerable to assault from more powerful societal influences (Bernal, 2014). Your entitlement to privacy empowers you to have authority over your own existence.

CHAPTER 6

CYBERCRIME AND TECHNOLOGY

Contents

Cybercrime is perpetrated by both individuals and collectives. Certain cybercriminals possess advanced technical skills, exhibit strong organizational abilities, and utilize state-of-the-art techniques (Moore, 2014). Some individuals lack expertise in hacking. This chapter will provide a comprehensive examination of various topics related to cybercrime, including: Technology and Cybercrime, Internet of Things (IoT) and Cybercrime, Artificial Intelligence (AI) and Cybercrime, Blockchain and Cybercrime, Cloud Computing and Cybercrime, Mobile Devices and Cybercrime, Social Engineering and Cybercrime, Ransomware and Cybercrime, and Phishing and Cybercrime.

6.1. THE INTERSECTION OF TECHNOLOGY AND CYBERCRIME

In the era of digitalization, information is disseminated to others using a diverse range of methods that utilize personal computers and associated technology. However, many organizations employ technology and computers to perpetrate criminal activities. These offenses encompass a wide range of activities, ranging from acquiring sensitive information for the purpose of gaining a competitive edge to unlawfully obtaining personal data from a computer. There exists a wide range of digital offenses, and prosecuting them can sometimes pose difficulties. These crimes can be diminished but not entirely eliminated through efficient law enforcement (Moore, 2014).

Crimes related to computers committed in foreign countries Across the globe, a multitude of fraudsters and hackers have employed diverse individuals and institutions to execute their illicit activities. These individuals or government intelligence units may be motivated by financial gain to engage in deceptive schemes aimed at stealing from others. Certain individuals are employing computers and online platforms to unlawfully acquire sensitive or confidential information. This could lead to the theft of information, fraudulent activities, and unauthorized access to other data sources, including organizational data. Due to these actions, it is imperative to comprehend the types of emails and data that can be obtained through personal computers. Both Internet and intranet companies are susceptible to attacks (Moore, 2014).

6.1.1. Using Computers for Criminal Activities

China has achieved notable success in its efforts to target businesses, institutions, and other countries, although it is not the sole nation to do so. Hackers can perpetrate their illicit activities utilizing a portable device, a personal computer, or an anonymous device. The utilization of specifically designed code is the most efficient technique for hacking. This can be utilized to perpetrate additional criminal activities, such as data theft, software or system alteration, acquisition of goods in exchange for money, or a variety of other unlawful acts. Hackers frequently exploit information to gain a financial edge over large corporations. The software can be utilized to replicate usernames and passwords, thereby enabling access to private or protected data. The expenses associated with the prevention and mitigation of cybercrimes have escalated in direct correlation with their proliferation. According to the information provided, data on legal actions against cybercrime reveals that an estimated amount of 134 billion dollars, equivalent to more than $410 per individual in the United States, was projected to be allocated for the purpose of preventing criminal activities in 2022 (Moore, 2014).

6.1.2. The Comparison Between Crime and Technology

When we discuss technology, what does it signify to you? Most individuals would contend that the objective was to enhance the convenience of our lives, and to a large extent, that remains true even now. Unfortunately, technology has also facilitated individuals to engage in clandestine criminal activities from the comfort of their own residences. Cybercrime refers to any illicit activity conducted online with the intent to cause harm to others, using a computer or electronic device. It is crucial to acknowledge that cybercrime manifests in various ways, and each instance must be approached with care. Instances such as credit card fraud, identity theft, cyberbullying, and sexual harassment are prevalent. These are the primary concerns that individuals worldwide may face at any given moment (Moore, 2014).

Based on projections by Cybercrime Magazine, the global economy is predicted to be the third largest in 2021, following the United States and China. The cost of cybercrime is anticipated to exceed $6 trillion. A cybercriminal is capable of engaging in any activity due to their ability to keep pace with technological advancements. This encompasses both the initial strategies derived from books and more intricate techniques that exploit contemporary technology. The recent hack of a Microsoft Exchange server resulted in the discovery of several zero-day vulnerabilities, making it one of the most damaging hacks in recent times. Microsoft identified the Proxy Logon vulnerabilities in January and subsequently resolved them in March. The initial entity to discover these issues was the hacker consortium known as Hafnium. Subsequently, after the Hafnium incident, other entities started focusing on vulnerable systems, resulting in the infiltration of numerous new companies (Moore, 2014).

In January 2021, Meet Mindful experienced a cybersecurity breach that led to the unauthorized access and pilferage of more than 2 million members' personal data. The hackers orchestrated the attack by gaining control over

Facebook account tokens and user information, which encompassed complete names (Moore, 2014). The pace of technological development surpasses the ability of law enforcement and potential victims to keep up with or even identify. Moreover, as technology advances, it will continue to generate novel methods of attack and broaden the scope of existing vulnerabilities. In order to combat the misuse and manipulation of emerging and existing technologies by criminals, law enforcement agencies must persistently utilize all available resources, tools, and opportunities. In order for law enforcement to effectively deter crime, it is crucial to establish collaborations between public and private entities, develop innovative technical solutions, implement preventive strategies, and enhance their capacity through training and development (Moore, 2014).

6.2. INTERNET OF THINGS (IOT) AND CYBERCRIME

In simple terms, the Internet of Things (IoT) encompasses any device or object that is connected to the internet. Nevertheless, the term is becoming more commonly used to describe technologies that are interconnected through networks and sensors, allowing for various actions to be performed. The applications of IoT-connected gadgets and technology are vast, with companies constantly striving to find innovative ways to enhance global connectivity. Based on a recent projection, the number of linked devices in use is expected to reach 14.2 billion in 2019 and 25 billion by 2027 (Hilt et al., 2019).

There is a wide range of examples to consider, starting with the more common ones such as sensors that control lights, and extending to more advanced technologies like smart watches, autonomous vehicles, health monitors, and the highly discussed “smart fridge.” The potential of the smart fridge goes beyond just keeping food fresh, as it could potentially facilitate grocery delivery by drone, eliminating the need for customers to manually create a shopping list. These advancements possess the potential to significantly boost productivity, elevate user satisfaction, and potentially even have life-saving implications. It is important to acknowledge the potential risks associated with the increasing interconnectedness and data recording capabilities of modern technologies (Hilt et al., 2019).

There are three significant risks that are commonly associated with the Internet of Things (IoT). To begin with, it is important to note that the convergence of personal data through the use of internet-connected devices has led to new and powerful possibilities. Enhanced customer experiences may arise as a consequence of this phenomenon. However, it is important to acknowledge that businesses, as well as potential wrongdoers, can glean a significant amount of information about individuals' behavior through seemingly innocuous devices. Take, for example, the data collected from your smart watch, the contents of your refrigerator, and the paths chosen by your self-driving car. When combined, these elements can provide a comprehensive overview of an individual's daily existence. One perspective to consider is that this approach can provide individuals with a means to influence the behavior of others. It is worth noting, however, that it can also be employed for marketing purposes or to provide strategies for enhancing one's daily life (Hilt et al., 2019).

On the other hand, IoT devices provide potential hackers with access to more than just user data and behaviors. In addition, they provide a solution to circumvent the fundamental structure of the internet. In 2016, a botnet was created with the purpose of taking advantage of a large number of Internet of Things devices. This was achieved by effectively scanning the internet for devices that still had default usernames and passwords. Subsequently, the devices became infected with a software called Mirai, which played a significant role in the largest DDoS attack to date. This attack resulted in the unavailability of popular platforms such as Twitter, CNN, and Netflix, as well as a significant portion of the internet.

Furthermore, as we delve into the concept of "smart cities," where the digital systems of entire cities are interconnected, the risks associated with IoT devices become increasingly significant. Now, we transition from discussing privacy concerns to exploring the potential physical dangers. As we delve into the topic, it becomes evident that there are already reports of both negative and positive effects on autonomous automobiles. With the increasing integration of the internet and offline worlds, the potential risks are expected to escalate (Hilt et al., 2019).

It is important to incorporate international standards into the design. Collaboration between governments and manufacturers is underway to create a cutting-edge technical framework that ensures the security of connected devices while maintaining a seamless consumer experience. The aim is to unlock the full potential of these devices in the future without burdening users with excessive costs or complicated processes.

There are a variety of programs currently being implemented to enhance consumer device security and promote the integration of security measures into device designs. A set of guidelines for securing consumer IoT devices has been recently approved by the European Technical Standards Institute (ETSI). The guidelines provided here build upon a UK code of practice for IoT security that was published in the previous year (Hilt et al., 2019). When purchasing internet-connected devices, it is crucial to consider three primary factors outlined in the ETSI specifications. These factors play a significant role in preventing various attacks. It is important to ensure that passwords on devices are not pre-set and are unique, as users are expected to change them. By implementing this solution, the customer would have been spared the inconvenience of having to change passwords and, more importantly, it could have played a crucial role in mitigating the Mirai attack (Hilt et al., 2019).

It is imperative for businesses that produce internet-connected products and services to provide a means for customers to report any issues they encounter. It enables businesses to effectively address and resolve any issues that may arise.

Software updates for linked devices should be fast and easy to apply. Ensuring the software remains free from bugs is crucial in order to prevent potential vulnerabilities that could be exploited by attackers. By promptly addressing any bugs that may arise, we can effectively mitigate the risk of security breaches.

In a significant development, California has become the pioneering state in the US to implement a specialized cybersecurity law for IoT. This law sets out the specific measures that device manufacturers are required to adhere to in order to guarantee the security of their devices. While there is still work to be done to ensure the security of the Internet of Things (Figure 6.1) and preserve the benefits of the Fourth Industrial Revolution, the collaboration shown in this recent effort is promising (Hilt et al., 2019).

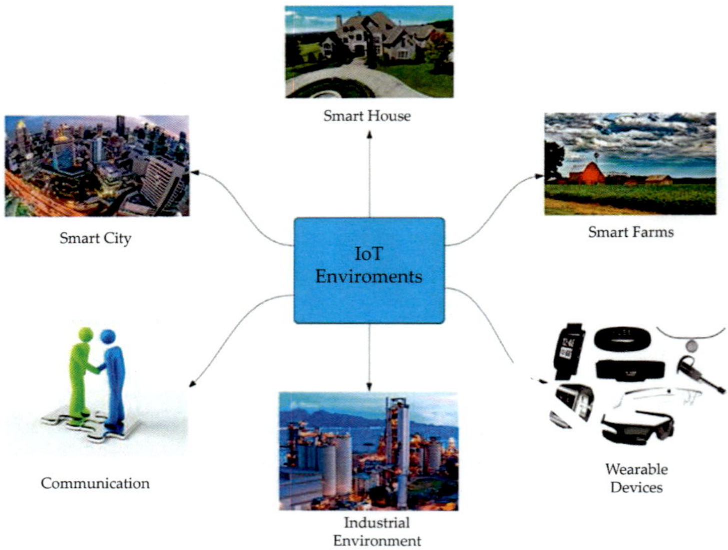

Figure 6.1. *Internet of things environments.*

Source: Obaidat et al. (2020).

6.3. ARTIFICIAL INTELLIGENCE (AI) AND CYBERCRIME

Artificial intelligence (AI) in cybersecurity involves the use of machine learning techniques, advanced algorithms, and intelligent software solutions to constantly monitor network environments and prevent cyber threats. Artificial Intelligence (AI) in cybersecurity emulates the reasoning and practices of cybersecurity specialists and system administrators (Dilek et al., 2015).

6.3.1. Fundamental Components of Security for AI

- Monitoring potential threats
- Analyzing patterns of behavior
- Addressing vulnerabilities
- Detecting fraudulent activity

Businesses in the banking and economic sectors can implement AI security solutions to ensure a robust and secure digital financial infrastructure and detect fraudulent activity, such as card fraud involving skimming and other techniques.

Identity theft, phishing campaigns, insurance fraud, money laundering, real estate fraud, phone bank fraud, financial manipulation, corruption, and transactions on the dark web are all serious issues that require our attention.

Security solutions that utilize artificial intelligence are currently being implemented. Businesses can effectively utilize AI in the field of cybersecurity by implementing various strategies and techniques. By leveraging AI algorithms and machine learning models, organizations can enhance their ability to detect and prevent cyber threats. Additionally, AI can be employed to analyze vast amounts of data in real-time, enabling businesses to identify patterns and anomalies that may indicate potential security breaches. Furthermore, AI-powered systems can automate routine security tasks, freeing up valuable time for cybersecurity professionals to focus on more complex and critical issues. Overall, the integration AI-driven cybersecurity solutions have become increasingly accessible to businesses of all sizes, including medium-sized and smaller ones. This affordability has opened up new possibilities for implementing custom AI technologies to enhance cybersecurity.

Artificial intelligence is being increasingly utilized by a growing number of mainstream companies, especially e-commerce platforms, to enhance their operations and mitigate the risks of fraud and hacking. AI technologies, such as those used by online retailers, have the ability to identify and report any abnormal shopping events that differ from typical consumer behaviors. This can be incredibly helpful in detecting unusually large orders or suspicious activities.

This method allows for the identification of various types of fraudulent activities such as account takeovers, chargeback fraud, credit card fraud, and merchant fraud. These fraudulent activities can result in significant financial losses for internet companies, amounting to millions of dollars (Dilek et al., 2015).

The incorporation of AI into cybersecurity systems offers several significant advantages for your company, such as real-time threat identification, automated reaction, scalability, cost-effectiveness, dark web monitoring, and insider threat monitoring.

Real-time cyber threat detection is a crucial aspect of modern security systems. It allows organizations to proactively identify and respond to potential threats before they can cause significant damage. By continuously monitoring network traffic and analyzing patterns, security teams can quickly detect and mitigate cyber-attacks. This proactive approach is essential in today's rapidly evolving threat landscape, where new threats emerge on a daily basis. Implementing real-time cyber threat detection is a key One of the key advantages of AI-managed cybersecurity technologies is the ability to detect threats instantaneously. In order to effectively combat the ever-evolving landscape of cyberattacks, it is imperative to possess a system that remains current with trends, considers previous encounters, and proactively identifies and mitigates risks before they manifest and result in significant damage. Artificial intelligence provides the necessary tools to quickly identify potential risks, such as malware, phishing scams, or unauthorized access, and promptly take the necessary measures to prevent them from posing a threat to your business (Dilek, Çakır, & Aydın, et al., 2015).

Reacting autonomously to online threats. One of the advantages of AI in cybersecurity is its ability to automatically respond to various types of threats, whether they are already known or not, whether they are predicted or hypothetical. One-way organizations can effectively address a range of cyber threats is by leveraging AI to automate security procedures (Dilek, Çakır, & Aydın, et al., 2015).

An economical cybersecurity strategy that utilizes AI technology. Through the automation of various tasks typically handled by human analysts, IT security consultants, or engineers, AI has the potential to significantly reduce the expenses associated with cybersecurity. By leveraging AI solutions, businesses can effectively decrease the workload of computer professionals without compromising the advantages of having a large team of cybersecurity specialists. Artificial intelligence, although not a substitute for a skilled cybersecurity administrator, empowers individuals to achieve significantly more than they would otherwise be capable of. With the assistance of an advanced AI/ML solution, a single IT administrator has the potential to reach productivity and capacity levels that rival, or even surpass, those of an entire cyber-security department (Dilek, Çakır, & Aydın, et al., 2015).

Technique for surveilling the dark web. The dark web is a hidden network of websites and services that cybercriminals often exploit to trade stolen data. This includes sensitive information like credit card numbers, login credentials, and other private data. Monitoring the dark web with AI support is a crucial element in the realm of cybersecurity. One important aspect is to conduct thorough searches for any references to an organization's name, personnel, or data on the dark web (Dilek, Çakır, & Aydın, et al., 2015).

6.3.2. The Potential Drawbacks and Potential Risks of AI in the Field of Cybersecurity

Each area has its own nuances, and cybersecurity with AI is certainly no exception. There are several drawbacks and potential hazards associated with AI applications in cybersecurity, which also raise important ethical and legal concerns.

- *AI Security Systems' Bias*: Artificial intelligence systems rely heavily on the data they are trained on, which means that their objectivity is directly influenced by the biases present in that data. This highlights the fact that bias is not solely a human issue. If the data is biased in any way, the AI system will generate results that are skewed. Discriminatory outcomes can arise from decision-making in the field of cybersecurity. It is reasonable to assume that renowned AI platforms such as Cylance and IBM Watson make continuous investments in rational machine learning training to minimize bias in their systems (Dilek, Çakır, & Aydın, et al., 2015).
- *There Seems to be a Misunderstanding:* Even the most advanced AI systems still experience instances of what can be referred to as "AI hallucinations." As a result, individuals may be prone to misinterpreting specific information and making judgments based on inaccurate or incomplete data that they were educated on. It is important to note that if threat assessments are inaccurate, there is a risk that attacks could go unnoticed. Additionally, there is a potential concern regarding the increased occurrence of false positives. This could potentially lead to the disruption of valid operations and the removal of authorized users.
- *The Problem of Over-Dependence*: Businesses and organizations might develop an excessive reliance on autonomous AI systems for cybersecurity as they seek more affordable IT services. This could

lead to a sense of complacency, a shortage of qualified oversight, and a lack of human support. Accumulation of AI mistakes in cybersecurity systems can lead to a substantial impact, especially in these "robotic mode" circumstances. These weaknesses further enhance the organization's vulnerability to new cyberattacks that exploit gaps in AI-managed barriers. It is important to note that cognitive computing still requires human proximity to achieve optimal results.

6.4. BLOCKCHAIN AND CYBERCRIME

Blockchain has made significant strides, evolving from its origins as a platform for cryptocurrencies to becoming a transformative technology. This represents a significant shift in our perspective on transaction integrity and data security. The foundation of blockchain technology lies in three core concepts: transparency, immutability, and decentralization. With the advent of safe digital transactions, a new era has begun, bringing with it a novel framework that has implications across various fields, particularly in the realm of cyber security. This groundbreaking innovation completely transforms the concept of data integrity and provides a robust safeguard against online attacks (Patmanathan et al., 2023).

6.4.1. The Use of Blockchain Technology in Transforming the Field of Cybersecurity

Blockchain is a technology that has the potential to revolutionize the field of cyber security. Decentralization and immutability are two key qualities that provide it with powerful tools to address existing security vulnerabilities. Blockchain technology has a multitude of applications in the field of cyber security, offering robust solutions for various aspects of security. Blockchain has proven its effectiveness in real-world applications by enhancing security protocols, showcasing its potential as a pivotal technology in bolstering cyber security measures (Patmanathan et al., 2023).

- *Using Blockchain Technology and Delocalization Methods to Combat Cybercrime:* Decentralization forms the core concept that underlies the security capabilities of blockchain. By distributing data over a network, blockchain effectively reduces the vulnerabilities found in centralized systems. The architecture is highly suitable for ensuring secure digital transactions and data storage. Its decentralized nature provides enhanced protection against cyberattacks, thereby significantly improving security.

- *Immutability:* This refers to the quality or state of being unchanging or unable to be altered. The protection of data integrity is primarily ensured by the immutability concept of the blockchain. Changing or tampering with data once it is stored on a blockchain can be quite challenging. This functionality is a fundamental aspect of blockchain's security features. It plays a crucial role in safeguarding against fraud and data breaches.
- *The Transparency and Traceability of Blockchain Technology:* Blockchain technology is highly regarded for its ability to enhance cyber security through its traceability and transparency. It provides a secure and transparent environment for transactions and operations, simplifying the process of tracking and monitoring. Blockchain is a crucial tool for maintaining the integrity of data and ensuring trust. It plays a vital role in identifying and preventing security breaches.
- *Smart Contracts: Leveraging Blockchain for Enhanced Security Automation:* Blockchain-based smart contracts offer a reliable and highly secure method for automating and enforcing security standards. They have become crucial in the fight against cybercrime due to their ability to provide a secure and automated platform for conducting various digital agreements and transactions.
- *Enhancing Personal Cybersecurity with Blockchain Technology:* It is crucial to consider the application of blockchain technology to individual cyber security. One of the potential benefits of this technology is the enhancement of identity protection and secure data storage. In order to showcase the versatility and ease of use of blockchain technology for personal purposes, this article provides users with practical tips on leveraging it for their digital security.
- *Blockchain in National Cybersecurity Strategies:* There is a growing recognition among federal governments of the potential benefits of blockchain technology in enhancing cyber security. There have been several case studies that showcase how different countries are incorporating blockchain technology into their national security strategies. These studies emphasize the effectiveness of blockchain in enhancing a nation's cyber security defenses.
- *Blockchain Education for Cybersecurity:* Understanding the importance of blockchain technology education for cyber security cannot be overstated. The objective of contemporary educational endeavors is to cultivate individuals who possess knowledge and proficiency in utilizing blockchain technology for the purpose of enhancing cyber security. Proper instruction is crucial in developing

well-informed professionals capable of utilizing blockchain technology to safeguard digital environments (Patmanathan, et al., 2023). To wrap things up, a significant advancement in our modern era revolves around the incorporation of blockchain technology in the realm of cyber security and the prevention of cybercrime. The unique characteristics of this solution offer compelling solutions to the ever-evolving challenges of cyber security, positioning it as a significant driver in shaping a more secure digital landscape (Figure 6.2).

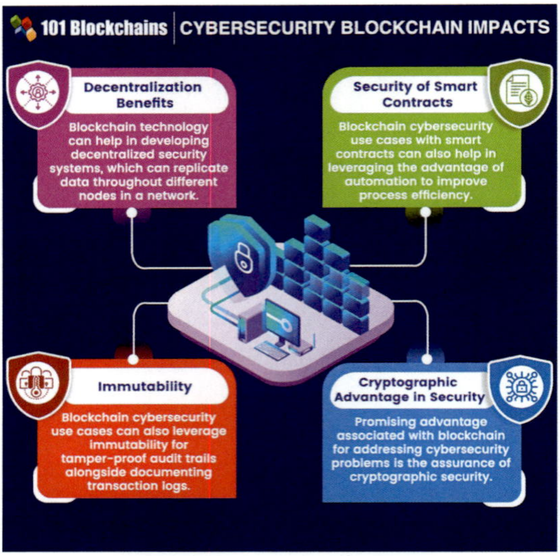

Figure 6.2. *Impact of blockchain on cybersecurity.*

Source: Howell (2023).

6.5. CLOUD COMPUTING AND CYBERCRIME

Due to the rapid expansion of cloud computing, the rise in cybercrimes targeting the cloud has become a significant cause for concern. It is important to stay vigilant against the ever-evolving tactics of cybercriminals in exploiting vulnerabilities in cloud computing systems. Their actions can lead to significant financial losses, unauthorized access to sensitive data, and breaches of privacy (Choo, 2010). There are several factors that contribute to cloud cybercrimes:

- *Insecure Passwords:* Weak passwords are a significant contributing factor to cloud cybercrimes. Many cloud users still rely on weak passwords such as "password123" or "123456," making it easy for cybercriminals to crack them using brute-force techniques. It is highly recommended for cloud users to generate robust and unique passwords that incorporate a mix of uppercase and lowercase letters, numbers, and special characters in order to prevent unauthorized access (Choo, 2010).

- *Lack of Multifactor Authentication:* Users are required to provide multiple forms of identification through multifactor authentication, or MFA, to gain access to cloud resources. It is important to be aware that cybercriminals have the ability to gain access to cloud services without multi-factor authentication. They employ various techniques, such as phishing attacks, to obtain user credentials. Enabling multi-factor authentication on each cloud account is crucial for preventing unauthorized access.
- *Software That Lacks Patches:* Another common cause of cybercrimes in the cloud is unpatched software. Malicious malware can be utilized by cybercriminals to exploit vulnerabilities in cloud software, enabling them to gain unauthorized access to cloud resources. In order to prevent such attacks, it is imperative for cloud users to promptly update their software and apply necessary security updates (Choo, 2010).
- *Inadequate Data security:* Data encryption plays a vital role in safeguarding sensitive information from the clutches of cybercriminals. It is crucial to ensure that data is properly encrypted during transmission or storage to prevent cybercriminals from intercepting and stealing it. It is crucial for cloud users to ensure that their data remains encrypted at all times, whether it is stored in the cloud or not.
- *Insufficient Security Measures:* Cyberattacks have the potential to focus on cloud resources as a result of security measures that are not up to par. This could include weak access controls or insufficient monitoring. Cloud users must implement strict security measures, such as role-based access controls and routine monitoring, to prevent unauthorized access and promptly identify and address potential threats.
- *Sixth-Party Dangers:* Many cloud users rely on external vendors to provide cloud services, which can introduce additional risks. Third-party vendors' systems may be more vulnerable to cyberattacks or have less stringent security measures. It is crucial for cloud customers to ensure that all third-party vendors have robust security measures in place. This can be achieved by conducting thorough screenings of these vendors.

6.6. MOBILE DEVICES AND CYBERCRIME

Cell phones and other mobile gadgets have completely transformed the way individuals interact with technology in their daily lives. Nowadays, phones have become incredibly versatile devices, allowing us to perform tasks that were once only possible on computers. These include sending and receiving emails, playing games, and even making payments. According to research findings, it is projected that by 2023, a staggering 270 million Americans, which accounts for approximately 81.6% of the population, will be in possession of a smartphone. Smartphones, tablets, and other mobile devices are increasingly becoming targets for cybercriminals. There are numerous software programs that are vulnerable to attacks, easily stolen, and contain significant amounts of personal data about the device owner.

Cellphones and tablets, in comparison to conventional computers, do not possess several of the advanced technical security features. The owner's decision-making has a significant impact on mobile device security, as highlighted by Alexandrou (2021). Here are a few strategies to protect your mobile devices, including smartphones, from malicious activity:

- *Employ a Pin, Password, or Pattern:* Implementing a password, personal identification number (PIN), or pattern can significantly enhance the level of security in case of theft or misplacement. In addition, utilizing a password manager to create and store unique passwords for each of your phone's accounts can provide protection against the potential compromise of personal data in case your device is lost or misplaced (Alexandrou, 2021).
- *Install Apps from Reliable Sources:* It is important to use a trustworthy source, such as Google Play or the program Store, when downloading apps, whether it is for entertainment purposes or for banking. Prior to permitting program downloads, both of these application marketplaces conduct thorough security checks.
- *Be Aware of App Permissions:* When apps are installed, they often request access to various services on your phone. Access to certain functions is often necessary for the programs to function properly. For example, a photo-editing program will require access to your camera roll. It is important to ensure that your microphone, along with other necessary components, can be easily accessed by a voice memo app. Some programs may request additional access beyond what is necessary for basic functionality. As an application's usage progresses, it may gain additional permissions. Access that has been granted originally remains unaltered unless you disable it.

- *Update Operating System and Apps Frequently:* Updates are essential for addressing security vulnerabilities. Installing updates is crucial for ensuring the security of your mobile device against online threats. Another benefit of these updates is the chance to explore new features and improve overall functionality.
- *When Using Wi-Fi and Bluetooth Connections, Please be Cautious:* It is important to note that Wi-Fi networks and Bluetooth connections can also pose a risk if they are not properly secured. Cybercriminals can exploit these entry points to gain unauthorized access. When utilizing public Wi-Fi networks, it is important to be aware of the potential risks involved (Figure 6.3). Cybercriminals have the ability to monitor your online activities and potentially expose sensitive personal information. Disabling Bluetooth when it's not being used can be quite beneficial in terms of minimizing the visibility of your device to potential thieves and unauthorized individuals who may try to pair devices. It is crucial to avoid handling sensitive information while using public Wi-Fi networks in order to maintain the security of your online activity. To establish a connection to a reliable network at your convenience, it is advisable to disable the automatic Wi-Fi connections on your device (Alexandrou, 2021).

It is important for individuals to remain vigilant about the potential security risks associated with mobile devices and the sensitive information they store, despite the undeniable convenience they offer in our everyday lives.

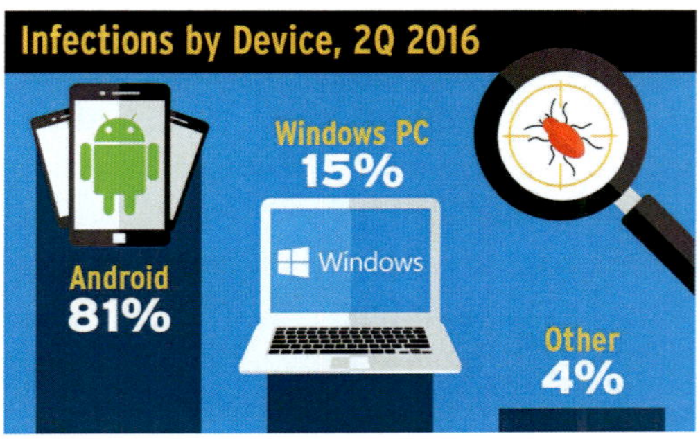

Figure 6.3. *Cybercrime, malware shift to mobile devices.*

Source: "Cybercrime, Malware Shift to Mobile Devices," (2017).

6.7. SOCIAL ENGINEERING AND CYBERCRIME

- Social engineering is a tactic employed by cybercriminals to exploit people's trust and obtain personal information, thereby facilitating further cybercrimes. They employ deceptive tactics, such as utilizing covert communication channels like emails or phone conversations, to trick individuals into revealing their passwords or personal information. For example, a cybercriminal may employ social engineering tactics to convince a worker to disclose their business credentials. Once the cybercriminal has successfully infiltrated corporate networks, they employ these credentials to pilfer data and introduce malware into the network (Breda, Barbosa, & Morais, 2017).

The cybercriminal can successfully deceive their target by impersonating a friend, coworker, or reputable business through means such as email, phone calls, or text messages. The cybercriminal may adopt a tone that is both familiar and urgent in order to convince the victim to update their banking details or provide their credit card information to claim their prize. Defending against social engineering is difficult due to the element of surprise and the unpredictable nature of individuals. The identification of individuals susceptible to social engineering tactics is inherently unpredictable (Breda, Barbosa, & Morais, 2017).

The inherent risk of social engineering lies in the fallibility of individuals. Individuals can be taken by surprise, despite being conscious of the need to be cautious regarding emails offering refunds or phone calls threatening immediate arrest unless they disclose their tax information (Breda, Barbosa, & Morais, 2017). Social engineering exploits human vulnerabilities, such as:

- **Lack of Comprehensive Knowledge Regarding Security Measures:** One of the major challenges that companies face in this field is the employees' lack of ability to identify and defend against social engineering attacks. Given that social engineering attacks exploit human vulnerabilities, the lack of awareness regarding security issues can have catastrophic consequences. Adversaries can acquire critical systems and data by convincing individuals to disclose confidential information or by downloading malicious software (Breda, Barbosa, & Morais, 2017).
- **Excessive Disclosure on Social Media Platforms:** Despite widespread awareness of the hazards associated with excessive disclosure on social media, a significant number of individuals still engage in this behavior. The reason for sharing life updates with friends and family is due to the convenience and enjoyment it brings. However, they often overlook the fact that excessive sharing can

make them and their loved ones susceptible to social engineering scams. Social engineers employ deceptive tactics and manipulate individuals into divulging confidential information or engaging in actions that go against their sound judgment. They may feign to be affiliated with a reputable organization, such as a financial institution or governmental entity, or they may disguise themselves as acquaintances or family members. In addition, they often target individuals who are more prone to disclosing personal information on social media platforms (Breda, Barbosa, & Morais, 2017).

- **Excessive Anxiety:** Generally, it is advisable to inquire; however, excessive curiosity can occasionally pose risks. If you possess a perpetual curiosity about the world and actively pursue new knowledge, you may be susceptible to social engineering. Social engineers manipulate and deceive individuals in order to manipulate them into fulfilling their own desires. They often target curious individuals because they can easily deceive them into revealing information or behaving inappropriately (Breda, Barbosa, & Morais, 2017).

6.7.1. Categories of Social Engineering Attacks

Various techniques can be employed to execute social engineering attacks. The following is a list of prevalent forms of social engineering:

- *Phishing:* This is a tactic employed to illicitly acquire confidential personal and corporate data. It encompasses the act of transmitting deceptive emails, text messages, and websites. Phishing scammers achieve success by carefully disguising themselves through the use of familiar emails and websites (Breda, Barbosa, & Morais, 2017).
- *Sealing Whaling:* This is a type of social engineering attack that specifically targets high-ranking executives or individuals with privileged access to confidential information. The attacker employs phishing and other tactics to dupe the target into revealing confidential information or engaging in actions that provide the attacker with access to the target's system. An organization may be vulnerable to whaling attacks, which can lead to the compromise of sensitive information or the disruption of critical business operations (Breda, Barbosa, & Morais, 2017).
- *Tailgating:* Tailgating refers to a form of physical social engineering where unauthorized access to a building or a secure area within a building is gained by exploiting trust. The perpetrator may simply shadow someone closely, circumvent security measures, or seek

permission to be granted access based on the pretext of misplacing their work swipe card. This instance of deception serves as a prompt for staff members to remain vigilant regarding individuals loitering near entrances and to confidently demand proof of identity.

- *Baiting:* The fundamental basis of baiting lies in the innate human desire for reward. Baiting is a form of social engineering attack that can take place in both offline and online settings. It involves enticing the victim with a reward in exchange for performing a specific action. For example, acquiring an attachment or inserting a USB key to obtain perpetual access to complimentary movie downloads. The program, known as a phishing tool, is designed to deceive users by sending fraudulent emails or acquiring their login credentials. Once installed, it can infect both the computer and potentially the entire network (Breda, Barbosa, & Morais, 2017).
- *Water-Holing:* This refers to a technique used by cyber attackers to compromise a targeted individual or organization by infecting websites that are frequently visited by the intended victims. Water-holing is a tactic that specifically targets a select group of individuals and the websites they regularly visit. The cybercriminal systematically investigates these websites for any vulnerabilities prior to injecting malware into them. Ultimately, the malware successfully infiltrates one of the individuals within the targeted group. The specific type of social engineering mentioned is challenging to detect and highly targeted.
- *Cheating:* Scammers employ voicemails to convince victims that they must promptly take action or else encounter peril or legal consequences. An example of a criminal act is when a thief sends a voicemail to the victim, instructing them to modify their banking information due to a security breach in their account.
- *Vishing:* This refers to the act of using voice communication, typically over the phone, to deceive individuals into revealing sensitive information or performing fraudulent actions. Vishing utilizes voicemails to deceive victims into taking immediate action or else face potential harm or legal consequences. For example, a criminal may leave a recorded message notifying the target that their account has been breached and advising them to update their banking information.
- *Pretexting*: This is a form of social engineering where individuals are deceived into revealing information through the use of a fabricated identity. For example, the cybercriminal may have knowledge that

the victim recently made a purchase from Apple. Therefore, the cybercriminal sends an email claiming to be an Apple customer support agent, asking for the victim's credit card details to be verified.

- *Quid Pro Quo:* Quid pro quo scams exploit information exchanges to manipulate their victims into taking action. This technique of social manipulation offers the target a service in exchange for a reward. A common strategy employed by the criminal is to impersonate an IT support staff member and contact individuals whose service requests are still unresolved. According to Breda, Barbosa, & Morais (2017), the cybercriminal guarantees a fast fix if the victim turns off their antivirus software or confirms their login credentials.
- *Malicious Software:* Malware tricks individuals into making payments to eliminate viruses, malware, or other harmful software from their computer systems. The victims are deceived into thinking that their computers are contaminated with malware or viruses, and that they can have it eliminated for a charge. The offender may utilize the victim's credit card information or introduce malicious software or ransomware into the device, depending on the nature of the deception (Breda, Barbosa, & Morais, 2017).
- *Deceptive Identity*: False identities are a crucial component of social engineering attacks. An assailant can gain the confidence of their victims, acquire confidential data, and execute other malicious actions by assuming a fraudulent persona. The most prevalent method of creating a fraudulent identity involves utilizing stolen or fabricated credentials, although there are alternative approaches available. This strategy can be executed by procuring illicitly obtained data from the underground market or by commencing from the beginning with openly available information to construct a fresh identity.

  After an attacker has successfully assumed a deceptive identity, they often exploit it to build trust with the target. An assailant possesses the capacity to participate in online forums and groups, initiate friend requests, and dispatch messages. Furthermore, hackers may exploit their fabricated identities to acquire sensitive information, such as bank account numbers or login credentials. Attackers sometimes exploit their fabricated identities to commit fraud or other criminal activities (Breda, Barbosa, & Morais, 2017).

CHAPTER 7

CYBERCRIME AND SOCIAL ENGINEERING

Contents

Social engineering is a tactic employed by cybercriminals to exploit people's trust and obtain personal information, thereby facilitating further cybercrimes. They employ deceptive tactics to elicit passwords or personal information from individuals through clandestine means such as emails or phone conversations. For example, a cybercriminal may employ social engineering tactics to convince an employee to disclose their business credentials. Once the cybercriminal has obtained entry into the corporate networks, they employ these credentials to pilfer data and contaminate the network with malware (Al-Mohannadi et al., 2016).

7.1. STEPS INVOLVED IN SOCIAL ENGINEERING

Adversaries employ social engineering tactics in an attempt to deceive individuals into revealing confidential information, such as banking information, login credentials, or access privileges. Social engineering involves four distinct steps (Figure 7.1).

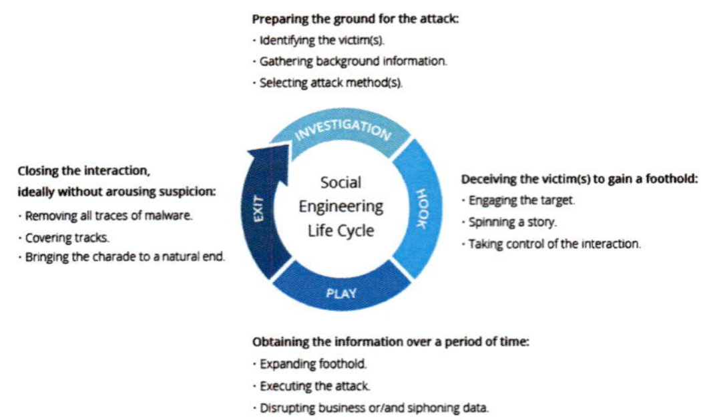

Figure 7.1. *Social engineering attack lifecycle.*

Source: Avital (2023).

1. *Preparatory Phase:* Attackers collect information on their targets by utilizing various means such as social media, phone calls, emails, texts, the dark web, and other sources.
2. *Infiltration Tactics:* Attackers typically employ infiltration tactics to approach victims, assuming the guise of trustworthy individuals or authorities, and leveraging the information they have gathered about their targets to gain their trust. This method can also be employed to obtain entry into more valuable targets, such as top-level executives, system administrators, or IT helpdesk personnel.
3. *Exploitation:* This refers to the act of an attacker manipulating or coercing a victim into revealing confidential information, such as passwords or payment account details. This information can be

utilized to initiate a cyber assault. This form of persuasion, which can include a website, social media quiz, attachment, or link, often exhibits subtlety.

4. *Disengagement:* This refers to the act of an attacker engaging in malicious behavior, then abruptly terminating contact with the victim and disappearing.

7.1.1. Techniques for Social Engineering

These are five of the most widely used social engineering attacks.

- **Phishing:** This refers to the fraudulent practice of attempting to obtain sensitive information, such as passwords or credit card details, by disguising oneself as a trustworthy entity in electronic communication. Phishing attacks employ email, social media, instant messaging apps, or SMS messages to deceive a target into clicking on a link leading to a harmful website or to extract sensitive information from them (Al-Mohannad et al., 2016).

  Phishing messages employ tactics such as curiosity, requests for assistance, or other emotional triggers to captivate a victim's attention and incite them to act. They often assume the identity of companies by utilizing their logos, images, or fonts to create the illusion that the communication is originating from a bank, colleague, or other authoritative source. Most phishing emails use a sense of urgency to deceive the victim into believing that there will be severe consequences if they do not quickly provide important information (Al-Mohannadi et al., 2016).

There several types of phishing attacks:

a. Email Phishing: This is a traditional form of phishing that involves sending emails to the target, urging them to respond or take further action. The email may contain hazardous attachments or links.

b. *Phishing by Voice:* It also referred to as vishing- this entails initiating a phone call, either by a human operator or an automated messaging system. By utilizing the telephone, the assailant has the ability to manipulate the victim into carrying out any action or obtain confidential information from them.

c. *SMS Phishing:* It is also referred to as smishing- this involves sending text messages or communications through mobile apps that may include harmful links or directly request the recipient to provide sensitive information.

d. *Angler Phishing:* This refers to the act of impersonating a reputable company's customer care representatives or social media account. By exploiting this vulnerability, the attacker gains the capability to intercept and monitor brand communications, transform them into confidential messages, and exploit them for spear phishing campaigns (Al-Mohannadi, Mirza et al., 2016).

e. *Search Engine Phishing:* The attackers employ search engine phishing as a strategy to present counterfeit websites prominently in search results. This objective could be achieved through the utilization of illicit black hat techniques, lawful search engine optimization strategies, or paid advertising.

f. *Session Phishing:* This refers to the act of attempting to disrupt normal online browsing by engaging in phishing activities during a client session. As an example, the perpetrator could direct the user to a harmful website or introduce a fake login interface.

g. *Spear Phishing:* Spear phishing also referred to as whaling- this is a form of targeted phishing that involves using any of the aforementioned methods to target a specific individual or department after conducting prior surveillance.

- **Deceptive Software Designed to Frighten or Intimidate Users:** Scareware is a malicious technique that aims to deceive individuals into downloading or purchasing software and updates that are infected with malware. Scareware attacks commonly trick individuals into thinking they need to download or install software that pretends to be a cybersecurity solution (Al-Mohannadi et al., 2016). Scareware is specifically crafted to coerce computer users into purchasing counterfeit software or exacerbating the infection of their system. Scareware commonly manifests as pop-up security notifications that mimic warnings from well-known antivirus vendors, falsely claiming that files are infected or the device is at risk. Additional variations encompass upgrades implemented through software or hardware, notifications regarding memory limitations, and services aimed at removing unused applications.

- **The Watering Hole:** A watering hole attack refers to the deployment or retrieval of malicious code from a reputable website that is frequently visited by the targeted victims of the attack. For example, hackers may infiltrate a news website that focuses on the financial sector, knowing that the users are likely to be professionals in that field and therefore an attractive target. Typically, a backdoor trojan is implanted by the compromised website, granting the attacker remote control over the victim's device (Al-Mohannadi et al., 2016). Watering hole attacks are typically carried out by skilled attackers who have discovered a zero-day exploit and are targeting a specific type of consumer as warned by Banks in 2017. These attackers may also be staff members of a particular organization who use a specific HR resource or tool.

- **An Attack Involving Whaling or Spear Phishing**: Spear phishing, also known as whaling, refers to targeted phishing attacks that aim at individuals with privileged system access or access to highly valuable sensitive information. Examples of potential targets for a whaling attack include network administrators, wealthy individuals, and senior executives (Al-Mohannadi et al., 2016). A whaling assault is a phishing attempt that is characterized by its advanced nature. Attackers conduct thorough research prior to formulating a message that will elicit specific targets to respond and engage in the desired activity. Phishing emails often masquerade as urgent business emails from someone the target knows, such as their manager, coworker, or colleague. These emails typically ask the victim to take immediate action (Al-Mohannadi et al., 2016).
- **Using a Pretext:** Pretexting attacks entail the fabrication of a deceptive persona by the perpetrator, which they subsequently exploit to deceive the target into revealing confidential information. For example, hackers may impersonate an external IT support company and request users' passwords and account information to assist them with a problem. Alternatively, scammers may impersonate the victim's financial institution and ask for confirmation of their bank account number or login credentials (Al-Mohannadi et al., 2016).

7.2. SOCIAL ENGINEERING PREVENTION

The elimination of security risks posed by social engineering may not be entirely achievable, however, the implementation of proactive measures can significantly diminish the likelihood of social engineering attacks.

Strategies to prevent social engineering attacks are discussed in the following subsections.

7.2.1. Two-Factor Authentication

Relying solely on a single factor is not advisable; even the most basic preventive measure guarantees the safety of one's account. While the password does offer security, we have discovered that it is insufficient by itself. Given the relative ease with which someone else can decode your password and gain access to your accounts. Social engineering can be employed to acquire passwords. Utilizing multi-factor authentication is imperative, encompassing methods such as one-time password (OTP) codes, security inquiries, or biometric authentication (Tulkarm, 2021).

7.2.2. Continuously Monitor Essential Systems

Maintain continuous monitoring of the system, which houses confidential information. Some exploitation techniques, like Trojan horses, sometimes depend on the system, which is vulnerable. Web application scanning is a technique that can be employed to examine both internal and external systems with the purpose of detecting vulnerabilities in one's system.

Furthermore, it is advisable to conduct a social engineering assessment at least once annually to ascertain the vulnerability of your employees to social engineering threats. If any fraudulent domains are detected, they can be promptly eliminated to prevent online copyright infringement (Tulkarm, 2021).

7.2.3. Use a Cloud-Based, Next-Generation Web Application Firewall (WAF)

While it is probable that your company already has a firewall implemented, a next-generation web application cloud-based firewall is specifically designed to provide the most effective protection against social engineering attacks. The conventional web application firewall (WAF) commonly employed by most businesses exhibits significant disparities when compared to the online WAF.

AppTrana has the capability to consistently monitor a website or web application for any abnormal activity or misconduct. Although social engineering attacks exploit human error, they serve as a preventive measure against attacks and provide notifications for attempted malware installations (Tulkarm, 2021). An effective approach to thwart social engineering attempts and potential breaches is to employ a risk-based Web Application Firewall (WAF).

7.2.4. Check the Identity of the Email Sender

Most scams employ the strategy of impersonating a trustworthy entity to deceitfully obtain the victim's personal information. Phishing attackers often impersonate trusted email senders, such as credit card companies, banks, social networking sites, or online retailers. The emails often employ narrative techniques to lure individuals into clicking on the deceptive, yet convincingly genuine, hyperlink.

Contact the alleged email sender to authenticate the source of the message and prevent potential harm from this form of social engineering fraud. It is important to remember that reputable banks do not send emails requesting authorized credentials or private information.

7.2.5. Identify the Key Assets That Attract Criminals

Many businesses prioritize protecting their assets from a strategic perspective. Cybercriminals may opt for an alternative approach to specifically target your enterprise. They consistently strive for the things that hold significance to them. When considering the perspective of the attacker, it is important to identify the assets that need to be safeguarded, while also considering resources beyond just your products, services, or intellectual property (Tulkarm, 2021).

7.2.6. Validate the SSL Certificate

To ensure the security of sensitive information, it is imperative to encrypt all forms of data, emails, and other communications. This precautionary measure serves to thwart potential hackers from gaining unauthorized access to intercepted information. This can be achieved by procuring SSL certificates from reputable sources.

Furthermore, it is imperative to verify the authenticity of the website prior to disclosing any crucial information. Inspect the URLs to verify the authenticity of the website. Websites that have the prefix "https://" are considered reliable and secure due to their encryption. Websites that have a "http://" prefix do not establish a secure connection (Tulkarm, 2021).

7.3. SOCIAL ENGINEERING AWARENESS

Incidents involving social engineering tactics present a growing threat to both individuals and businesses. The objective of these attacks is to trick individuals into revealing confidential information, such as personal details, financial data, or login credentials. Social engineering attacks can manifest in several forms, such as phishing emails, phone calls, and text messages, and they have the potential to be highly effective. According to the 2022 Verizon Data Breach Investigations Report, 82% of data breaches that involve human participation are caused by social engineering attacks (Aldawood & Skinner, 2019). However, there are methods to prevent these attacks, and one crucial approach is through information security awareness training.

Information security awareness training can help prevent social engineering attacks through the following methods:

- *Develop the Capacity to Identify Indicators of Social Engineering Attacks:* Employees can acquire the ability to identify indicators of social engineering attacks by participating in information security awareness training. This training covers topics such as unsolicited emails or messages, requests for confidential information, and language that appears urgent or threatening. Employees can avoid becoming targets of social engineering attacks by being vigilant of these warning signs.
- *Implement Comprehensive Information Security Protocols:* Information security awareness training can educate staff members on effective security practices, such as generating robust and unique passwords, enabling two-factor authentication, and regularly updating software. It is imperative to avoid using the same password for multiple accounts, as this can enable fraudsters to gain access to multiple accounts using just one password. These procedures enhance the defense against social engineering attacks by augmenting the level of difficulty for hackers to acquire sensitive data.
- *Conduct Phishing Simulations:* Phishing simulations are an effective method for assessing employees' susceptibility to social engineering attacks. Incorporating phishing simulations that replicate real attacks into information security awareness training can be used to assess employees' responses. Through enhancing overall security consciousness, these simulations can aid in pinpointing areas that necessitate additional training. Aldawood and Skinner (2019) have demonstrated that AwareGO's Human Risk Assessment is effective in addressing this issue. The program assesses and instructs employees on cybersecurity protocols by simulating real-life situations within a secure environment that does not assign blame.
- *Encourage the Disclosure of Illicit Activities:* Employees who undergo information security awareness training may also be incentivized to report any suspicious activity, such as phishing emails or phone calls. One can detect and prevent social engineering attacks that may harm individuals by reporting any suspicious activities.

7.4. SOCIAL ENGINEERING RISKS

A social engineering attack can have severe consequences for a business.

- *Data Exfiltration of Sensitive Information*: A prevalent objective of social engineering attacks is to obtain confidential data. Successful completion of this task could potentially lead to the exposure of confidential data pertaining to clients, employees, financial matters, or proprietary information.

- *Financial Loss*: Via fraud, unlawful financial transfers, or payments to dishonest vendors, cybercriminals can utilize social engineering to cheat the business of money.
- *Damage to a Company's Reputation*: Successful social engineering attacks can cause significant damage to a company's reputation. Revealing confidential data or being linked to fraudulent activities can lead to a decrease in trust from clients and business partners.
- *Operational Disruption*: A specific objective of some social engineering attacks is to disrupt the functioning of a business. This could result in decreased productivity, service disruptions, and significant expenses for restoration.
- *Legal Liability*: This can arise for businesses when they are responsible for privacy breaches affecting their clients or when they incur financial losses due to a successful social engineering attack. There may be legal consequences as a result of this.
- *Network and System Infiltration*: Social engineering attacks grant hackers entry into corporate networks and systems, thereby facilitating the theft of intellectual property, cyber espionage, and various other forms of incursion.
- *Malware Propagation*: Through the use of social engineering tactics, attackers can manipulate staff members into downloading malicious software, thereby posing a threat to the security of data and IT systems.
- *Financial or Accounting Data Loss*: Social engineering attacks can specifically target individuals responsible for financial or accounting tasks, leading to the fraudulent alteration or loss of critical financial data.

The telecommuting trend has brought about a significant shift in how employees interact with the IT infrastructure and systems of their respective companies. While teleworking presents various advantages, it can also increase the likelihood of social engineering attacks for several reasons. Due to their frequent solitude while working remotely, employees may be more vulnerable to social engineering scams.

Detecting attempted scams can become more difficult in the absence of nearby colleagues to consult or verify information. In addition, certain employees may engage in remote work using their personal computers, which may not offer the same level of security as the PCs provided by the company (Salahdine

& Kaabouch, 2019). These gadgets can serve as a means for cybercriminals to launch attacks. The main modes of communication utilized in teleworking are emails, online messages, and virtual meetings.

Cybercriminals utilize these platforms to disseminate harmful collaboration messages, phishing emails, and fraudulent meeting invitations, along with other forms of social engineering attacks. Remote employees often have limited exposure to hazard awareness and IT security training. As a result, they have a lower ability to identify and report cases of social engineering. Using public or unprotected Wi-Fi networks raises the likelihood of telecommuting staff eavesdropping on or observing communications. In order to mitigate these risks, companies should implement telecommuting-specific security measures such as personal computer security policies, telecommuting-specific security training, and email security systems capable of detecting and preventing social engineering attempts. Employee comprehension of cybersecurity threats and optimal strategies is indispensable in thwarting social engineering attacks (Salahdine & Kaabouch, 2019).

7.4.1. Social Engineering Attacks That Have Occurred in the Past Few Years

1. In 2022, Uber experienced a social engineering attack. The individual confessed to the New York Times that they had utilized social engineering, a widely-used phishing method that exploits individuals' inclination to disclose personal information to unfamiliar individuals. The hacker employed a deceptive tactic by assuming the identity of an Uber IT representative and utilized WhatsApp to contact an employee, manipulating them into accessing a counterfeit Uber website. Consequently, the hacker managed to acquire the worker's password and manipulate him into utilizing the company's Multi-Factor Authentication (MFA) program for verifying his access.
2. In 2020, Twitter experienced a vishing attack. Due to the cyber-attack, users of the platform experienced a loss of approximately $118,000 worth of bitcoins. Around 130 authenticated Twitter accounts, all belonging to prominent individuals, were breached. Warren Buffet, Kim Kardashian, Barack Obama, and Elon Musk were among the prominent individuals who were affected. The attackers employed a phishing campaign to entice victims into transferring bitcoin payments to a specific wallet, under the false pretense of receiving double the amount sent. The fraudsters employed a two-step process to acquire the administrative particulars for these

authenticated accounts. The perpetrators initiated their operation by utilizing a strategy commonly referred to as "vishing," wherein they targeted Twitter employees in lower-ranking positions who did not possess the necessary privileges to access administrative tools. These workers inadvertently provided the hackers with their login information, enabling the hackers to contact more senior employees who had the necessary permissions.

3. In 2017, Facebook and Google were targeted by spear-phishing and "BEC" (Business E-mail Compromise) attacks. An individual from Lithuania managed to deceive both Google and Facebook. In order to accomplish his task, he assumed the identity of a Quanta Computer employee, as the two companies had a history of collaboration. The hacker acquired $100 million through the utilization of counterfeit contracts, invoices, and reminders directed towards accounting departments. The individual went as far as to establish bank accounts in Taiwan in order to avoid attracting suspicion.

7.5. SOCIAL ENGINEERING PSYCHOLOGY

1. Social engineering refers to the act of persuading someone to engage in an action that may or may not be advantageous to them. Emotions serve as a strategic method used by malicious individuals to manipulate their victims into taking actions they would not normally take. Being the recipient of such an attack does not indicate a deficiency in intelligence or expertise (Crisp, Turner, & Meleady, 2024). During an adversarial simulation conducted by Social-Engineer, LLC (SECOM), cyber security experts themselves disclosed confidential information in a vishing test. Why are these attacks still effective against professionals in the field? The crux of the matter lies in the impact of emotions on human behavior. Unscrupulous individuals use tactics of influence to provoke strong emotions such as terror, resulting in a "amygdala hijack" where emotional reactions override rational thinking (Crisp, Turner, & Meleady, 2024). This induces individuals to engage in behaviors that deviate from their typical conduct. Here are a few examples:

2. *Fear or Apprehension*: Fear is a distressing and often intense emotion that arises from awareness or expectation of danger. Fear, being a potent human emotion, is commonly exploited by malicious individuals to manipulate their targets. Moreover, it is effortless to provoke fear. Take, for instance, receiving a counterfeit email with the subject line "Attention." There has been fraudulent activity

detected on your account. Without delay, alter your password. What is your opinion? The occurrence of a "virtual kidnapping" scam, wherein the victim is notified of the alleged abduction of a family member, represents a significantly more alarming form of attack. The malicious individuals employ intimidation and deception to coerce the victims into making a ransom payment.

3. *Greed:* The Cambridge Dictionary defines greed as "an intense longing to acquire more of a particular resource, particularly wealth." Given that greed is an inherent human emotion, social engineers perceive it as an exceedingly advantageous instrument. This is demonstrated by the "419 Nigerian scam." Cybercriminals employ phone calls or emails to impersonate wealthy individuals from foreign countries who seek aid in transferring millions of dollars out of their nation. For a nominal fee, they ensure a significant share of the wealth. Driven by a strong desire for financial gain, the individual willingly reveals the specific information regarding their bank account with the expectation of receiving a reward (Crisp, Turner, & Meleady, 2024).
4. *Providing Aid or Support:* From an early age, we are taught that displaying kindness and obedience is the key to being perceived as a respectable individual. Hostile assailants can exploit this willingness to assist others. Threat actors often focus on newly hired individuals due to their inclination to be cooperative and excel in their fresh positions. The majority of cultures imbue in us the importance of showing deference to authority figures and individuals of higher rank. Hence, there will be minimal opposition to the validity of a request made by an individual in a position of power. Consequently, unscrupulous individuals may impersonate the employer in a phishing email and request a straightforward favor. The "favor" may involve soliciting confidential information such as business details, login credentials, gift cards, account numbers, or financial data.
5. *Need for Urgency:* A social engineering attack often incorporates a sense of urgency. In situations of urgency, the victim may act spontaneously without taking time to reflect. Instances may involve receiving a pressing demand from your employer, whom you are presently unable to contact, or uncovering a suspicious transaction on your account that necessitates your immediate focus (Crisp, Turner, & Meleady, 2024).
6. *Curiosity:* This is another strategy employed in social engineering. In order to deceive their victims, the attackers employ alluring or

advantageous pledges. Engaging in a cyber-attack could involve sending an email with the subject line "Your Amazon purchase for the sum of $800.00 is prepared for shipment." Please click on the provided link to view your order. The recipient of such an email or text message may develop a sense of curiosity and a feeling of obligation to click on the provided link (Crisp, Turner, & Meleady, 2024).

7.6. SOCIAL ENGINEERING TOOLS

Social engineering refers to the ability to manipulate individuals into voluntarily revealing confidential information. It exploits individuals' trust through psychological manipulation in order to extract sensitive information, such as passwords, bank account details, and even system login credentials, without arousing suspicion. Phishing attacks, such as fraudulent websites and deceptive emails, are the most prevalent methods of social engineering. These tactics imitate legitimate channels of genuine companies with the intention of acquiring personal information (Maaz et al., 2023).

- *Maltego*: This is a social engineering tool specifically designed for Kali Linux. Maltego is an open-source intelligence (OSINT) research tool that visually represents the relationships between different pieces of information. Maltego is a tool that allows you to uncover relationships between people and various types of information resources, such as social media profiles, screen names, email addresses, and other details that link an individual to a business or service. To evaluate your staff members' security awareness, you can simulate a social engineering attack using the information you have acquired.
- *The Social Engineering Toolkit (SET):* This is a social engineering tool specifically designed for Kali Linux. The Social Engineering Toolkit, also referred to as SET, is a Python-based toolkit that is open-source and specifically created for conducting penetration testing focused on social engineering. By utilizing SET's diverse range of distinctive assault vectors, you can efficiently assemble a persuasive attack. The website tool included with SET has the ability to turn your Kali computer into a web server, which can be used to exploit vulnerabilities in a wide range of browsers. The objective is to provide a hyperlink to your website that will automatically download and execute the exploit on the computer of your intended target (Maaz et al., 2023).

In order to enhance the credibility of the exploit, you can replicate a legitimate website by utilizing the pre-designed templates available in SET. The Social Engineering Toolkit (SET) offers pre-configured phishing pages for popular websites like Facebook, Twitter, Google, and Yahoo.

- *Wifi Phisher:* This is a cutting-edge social engineering tool that automates phishing attacks on Wi-Fi networks with the goal of acquiring the WPA/WPA2 passwords of a specific user group. The tool has the capability to choose and disrupt any nearby Wi-Fi access point by de-authenticating all users. Additionally, it can create a duplicate access point that can be joined without requiring a password. The apparent phishing page that emerges when an individual connects to the deceptive open network requests the Wi-Fi password to facilitate the download of a firmware upgrade, purportedly responsible for the malfunctioning of the Wi-Fi connection. The WIFI phisher delays sending an alert after the targets enter a password. Upon transmitting the gathered password, the system will display a deceptive update screen and a counterfeit reboot timer, providing you with additional time to test it. This tool is valuable for evaluating the effectiveness of your security measures in protecting against social engineering attacks conducted through Wi-Fi (Maaz et al., 2023).
- *Metasploit MSF:* This is a penetration testing tool that aids in the discovery, exploitation, and verification of vulnerabilities. The platform offers the necessary infrastructure, tools, and content to conduct comprehensive security audits and penetration tests (Maaz et al., 2023). One of the most powerful features of Metasploit is its ability to set up a simulated SMB server. Consequently, when a user tries to connect to the server over the network, their machine will be required to exhibit their login details in the shape of their "domain password hash." If users attempt to authenticate with the SMB server, it is possible to obtain domain credentials by exercising patience. To acquire the domain credentials of the target, you can send them an embedded UNC path that they can click on to gain access. As soon as the creators of new exploits make them available, they are promptly updated, and MSF is regularly updated as well.
- *MSFvenom Payload Creator (MSFPC):* This is a user-friendly tool that simplifies the process of generating basic payloads. This tool facilitates users in creating payloads without the need to manually enter lengthy msfvenom commands. This generator allows you to create payloads that necessitate a minimum of one argument. MSFPC can be used to create payloads for Windows, Linux, and Android

operating systems. The script is highly efficient when you require rapid construction of fundamental payloads, resulting in significant time savings. Acquiring knowledge can still be beneficial, even if it does not necessitate encoding in order to bypass antivirus software. Occasionally, there are instances when your sole objective is to promptly construct a payload, transport it to a specific location, and proceed with your tasks. These types of scenarios are where msfpc.sh can prove to be beneficial. To utilize MSFPC, simply specify the desired payload by choosing either the file extension or the platform on which it should be deployed.

7.7. SOCIAL ENGINEERING COUNTERMEASURES

In a social engineering engagement, a threat actor usually exploits social skills and human error to acquire or compromise an organization's assets. The primary objective of countermeasures against social engineering attacks is to eliminate human error. Various countermeasure types can be classified into three distinct categories: a) Standards and procedures b) Workers' awareness c) Technical activities

7.7.1. Standards and Procedures

Implementing suitable policies, protocols, and procedures ensures that staff members are adequately prepared for potentially hazardous situations. Humans inherently experience feelings of guilt when they refuse or decline. Nevertheless, if there are clearly established protocols in place for managing situations that deviate from the usual, your employee will feel more at ease refusing and following corporate policies in potentially hazardous circumstances (Adewole et al., 2015). In order to address the problem of social engineering targeting your company, please review the following set of policies:

1. *Internet Usage*: Discusses the proper and suitable ways to use the Internet. For example, usage that is exclusively applicable to work may be permitted. This measure could protect employees from receiving phishing emails that are unrelated to their job responsibilities.
2. *The Software Policy:* This outlines the software that is allowed to be used and the individuals who have the authority to install or update software. Consider implementing restrictions on the installation of software on computers. Implementing this measure could effectively prevent a social engineer from executing a vishing attack, in which the attacker manipulates the victim into installing malicious software on their computer.

3. *The Hardware Policy:* This defines the acceptable usage and recommended hardware. USB flash drives, for example, may be prohibited. This measure could deter employees from inserting potentially dangerous USB devices into their work computers, which they discovered in the company's parking lot.
4. *Segregation of Duties*: Establishes the specific responsibilities and authorizations assigned to each individual. An employee's access and actions may be significantly restricted if they become a victim of a social engineering attack.
5. *Password Policy*: Offers clear instructions on the specifications for creating new passwords (including character count, length, and other relevant factors), managing passwords (such as avoiding sharing or reusing them), resetting passwords, and additional related guidelines. Adhering to the rule of never sharing one's password can discourage certain employees from revealing their password during a vishing attempt, where social engineering is used to impersonate an IT staff member.
6. *Policy Regarding Physical Access*: This document provides a set of instructions for physical access, which include the requirement to always wear an identity badge, the prohibition of individuals from following you through locked doors, the verification of guests' identities, and the necessity for them to be accompanied by chaperones (Adewole et al., 2015).

7.7.2. Workers' Awareness

As threat actors constantly adapt their strategies, it is crucial for your team to undergo training in order to detect attacks or, at the very least, recognize abnormal occurrences during regular operations. Skills that have been acquired may gradually fade from memory as time passes. However, the strategies and tactics employed by our adversaries are continually evolving. It is imperative that all staff members receive timely and consistent training.

Effective training programs should include comprehensive social engineering exercises, regular simulated phishing tests, and overall security awareness training. It is imperative that staff members possess a comprehensive understanding of the sensitivity and classification of assets and information. The staff must recognize that dealing with highly sensitive information necessitates a higher level of skepticism compared to handling less significant assets (Adewole et al., 2015).

7.7.3. Technical Activities

The objective of technical countermeasures is to mitigate the issue and prevent its escalation. The objective is to eliminate potential dangers prior to their ability to take advantage of human tendencies. Various options are offered in this context, including individual authentication, advanced access cards, secure physical access systems (such as gates and doors), confidential waste disposal, and guest supervision.

CHAPTER 8

CYBERCRIME AND FINANCIAL FRAUD

Contents

Due to human fallibility, the ability to remain anonymous on the internet, and the interconnectedness of global financial systems, cybercrime and financial fraud have become closely linked in the modern world. Cybercriminals employ advanced fraudulent techniques to bypass standard security systems in order to target individuals and organizations, with the intention of stealing ransom money (Hasham et al., 2019).

8.1. FINANCIAL FRAUD IN CYBERCRIME

Technological advancements, increased cloud usage, and innovative working practices are causing sensitive data to be more widely distributed, often outside of businesses' direct control. As a consequence, they become increasingly vulnerable to financial fraud and the growing prevalence of cybercrime. Furthermore, the digitization of financial services has led to an escalation in the risks associated with data loss and financial harm. Amidst the challenging circumstances, it is imperative for experts to skillfully guide their companies to secure positions through the turbulent online landscape (Hasham et al., 2019). The resourcefulness and tenacity of cybercriminals are exemplified by the current threat landscape. Financial fraud is a significant problem that affects all sectors. Due to the rapid pace of digitalization in enterprises and the frequent inadequacy of cybersecurity measures, fraud results in a loss of approximately 5% of annual revenue for businesses.

8.1.1. Fraudulent Strategies

Financial institutions must stay vigilant about the patterns of fraudulent activity, including its origin and target. Gaining comprehension of the potential risks and their potential consequences is crucial as it empowers businesses to establish countermeasures against cyberattacks. Cybercriminals frequently employ various techniques such as phishing, vishing, smishing, and sophisticated spear phishing to target unsuspecting individuals and bank clients. Scammers employ state-of-the-art artificial intelligence technologies to create alluring schemes that are extremely difficult to uncover (Hasham et al., 2019). According to the FBI, the Business email compromise (BEC) is a highly financially detrimental and rapidly growing criminal activity, resulting in losses exceeding $43 billion. During business email compromise (BEC) attacks, criminals employ persuasive emails that mimic those of high-ranking executives in order to deceive the company and commit fraud. Due to their possession of insider knowledge, criminal actors pose a significant risk in conducting BEC attacks.

Despite their age, tech support scams continue to exploit the fear, anxiety, and limited technical knowledge of their victims (Hasham et al., 2019).

Cybercriminals assume the role of tech support specialists when contacting individuals regarding computer issues, with the intention of gaining remote control over the victim's device and either installing malicious software or pilfering data. Fraud and cybercrime are interconnected due to human error, internet anonymity, and the global interdependence of money. Cybercriminals employ advanced fraudulent techniques to breach standard security systems and pilfer ransom funds from individuals and organizations. As a result of this convergence, the methods employed to undermine the security of financial systems have progressed from simple scams to complex, multi-faceted attacks (Hasham et al., 2019). Cryptocurrencies and online banking further obscure the barriers, providing criminals with additional channels for money laundering.

8.1.2. Optimal Security Protocols

Preemptive measures are more desirable than corrective ones, especially in the context of cyber fraud, where risks and response protocols need to be constantly reassessed. It is important for companies to regularly evaluate the potential risks they face and make any necessary changes. Businesses must incorporate the following crucial actions into their cybersecurity strategy:

- *Education*: Regular training on identifying and handling cyber risks is essential in order to minimize human error and enhance security awareness among staff, clients, and consumers.
- *Cyber Hygiene*: This involves implementing robust password policies, utilizing two-factor or multi-factor authentication, regularly updating software, conducting security audits, and continuously monitoring for potential threats in order to prevent attacks that exploit security vulnerabilities.
- *Security Strategy*: Implement a multi-layered security approach that incorporates intrusion detection systems, firewalls, and routine security audits to effectively deter hackers.
- *Response Planning*: In order to minimize harm and recover quickly from security breaches, it is important to Have a well-rehearsed incident response strategy.
- *Advanced Technologies*: Stay ahead of potential threats by utilizing machine learning and artificial intelligence to detect anomalies and conduct predictive analysis.
- *Compliance*: Compliance with regulations such as PSD2, NIS2, and DORA provides a structure for preventing fraud. However, firms must prioritize compliance because they may face significant regulatory fines if they fail to comply.

- *Cooperation*: This involves the exchange of perilous information among organizations and the establishment of collaborations between the public and private sectors, can yield significant outcomes.

An adaptive and versatile approach to cybersecurity is necessary in response to the ever-changing nature of fraud and cybercrime. Preserving trust, credibility, and the underlying framework that sustains financial systems is equally crucial to safeguarding money. Technological advancements must be accompanied by corresponding measures to mitigate these risks.

8.2. ONLINE BANKING FRAUD

The prevalence of online banking fraud has risen in tandem with the adoption of online banking services. Currently, bank phishing schemes are one of the most widespread forms of criminal activity on the internet. Cybercriminals engage in the theft of credit and debit card information, as well as bank account login credentials, with the intention of gaining financial profit. Nevertheless, what are the precise mechanisms underlying these cybercrimes and what are the individual repercussions that ensue from them?

Online bank fraud refers to the unauthorized acquisition of an individual's or organization's digital banking credentials and sensitive financial information by a cybercriminal. Subsequently, they exploit this situation by promptly withdrawing funds from their account or participating in diverse financial fraudulent activities. From a legal standpoint, any illicit behavior carried out through a financial institution's website or application is considered online banking fraud. This refers to the act of illicitly accessing someone else's account with the intention of managing or transferring their funds (Williamson & Money-America's, 2006).

The extensive digitalization of modern banking offers attackers multiple avenues to perpetrate these crimes. Despite banks' increasing efforts to protect their digital services and customers' accounts, the prevention of fraud is becoming increasingly challenging due to the growing sophistication of these attacks.

8.2.1. Operational Mechanisms of Bank Scams

Cybercriminals are utilizing increasingly sophisticated tactics to deceive unsuspecting individuals into inadvertently revealing their banking details and perpetrating online banking fraud. These attacks are frequently complex and employ various strategies, which makes their identification difficult. Therefore, it is crucial for all individuals utilizing online financial services to be cognizant of these dangers in order to avoid them (Williamson & Money-America's, 2006).

Online banking fraud can be classified into two main categories: Automatic Transfer Systems (ATS) and Account Takeovers (ATO).

Below are some of the most prevalent methods employed by cybercriminals to execute Account Takeovers (ATOs) and online banking fraud:

1. *Phishing*: In bank phishing schemes, the perpetrator impersonates the victim's reputable financial institution and sends an email requesting the recipient to verify their login credentials. The phisher can acquire login credentials by inputting them on a fraudulent website that replicates the official website of the bank, usually accessed through a link provided in the email. Financial institutions regularly inform their customers that they will never ask for sensitive information, such as passwords or personal identification numbers (PINs).
2. *Vishing*: This refers to phishing attacks conducted through phone calls rather than email. During a telephonic conversation, the assailant impersonates the victim's financial institution and deceives them into divulging their login credentials and account details. Consequently, the attacker now possesses full authorization and authority over the account. Occasionally, the assailant endeavors to acquire particular personal information from the target with the intention of employing it in subsequent online banking fraud schemes, or they manipulate the target into directly transferring money to them (Williamson & Money-America's, 2006).
3. *Keyloggers*: These are a type of malware, specifically Trojans, that monitor and record keystrokes on a computer. It captures keystrokes when it detects that the user is accessing a pre-determined list of banking websites. This action essentially involves illicitly obtaining the login credentials for a bank account, thereby granting the attacker unauthorized access to the account and the ability to withdraw funds from it (Williamson & Money-America's, 2006).
4. *Password Theft*: Bank login scams sometimes employ brute force and dictionary attacks. These programs systematically attempt different passwords until they find the correct one, which the attacker can then use to gain unauthorized access to the linked bank account (Williamson & Money-America's, 2006).
5. *Exploiting Wi-Fi Networks*: Cybercriminals possess the capability to compromise numerous internet connections. This is especially accurate for public Wi-Fi networks that are not safeguarded and do not have sufficient security protocols in place. The assailants can exploit any transmitted data, such as bank account information, by infiltrating these networks.

8.2.2. Automate Transfer Systems

The progress in technology and cybersecurity has significantly increased the level of difficulty in carrying out ATO attacks. Cybercriminals have devised novel, automated methods to execute attacks efficiently and with reduced chances of detection, aiming to bypass security measures and perpetrate online banking fraud while minimizing the risk of being identified as identity thieves. These systems are referred to as Automatic Transfer Systems (ATMs) and they eliminate the necessity of bank login scams as a method of attack. Instead, these automated programs monitor the actions of a computer user. This malware surreptitiously injects a script into the legitimate website when the user logs into their bank account, initiating unauthorized money transfers that go unnoticed by the user until it is too late. As a result, the attacker no longer needs to acquire user data or bypass multifactor authentication systems (Williamson & Money-America's, 2006).

8.3. CREDIT CARD FRAUD

Credit card fraud refers to the illicit utilization of a debit or credit card for the purpose of making purchases or withdrawing cash. As reported by the Federal Trade Commission, there were 389,845 cases of identity theft in the United States in 2021 that were attributed to credit card fraud. The majority of victims fell within the age range of 20 to 39 (Delamaire, Abdou, & Pointon, 2009).

8.3.1. Mechanisms Behind Credit Card Fraud

Credit card fraud previously occurred when an individual unlawfully obtained the physical card from its rightful owner. In contemporary times, the occurrence of credit card fraud has increased the likelihood of criminals obtaining a victim's credit card information without physical possession of the card (Delamaire, Abdou, & Pointon, 2009).

8.3.2. Instances of Credit Card Fraud

Credit card fraud can be classified into two main categories:

1. **Card-Not-Present (CNP) Fraud:** This refers to fraudulent activities where a credit or debit card is used for a transaction without the physical presence of the card.

With the increasing prevalence of digital payments, occurrences of this are becoming more frequent. After obtaining stolen credit card details, the fraudster can engage in further fraudulent activities, typically involving online transactions. When a criminal acts swiftly to optimize the duration before the fraud is detected, they may engage in substantial online purchases or acquire large quantities of the same item. This is an instance of digital card-not-present (CNP) fraud. Offline card-not-present (CNP) fraud can occur when a fraudster utilizes the credit card information they have acquired to complete a payment form and submit it to a physical store. It can also occur via telephone (Delamaire, Abdou, & Pointon, 2009).

Instances that could lead to the occurrence of CNP credit card theft include the following:

- Credit card data compromised at a retail establishment or restaurant.
- Credit card information is obtained through fraudulent means such as phishing, which can occur via SMS or email.
- Information overheard during a phone conversation in a public environment.
- A compromised public WiFi network is being used to make transactions with a credit card.
- The perpetrator obtained the victim's credit card information from documents that were not properly shredded.
- Credit card abuse through exploiting or deceiving a susceptible individual into revealing their credit card details (Delamaire, Abdou, & Pointon, 2009).

2. **Card-Present Fraud:** The implementation of chips and PINs has reduced the frequency of this occurrence. Card-present fraud can occur when:

- Credit cards are stolen from your person or residence.
- Misplaced credit card—assuming it is inadvertently left behind in the rear of a taxi.
- Engaging in credit card skimming at an ATM, store, or restaurant to create copies of credit cards.
- Intercepting a newly issued or replacement credit card during the mailing process.

8.3.3. The Impact on Financial Institutions

Financial institutions should prioritize the prevention of credit card fraud due to its potential to greatly impact staff productivity, financial resources, and reputation. If unresolved disagreements persist and the client lodges a complaint against the organization with the Ombudsman or a similar authority, the repercussions could be significantly more serious. Under the Fair Credit Billing Act in the United States, credit card companies are obligated to compensate customers for any unauthorized purchases that exceed $50 before the fraud is detected and reported. Some card issuers have regulations that reduce this amount to zero. According to Delamaire, Abdou, & Pointon (2009), the customer is required to inform the card company of any fraudulent transaction within 60 days. The card company then has a maximum of ten days to respond.

In the UK, the regulations are similar. While certain banks may choose not to reimburse the initial £50 if they determine that the consumer failed to maintain the security of their credit card information, customers are not legally responsible for any unauthorized transactions made with their credit card according to the Consumer Credit Act. As a financial institution, it is incumbent upon you to prove that the client neglected to safeguard their personal information (Delamaire, Abdou, & Pointon, 2009).

8.3.4. Strategies Businesses Can Employ to Detect and Prevent Credit Card Fraud

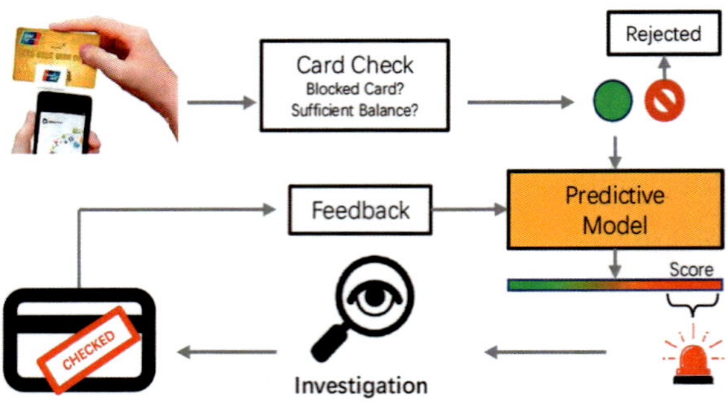

Figure 8.1. *The framework of credit card fraud detection.*

Source: Cheng et al. (2020).

Criminals engaged in credit card fraud will continuously innovate their methods, however, businesses have the ability to equip their customers with the necessary resources to avoid becoming targets.

- Customers should promptly report incidents of credit card fraud once they become aware of them.
- Businesses should encourage credit card users to utilize strong customer authentication methods, including multi-factor authentication, one-time passwords (OTPs), in-app approval, and biometrics, such as speech and language recognition.
- Consistently examine their statements and establish transaction alerts. 3. Refrain from documenting their PIN; instead, maintain its confidentiality.

8.6.1. The Process of Money Laundering

Money laundering is essential for criminal organizations that utilize illegally obtained funds. In order to create the illusion of legitimacy, criminals deposit funds into reputable financial institutions (Levi & Reuter, 2006).

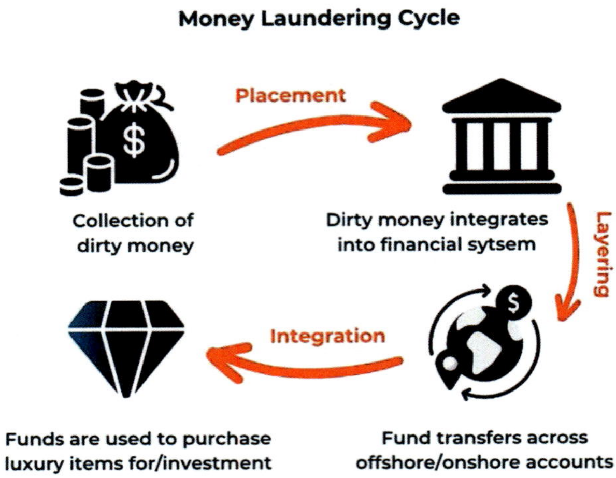

Figure 8.3. *Stages of money laundering.*

Source: Leal (2023).

Money laundering typically involves three distinct steps (Figure 8.3), although there is potential for these steps to be combined or repeated.

- *Placement*: Involves the authorized introduction of illicit funds into the banking system.
- *Layering*: Involves employing a series of financial transactions and deceptive accounting techniques to obscure the origin of the funds.
- *Integration*: Laundered funds are transferred from the legitimate account.

8.6.2. Types of Transactions

- *Smurfing or Structuring*: This refers to the process of illegally obtaining large amounts of money and then distributing it across multiple accounts by dividing it into smaller deposits.
- *Currency Smugglers, also Known as "Mules:"* They engage in the illegal transfer of money between countries, depositing it into offshore accounts.
- *Engaging in Commodity investments*: Utilizing highly portable gold and jewels that can be easily transferred across international borders.

- Avoid carrying your national insurance number or social security number with you.
- Avoid storing their credit card details on the internet, particularly the Card Verification Value (CVV) code.
- Opting for guest checkout is often more secure, particularly on less trustworthy e-commerce platforms.
- Avoid using public Wi-Fi networks for conducting financial transactions.
- Confirm that online store websites commence with "https://" to signify their security
- Be vigilant for signs of ATM tampering.

Integrating artificial intelligence (AI) and machine learning (ML) into fraud detection software can greatly enhance the prevention and identification of credit card fraud (Figure 8.1). ML technologies enable rapid and precise processing of large amounts of data. Machine learning has the capability to predict future behavior and assess the likelihood of a transaction being fraudulent by utilizing sophisticated transaction monitoring tools (Delamaire, Abdou, & Pointon, 2009). Moreover, ML can aid businesses in tracking trends and maintaining a competitive edge by anticipating novel advancements in credit card fraud schemes. It is essential for businesses to prioritize the maintenance of customer trust, brand reputation, and the reduction of costly chargebacks.

8.4. IDENTITY THEFT

Identity theft refers to the fraudulent utilization of someone else's financial or personal data to engage in unauthorized transactions or purchases. Identity theft encompasses a wide range of methods, and its victims typically experience negative effects on their reputation, financial status, and creditworthiness (Anderson et al., 2008).

8.4.1. Types of Identity Theft

Identity theft manifests in various forms, which encompass:

a. *Financial Identity Theft:* Financial identity theft refers to the act of using another person's name or information to obtain credit, goods, services, or advantages. The most common form of identity theft is this particular type.

b. *Social Security Identity Theft:* Identity thieves can exploit an individual's Social Security number to fraudulently obtain credit cards and loans, enabling them to evade repayment of any outstanding debts. Scammers can exploit their phone number to fraudulently obtain additional advantages, such as disability and health insurance.

c. *Medical Identity Theft:* To obtain complimentary medical treatment, an individual engages in the act of medical identity theft.

d. *Synthetic Identity Theft*: Synthetic identity theft is a form of fraud where a criminal fabricates a new identity by counterfeiting and utilizing genuine information, typically obtained through theft. The objective of this newly created persona is to establish fraudulent accounts and engage in unauthorized transactions. Through the utilization of an alias, an individual with malicious intent can fraudulently acquire credit from financial institutions and credit card companies, thereby embezzling funds from them (Anderson et al., 2008).

e. *Child Identity Theft:* Child and teenage identity theft refers to the exploitation of a minor's personal information for various self-centered motives. This is a common occurrence as children often lack the cognitive ability to engage in actions that would create obstacles in the offender's life. By utilizing the child's name and Social Security number, the perpetrator can secure employment, acquire housing, obtain loans, and shield themselves from apprehension due to outstanding warrants. The victim of the offender is often a family member, a child of a friend, or someone else who is close to them. Some individuals are known to steal even the personal information of deceased individuals (Anderson et al., 2008).

f. *Tax-Related Identity Theft:* Tax identity theft refers to the act of someone submitting a fraudulent state or federal tax return using your personal information and subsequently receiving a refund. This occurs when an individual utilizes your personal information, such as your Social Security number.

g. *Criminal Identity Theft:* When an individual engages in criminal identity theft, they may assume a false identity when being arrested in order to avoid receiving a summons, prevent the discovery of a warrant issued under their real name, or evade arrest or having their criminal record expunged (Anderson et al., 2008).

8.4.2. Instances of Identity Theft

Regularly examining one's bank statements is crucial in order to ascertain if one has fallen prey to identity theft. Here are some clear indications of identity theft:

- Unauthorized charges appearing on credit card statements, online platforms, or invoices received via email or postal mail for items that were not purchased by the individual.
- Phone calls from debt collectors regarding accounts that have not been opened by the individual.
- Rejected loan applications despite having a positive credit history.
- Dishonored checks.
- A warrant for arrest
- Erroneous medical invoices and insurance company explanations of benefits (EOBs)
- Discontinuing utility services and being unable to access accounts
- Intensive investigations into one's credit report without any clear justification
- Receiving newly issued credit cards in one's name without having applied for them

Individuals who may have had their personal information stolen or used without their consent, potentially resulting in identity theft.

Identity theft is a potential risk that can occur to individuals regardless of their circumstances or timing. However, the elderly and children are particularly vulnerable. They may not fully understand specific circumstances or documents, such as bills. In addition, their finances and care are often overseen by individuals who may not regularly provide them with updates or closely monitor their accounts (Anderson et al., 2008). Children who encounter identity theft may not become aware of it until they reach adulthood. Adults requiring medical attention often have to repeatedly provide a significant amount of personal information to healthcare organizations, hospitals, clinics, and doctor's offices. This indicates that the aforementioned information can be intentionally and unlawfully obtained from various sources (Anderson et al., 2008).

8.5. INVESTMENT FRAUD

Investment fraud refers to deliberate efforts to deceive individuals into investing money. They may encourage him to invest in cash, commodities, notes, stocks, bonds, and even real estate. An individual engaging in fraudulent activities may falsify information or intentionally deceive others in relation to a genuine investment opportunity. They have the ability to create a false investment opportunity. Individuals who engage in investment fraud may impersonate financial advisors or telemarketers. They radiate charisma, intellect, and affability. They may notify someone about a pressing investment opportunity. To expedite the process of providing funds to an individual and minimize inquiries, the objective is to establish a sense of trust with them (Reurink, 2019).

8.5.1. Common Investment Scams

- *Affinity Fraud*: This refers to the fraudulent activities where scammers intentionally deceive individuals who are part of a specific group based on a common characteristic, such as age, race, or religion. In order to establish trust with the leader and members of the group, swindlers assume the identities of group members. Scammers hold the belief that if the leader of a group makes an investment, then others will be inclined to do the same (Reurink, 2019).
- *High Yield Investment Programs*: This involve fraudsters making false promises to investors regarding substantial profits from their investments. It is believed that the investment will yield substantial profits. These investments are often deceptive or, to be more precise, stocks that are being sold for a very low price.
- *Pyramid Schemes*: This involve fraudulent individuals who falsely promise substantial returns or payouts in exchange for a small initial investment. Additionally, they must also identify and secure additional investors. Essentially, the "profit" they obtain is simply the funds that other investors have contributed. Once the con artist exhausts all potential victims or absconds with the entire sum of money, the scheme disintegrates (Reurink, 2019) (Figure 8.2).

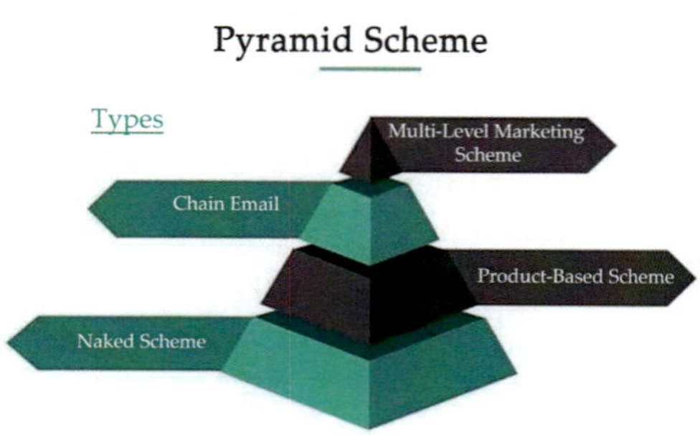

Figure 8.2. *Common types of pyramid schemes.*

Source: wallstreetmojo.com/ (2024).

- *Ponzi Schemes*: Generally, a fraudster impersonates a portfolio manager and guarantees to invest a victim's funds, resulting in substantial returns. Nevertheless, the funds they obtain in return are essentially derived from the payments made by other investors. Once the con artists exhaust their options in finding additional investors who are willing to provide them with funds, their plan collapses abruptly (Reurink, 2019).

- *Pump and Dump*: Fraudsters acquire low-priced stocks and artificially increase their worth by deceiving potential buyers about the quality of the securities. Investors may choose to buy the stocks at a higher price than their current value because they have confidence in their potential for profitable returns. Following the fraudster's sale of the stocks at an inflated price, the stock price experiences a decline, resulting in the individual being left with stocks that have no value.
- *Recovery Room Schemes*: Scammers request upfront payment in return for their aid in recovering funds lost from previous investment schemes. Once they receive payment, they become inactive or unproductive.

8.5.2. Indicators of Potential Scam or Fraud

- Guarantees of consistent and substantial returns on investment.
- Individuals who do not possess a securities sales license.
- Engaging in the trading of unregistered securities.
- Individuals who deceive others and falsely assert their expertise in investment and retirement matters.
- Absence of the necessary paperwork that provides a comprehensive explanation of the investment, such as a circular for bonds and a prospectus for stocks/mutual funds.
- Salespeople who are assertive and persistent in their pursuit of your payment, response, or endorsement.

8.6. MONEY LAUNDERING

Money laundering refers to the illegal process of disguising large amounts of money acquired through criminal activities, such as financing terrorism or drug trafficking, to make it appear as if it came from a legitimate source.

Illegally acquired funds are considered tainted and undergo a process known as "money laundering" to give the appearance of legitimacy. Financial institutions utilize anti-money laundering (AML) regulations to detect and prevent such illicit activities (Levi & Reuter, 2006).

- *Acquisition and Disposition*: Allocating capital for swift investments in assets such as boats, vehicles, and real estate.
- *Casino Transactions:* Money laundering facilitated through casino transactions.
- *Shell Companies*: Establishing inactive businesses or corporations that solely exist in documentation.

8.6.3. Cyber-Enabled Money Laundering

The proliferation of peer-to-peer (P2P) mobile money transfers, anonymous internet payment systems, and online banking has increased the difficulty in detecting illicit financial transactions. The identification of the third component of money laundering, integration, becomes more difficult due to the use of proxy servers and anonymous software. This allows funds to be transferred or withdrawn without leaving any trace of an Internet protocol (IP) address (Levi & Reuter, 2006).

Online sales and auctions, gambling websites, and virtual gaming platforms are susceptible to being used for money laundering. These websites facilitate the conversion of illegal profits into in-game currency, which can then be converted back into real, spendable, and untraceable "clean" money. Bitcoin and other cryptocurrencies have the potential to be utilized for the purpose of money laundering. While not completely anonymous, the comparative level of secrecy associated with cryptocurrencies, as opposed to traditional fiat currency, renders them valuable in facilitating drug trafficking, blackmail schemes, and other illicit activities (Levi &Reuter, 2006).

8.6.4. Indicators of Money Laundering

Indicators of money laundering include:

- An individual's dubious or uncommunicative conduct regarding financial affairs
- Significant cash dealings
- Possession of a seemingly purposeless company
- Excessively intricate transactions, or multiple transactions that narrowly avoid the reporting limit.

8.6.5. The Function of Cryptocurrencies in Facilitating Money Laundering

According to a June 2021 study conducted by the Financial Crimes Enforcement Network (FinCEN) of the United States, convertible virtual currencies (CVCs), also known as cryptocurrencies, are the most commonly used method of payment for various illegal activities conducted online. CVCs possess the capacity to obscure the origin of funds acquired through illegal activities by engaging in a series of complex transactions. Criminals utilize various money-laundering techniques in the realm of cryptocurrency, including "mixers" and "tumblers," which sever the connection between the sender's address or cryptocurrency "wallet" and the recipient's address (Levi & Reuter, 2006).

Money laundering is used to conceal illegally acquired financial assets. Financial institutions and governments worldwide implement anti-money laundering policies. The prevalence of money laundering has surged as a result of the proliferation of digital assets and online activities.

8.7. CRYPTOCURRENCY FRAUD

Cryptocurrency is a specific form of currency that exists within the realm of digital finance. Cryptocurrencies, unlike traditional fiat money, exist solely in digital form. Individuals have the option to acquire these digital assets through various channels, such as mobile devices, personal computers, or bitcoin ATMs. While the cryptocurrency market provides a diverse range of options, including frequent additions, prominent examples of cryptocurrencies include Bitcoin and Ether. Digital currencies operate on decentralized networks, which offer both opportunities and challenges in the ever-evolving field of financial technology (Kutera, 2022).

People use cryptocurrencies for several reasons, such as fast payments, avoiding transaction fees imposed by conventional banks, and maintaining some level of anonymity. Many individuals hold cryptocurrencies with the expectation that its value will appreciate, making it a lucrative investment.

A cryptocurrency ATM, website, app, or exchange are all platforms where you can acquire cryptocurrencies. Bitcoin is acquired by certain individuals through a demanding procedure referred to as "mining," which involves the use of advanced computer hardware to solve highly difficult mathematical puzzles (Kutera, 2022).

Digital wallets provide secure storage for cryptocurrency within the vast realm of the internet. These wallets can be accessed using computers, external hard drives, and internet platforms.

A digital wallet's address typically consists of an intricate combination of alphanumeric characters. Users should exercise prudence, as recovering lost funds may prove challenging. In the event of unforeseen circumstances such as platform shutdown, erroneous transactions, password loss, theft, or compromise, it is often impossible to recover your cryptocurrency. Ensuring security and maintaining constant awareness are essential in the dynamic realm of digital finance (Kutera, 2022). The primary differentiation between cryptocurrencies and traditional currencies, such as US dollars, lies in the fact that cryptocurrencies are solely accessible through online platforms. Cryptocurrency accounts do not receive any guarantees from the government. Cryptocurrency held in accounts is not protected by the government, unlike US dollars deposited in a bank account insured by the FDIC. The government has no obligation to intervene or provide assistance in the event of any loss or damage to your account or cryptocurrency funds, such as a hack or the closure of the business that holds your wallet (Kutera, 2022).

Cryptocurrencies experience daily fluctuations in value. The value of a cryptocurrency can experience significant fluctuations, occasionally even on an hourly basis. Moreover, there could be a significant disparity in quantity. Multiple factors, including supply and demand, exert an influence on it. When comparing cryptocurrencies to traditional investments such as stocks and bonds, cryptocurrencies are generally characterized by higher levels of volatility. An investment of one thousand dollars today may only yield a value of a few hundred dollars tomorrow. Furthermore, there is no guarantee that the value will increase after it decreases (Kutera, 2022).

In the ever-evolving realm of cryptocurrency, swindlers are perpetually devising novel methods to exploit susceptible individuals. Here are essential guidelines to prevent falling prey to bitcoin scams:

- *Be Cautious of Requests*: Typically, scammers are the ones who make requests for cryptocurrency payments. Reputable enterprises never solicit upfront cryptocurrency payments, whether for transactions or to safeguard your funds. Exercise caution when encountering such solicitations, as they are likely to be associated with fraudulent activities.
- *Profit Guarantees*: Scammers often make grandiose or substantial profit or return guarantees. Avoid anyone who claims that you can make quick and effortless profits from the cryptocurrency markets. Typically, these assurances are deceptive.
- *It is Advisable to Maintain a Clear Distinction Between Online Dating and Investment Advice:* Exercise utmost vigilance if you encounter an individual on a dating platform or application who abruptly begins proffering guidance on bitcoin investments or solicits transfers of cryptocurrency. The combination of romantic and financial decision-making can lead to scams.

8.8. FRAUDULENT SCHEMES

News reports frequently emphasize cases of fraud in the collective awareness, although individuals tend to hold the belief that such occurrences will not have a direct impact on them personally. Nevertheless, this assumption can be misleading. Modern fraudsters have become more advanced, surprising even the most watchful individuals (Sanusi, Rameli, & Isa, 2015). Here are common fraudulent schemes that everyone should be cautious of:

- *An Unentered Lottery or Contest:* The methods by which they manipulate and mislead you. "Congratulations!" Congratulations! You have just become the lucky winner of the lottery in Jamaica!Prior to disbursing your winnings, they will request that you settle the tax obligations. The key takeaway from this. Prior to accessing your wealth, you will need to make an additional payment. Ultimately, you will not be refunded the money(Sanusi, Rameli, & Isa, 2015). How can one prevent or circumvent this particular situation?

  Avoid scams that seem excessively remarkable as they are false. To prevent future responses, ensure that you block the phone number or email address that is being used to contact you.
- *Assistance Required by Prince or Governing Body:* An individual contacts you via email, social media, text message, or phone call and requests your aid. They will openly acknowledge their wealth and offer you compensation to transfer their funds out of the country. The con artist will request a monetary transfer from you in return for a portion of their riches (Sanusi, Rameli, & Isa, 2015).Corruption and extortion will persist indefinitely. Contrary to what you believe, this individual will not be sharing any part of your wealth with you, and you will end up losing all the money you gave them. How can one prevent or circumvent this particular situation? Notify your service provider and utilize the option to block the contact method.
- *Import/Export Customs Clearance Fee:* An acquaintance has sent an electronic message asking for financial assistance to cover the expenses associated with customs clearance and the acquisition of a highly prized item. You are required to pay a customs fee, which will be refunded to you. It is possible that they have transmitted counterfeit documents in order to "demonstrate" their need for aid, and the email appears to be genuine. You will probably be informed about the existence of extra expenses and the extent to which your friend values your help. Despite the emails' official appearance, they are in fact not genuine. The fraudulent individual will employ

an indistinguishable email account and emblem in order to deceive you. Minor modifications to the email and logo, if detected, could suggest that it is counterfeit (Sanusi, Rameli, & Isa, 2015).

- *E-Commerce Vendor:* You attempt to market your vehicle through a reliable online platform. Someone is considering purchasing your car, but they mistakenly sent you a cashier's check for $15,000 instead of the correct amount of $10,000. Simply deposit the surplus funds back to them (Sanusi, Rameli, & Isa, 2015). Upon delivering the vehicle to the buyer, you proceed to deposit the remaining funds to be returned to them. Currently, the initial payment is returned due to insufficient funds, and the buyer is disregarding any efforts to communicate with you. You have incurred an additional loss of $5,000 in cash, in addition to the loss of your car.
- *Internet-Based Borrowing:* You require financial resources, however, obtaining a loan from a bank is not feasible due to your credit history. Alternatively, you can submit an application on a website that appears to be genuine, and in return, they provide you with a check for a fraction of the total loan amount. Prior to receiving the full loan amount, the lender mandates that you repay a small sum as a demonstration of your trustworthiness. Once the money is sent, your check for the full amount will be sent promptly (Sanusi, Rameli, & Isa, 2015). The money you sent in "good faith" is lost when the loan check is returned unpaid. The lender is unidentifiable and will not acknowledge any of your efforts to contact them.
- *Internet-Based Job opportunities:* During your online search, you discover a job opening for the role of an assistant at an international company. In order to facilitate the transfer of funds to clients in different geographical areas, it is necessary for you to establish a bank account (Sanusi, Rameli, & Isa, 2015). You observe transactions in your account and are directed to transfer the funds to a different destination. The organization you are employed by is, in fact, fraudulent, and the remuneration you have received is entirely derived from illicit means. You are now responsible for the theft, distribution, and current absence of the money.
- *Love and Affection Between Two Individuals:* An individual from a foreign country establishes a friendship with you, and the two of you initiate a conversation. After engaging in authentic communication, you may form a relationship and potentially even become engaged with this person. The individuals will claim to be employed by a legitimate corporation, and there is a possibility that

you can engage in a video conference with them. Unfortunately, due to travel restrictions, they are unable to come and meet you. With a compassionate mindset, you extend an offer to provide financial assistance to help them cover the costs of hiring a lawyer or purchasing a plane ticket.

Over time, they will progressively insist on receiving larger amounts of money from you. The fraudulent individual will request that you refrain from providing your banking details or granting access to this information to your family members. They can assert that they are the sole individuals who are acquainted with and aware of you. You are, indeed, being deceived. Once you cease providing financial support, this individual will no longer initiate communication with you.

- *Social Interaction and the Presence of others:* An individual whom you have not previously encountered establishes a friendship with you on the internet. However, after engaging in several conversations, they request your aid. The parents inform you that their daughter is unwell and in need of surgery, however, the medical professionals and hospital demand upfront payment. Their daughter's survival is contingent upon the procedure and your assistance. Your acquaintance persistently solicits additional funds from you due to their daughter's predicaments. Despite not having an actual sick child, they consistently express dissatisfaction and claim that they require additional funds for medical professionals (Sanusi, Rameli, & Isa, 2015). You are completely unaware of the identity and location of this individual, yet they have absconded with your funds.
- *Grandchildren in a State of Profound Sadness and Grief:* Upon receiving a call, your grandchild informs you that they are facing a challenging situation and require your assistance. They desire to wed discreetly and wish to keep their parents unaware of their incarceration, hospitalization, or both. In order to aid them, you are requested to promptly transmit the funds (Sanusi, Rameli, & Isa, 2015). Your cherished grandson is not in any danger and is not contacting you. Instead, you are communicating with and sending money to a fraudulent individual, who is likely situated in another country. To verify the account, promptly contact the parents of your grandchild.

8.9. FINANCIAL FRAUD PREVENTION

Fraud prevention refers to the implementation of a systematic approach to detect and prevent fraudulent transactions or banking activities, thereby safeguarding the financial well-being and reputation of both the customer and the financial institution (FI). The importance of a strong fraud protection strategy will increase as financial institutions (FIs) further adopt digital technologies and online and mobile banking become more popular (Bănărescu, 2015).

The fields of cybercrime and fraud prevention are closely interconnected and constantly evolving. While fraud prevention experts develop advanced authentication and fraud detection systems, criminals are actively collaborating, generating profits, and exchanging information on the dark web. In modern times, criminals employ malicious software and sophisticated strategies to execute their deceitful plans. Although fraud protection technology is continuously advancing and has made significant progress, it remains crucial to identify fraudulent tactics and understand how to evade them.

To mitigate the risk of fraud in your company, it is advisable to endorse these measures.

- *Ensure the Execution of Payments with enhanced Security Measures:* Although online banking is becoming increasingly popular, it is important to exercise caution when making purchases or transferring money online. Varied patterns of online expenditure may result in differing levels of susceptibility to fraudulent activity. Websites that lack robust security measures are vulnerable to cybercriminals who can infiltrate the site and acquire sensitive payment information. These factors necessitate the need for exercising prudence when making an online purchase of goods or services. Stick with established and trustworthy payment networks, such as PayPal (Bănărescu, 2015).
- *Safeguard Personal Information Personalized Data is Highly Valuable:* Prevent your clients from easily sharing it, even if the individual making the request claims to be employed by a reputable organization. Utilizing a user's personal information can lead to significant consequences. Attackers can exploit it to engage in account takeover fraud, establish new credit lines, or transfer funds to an untraceable account.
- *Conduct Periodic Examinations of Your Credit Reports:* Encourage your clients to vigilantly monitor their credit report throughout the entire year. Individuals can track their credit score through various applications and financial services without undergoing a

formal credit check. These resources will help identify fraudulent transactions or unauthorized credit activity associated with the user's name, potentially impacting their credit rating unexpectedly. Customers have the option to receive a credit alert from any of the three main credit agencies, Experian, Equifax, and TransUnion, if they lose their credit card or encounter a security breach.

- *Conduct Online Searches:* Online shoppers are at risk of becoming victims of fraud. Prior to making a purchase from an online company, consumers should promptly consult online evaluations on reputable review platforms, such as Google and Yelp. The mentioned corporation does not possess jurisdiction over these review platforms and therefore cannot eradicate unfavorable reviews. If a user can only find negative reviews or no reviews at all, it is advisable for them to reassess the risk associated with conducting business with this company. In addition, it is advisable for users to restrict their usage of financial applications to those that possess robust security measures, such as the OneSpan Mobile Security Suite.

CHAPTER 9

CYBERCRIME AND NATIONAL SECURITY

Contents

For over four decades, cybercrime has presented a threat of unauthorized access to national security information and its associated information systems (Patel & Chudasama, 2021). Currently, the proliferation of highly profitable international cybercrime networks raises the level of danger. These transnational criminal networks have had an impact on the functioning of essential services and critical infrastructure by engaging in and facilitating highly disruptive cyber incidents. These criminal networks can serve as proxies for malicious activities conducted by foreign governments or provide a certain level of plausible deniability for foreign government security agencies involved in their own malicious cyber operations.

9.1. NATIONAL SECURITY THREATS

Cyberattacks have transitioned from being a fictional concept to a tangible and present threat. The perpetrators typically focus on countries with strong economies and functioning democracies. The risks encompass a wide spectrum, such as identity theft, corporate surveillance, destruction of critical infrastructure, and manipulation of political and official communication channels.

What is the underlying motivation of the offenders? Cybercrime is a highly profitable industry. Occasionally, contemporary wrongdoers generate higher income than individuals engaged in the worldwide illicit drug business. Nevertheless, numerous cyberattacks are driven by political motives (Patel & Chudasama, 2021).

The increasing prevalence of online services has also attracted a significant amount of illicit behavior. They employ deceptive emails and websites in order to acquire sensitive information, including credit card numbers, passwords, and access credentials. Phishing attempts refer to these activities. Personal information such as passwords, addresses, and birth dates are either directly exploited by criminals or sold at a high price on the illegal market.

The increasing digital mobility and networking come with inherent security risks and cyber threats. There has been a significant rise in the frequency of deliberate cyberattacks targeting individuals, businesses, and governments (Patel & Chudasama, 2021).

Despite its advanced sophistication, even the most advanced anti-virus software is incapable of preventing the infection. Moreover, the attacks are highly disguised, rendering it arduous to ascertain the primary origin, thereby exacerbating the low detection rate. In order to address the dangers presented by cyberattacks, various national and international organizations are working together.

9.1.1. The Prevalence of Security Risks

Cybercriminals possess a worldwide reach and focus on acquiring sensitive information and attacking critical infrastructure during their assaults on computer systems. Their cyberattacks are often motivated by criminal or political factors. During a ransomware attack, perpetrators seize control of sensitive information and demand a monetary payment (Patel & Chudasama, 2021).

Utility service providers, such as banks, hospitals, transportation companies, and power providers, increasingly rely on information and communications technology for their operations. Consequently, these establishments and organizations are commonly referred to as "critical infrastructure," and they are specifically targeted by cyberterrorists. Targeting these infrastructures would have severe consequences for all parties involved. An unprecedented cyberattack was initiated by executing a double click on an email attachment, a scenario that was previously inconceivable. A malicious software designed to propagate across the system and encrypt data was transmitted through a connection.

9.1.2. Cybercrime Transcends National Borders

Cybercrime is a global problem that surpasses geographical and personal limitations. Cybersecurity breaches can transpire in any location where individuals utilize computers and smartphones. Tracing the origin of attacks can be challenging due to the attackers' ability to operate from virtually any location worldwide. The proliferation of malware programs is increasing, while hackers are also enhancing their expertise and hacking skills (Patel & Chudasama, 2021).

Politicians, federal officials, and businesses are susceptible to being targeted by attacks. Efficient intelligence-gathering activities possess the capability to inflict significant financial and economic damage.

9.1.3. Federal Government Funds Allocation for Improving Cybersecurity

Indeed, federal ministries ensure that there will be a significant and continuous increase in spending on cyber security. This encompasses protection against potential cyberwarfare, industrial espionage, and security breaches on critical infrastructure. Each individual has a specific responsibility in the realm of cybersecurity.

Reports indicate that home offices and the integration of personal devices into business networks pose additional issues and security risks. Unfortunately, many individuals neglect to implement necessary measures (Patel & Chudasama, 2021). In order to fully exploit the extensive advantages and possibilities offered by digitization, countries must implement a proactive cyber security policy. This task necessitates inter-ministerial collaboration. In light of this, various government departments and agencies are working together in close cooperation to address and counteract cyber threats (Patel & Chudasama, 2021).

9.2. CYBER WARFARE

Cyberwarfare is defined as a cyberattack or a series of cyberattacks specifically aimed at a nation. It has the potential to incapacitate critical systems and cause extensive damage to both public and private infrastructure, resulting in harm to the state and potentially even loss of life.

Cyberwarfare typically involves a nation-state initiating cyberattacks against another nation-state. However, it is also possible for terrorist groups or non-state actors to carry out cyberattacks with the intention of furthering the goals of an opposing state. While there have been numerous documented instances of cyberwarfare in recent years, there is currently no universally recognized and officially defined criteria for classifying a cyberattack as an act of war (Basholli, 2022).

9.2.1. Categories of Cyber Warfare Attacks

The following are the 7 types of cyberwarfare attacks (Figure 9.1):

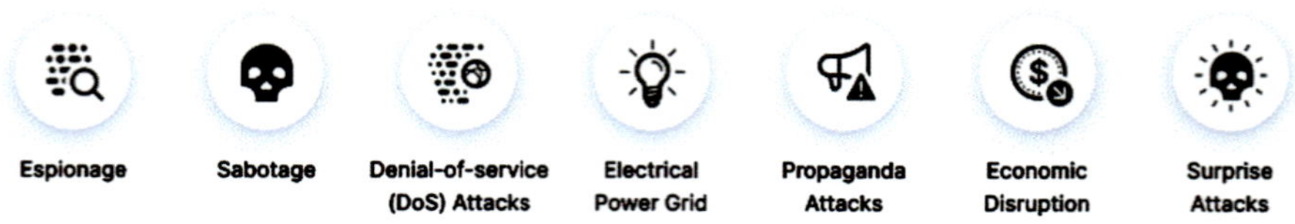

Figure 9.1. *Types of cyber warfare attacks.*

Source: Avital (2023).

- *Espionage:* This refers to the act of surveilling other nations with the intention of acquiring confidential information. In the realm of cyberwarfare, this involves gaining unauthorized access to vulnerable computer systems through techniques such as spear phishing or botnets, and subsequently extracting valuable and confidential information.

- *Sabotage*: This refers to the deliberate act of causing damage, disruption, or harm to something or someone, typically with the intention of undermining their success or progress

  Government agencies must ascertain sensitive data and assess the potential ramifications of a breach. Insider threats, including dissatisfied or careless employees, or government personnel with affiliations to the attacking country, can be utilized by terrorists or hostile governments to pilfer or obliterate information.

- *Denial-of-Service (DoS) Attacks:* Denial-of-service (DoS) attacks hinder legitimate visitors from accessing a website by overwhelming it with fake requests and forcing it to respond to them. This type of attack has the capability to disrupt critical processes and systems, impeding citizens, law enforcement, and research organizations from accessing private websites.
- *Electric Power Grid:* Adversaries have the potential to inflict bodily harm, disrupt critical infrastructure, and annihilate essential services by focusing on the electrical grid. Power grid attacks not only disrupt communication but also have the capacity to render text messaging and other services ineffective.
- *Propaganda Assaults:* Efforts to manipulate and dominate the minds and emotions of individuals who are either citizens or combatants of a specific country. Propaganda can be employed to elicit sympathy for their adversaries, disseminate falsehoods to erode public trust in their country, or expose inconvenient realities.
- *Economic Disruption:* This refers to a significant disturbance or interruption in the normal functioning of an economy.

  The utilization of computers is prevalent in the majority of contemporary economic systems. Adversaries have the capability to target the computer networks of financial institutions, such as banks, stock exchanges, and payment processors, with the intention of pilfering funds or obstructing users from accessing essential funds (Basholli, 2022).

- *Surprise Offensives:* These attacks are equivalent to the 9/11 and Pearl Harbor of cyber warfare. The concept is to catch the opponent off guard with a substantial assault that will enable the aggressor to breach their defensive measures. Within the framework of hybrid warfare, this action may be undertaken to prepare for a tangible assault (Basholli, 2022).

9.2.2. Examples of Cyberwarfare Operations

Below are some notable cases of cyberwarfare that have occurred in recent years.

- *The Stuxnet Virus:* The Stuxnet malware specifically aimed at disrupting Iran's nuclear program. This cyberattack is considered to be one of the most sophisticated and advanced attacks to date. The malware specifically focused on supervisory control and data acquisition systems, spreading through infected Universal Serial Bus devices. According to most sources, the attack significantly impaired Iran's ability to manufacture nuclear weapons.
- *Sony Pictures Cyberattack:* After the release of the film "The Interview," which portrayed Kim Jong Un in a negative light, Sony Pictures was targeted in an attack. The attack is attributed to hackers employed by the North Korean government. The FBI determined that the code, encryption techniques, and data erasure mechanisms were similar to previous cyberattacks conducted by North Koreans.
- *Bronze Soldier:* In 2007, Estonia relocated a Soviet-era monument called the Bronze Soldier from the city's center to a military cemetery located outside of Tallinn. During the subsequent months, Estonia experienced a series of severe cyberattacks. Estonia experienced a significant influx of traffic due to deliberate and extensive denial of service (DoS) attacks, resulting in the disruption and unavailability of banks, media, and government websites.
- *Fancy Bear:* Between 2014 and 2016, the Russian group Fancy Bear conducted systematic cyber-attacks on Ukrainian artillery and rocket units, as reported by CrowdStrike. The D-30 Howitzer artillery unit utilized a contaminated Android application to handle targeting data, thereby facilitating the spread of the malware. The X-Agent malware was detected in the application, which had extensive usage among Ukrainian officials. The attack has been deemed highly successful, as it resulted in the destruction of more than 80% of Ukraine's D-30 Howitzers.

9.3. CRITICAL INFRASTRUCTURE PROTECTION

Modern businesses operate within a tightly interconnected and ever-changing global environment. Due to the exponential expansion of digital technologies, businesses are now required to operate within a 24/7 digital economy. These advances have also given rise to cyberattacks and other emerging threats. Ensuring the security of critical infrastructure is an essential initial measure. It involves protecting and defending against cyberattacks that have the potential to jeopardize or disrupt the delivery of essential services by vital infrastructures. Safeguarding essential infrastructure entails both preventing potential cyber assaults and being prepared to manage them when they inevitably transpire. The response should be immediate, rational, and commensurate.

Critical infrastructure refers to the computers and networks responsible for managing essential services such as energy production, telecommunication, banking, and healthcare. The system encompasses the management and surveillance of critical infrastructure, such as climate control systems, urban development, and sensory devices. Crucial infrastructure security is synonymous with critical infrastructure. For example, the Australian Federal Government recently passed a crucial infrastructure bill that mandates industry-specific risk management programs to be developed by owners and operators of essential infrastructure. These programs must go beyond existing legal frameworks. The legislation confers upon the government the power to classify specific systems as having national significance and to enforce more stringent cybersecurity obligations on business proprietors.

Gaining insight into the vulnerabilities that your company is exposed to and determining the specific safeguards necessary is the initial stage in formulating a robust cybersecurity strategy.

The field of cybersecurity is in a constant state of flux, with new threats emerging on a daily basis. In order to prevent unauthorized access to their networks, modern businesses must ensure that their cybersecurity defenses are regularly updated. However, even though the field of cybersecurity is constantly changing, there are certain cybersecurity concepts that remain relevant and unchanging. These factors encompass the need for being conscious, the importance of fostering a culture of security, and the demand for strong cybersecurity protocols. These concepts are indispensable irrespective of the sector in which you are employed. They can help you protect your company from both internal and external risks.

9.4. GOVERNMENT CYBERSECURITY

For many reasons, the government sector is a popular target for cyberattacks. Among the most prevalent are the fact that governments are in charge of vital infrastructure that is susceptible to cyberattacks and have access to extremely sensitive data. Additionally, politically motivated hacktivists may target government agencies. Cyberattacks have become a more common weapon of war in recent years. One of the best examples of this is the conflict between Russia and Ukraine, where Russian-affiliated hackers have attacked Ukraine and its allies in an attempt to interfere with their daily lives and military activities. The frequency of these attacks is increasing the security dangers for government agencies (Norris et al., 2021).

9.4.1. Cybersecurity's Significance for Governmental Organizations

Important responsibilities and sensitive data are assigned to government institutions. A disruptive cyberattack or data breach has the potential to seriously harm the firm and its stakeholders. Government organizations therefore have a big duty to put robust cybersecurity in place to fend off these threats. Governmental organizations must have defenses in place against a variety of possible dangers. They need the following kinds of protections, to name a few:

- *Internet of Things (IoT)*: IoT devices are frequently used to operate and control critical infrastructure, and because of unpatched vulnerabilities and other issues, they can seriously jeopardize government cybersecurity. IoT devices need to be carefully maintained to make sure they aren't utilized as agency network access points or compromised by botnet software.
- *Data Security*: A significant amount of sensitive data, including personal and classified information about citizens, is accessible to government entities. For the sake of the security of the nation and its residents, this data must be shielded from ransomware and data breaches.
- *Cloud Security*: Because of the scalability, resilience, and other advantages that cloud infrastructure provides, businesses and government organizations are embracing it quickly. However, mismanagement of third-party risk, setup, and access control can leave data or apps stored in the cloud vulnerable to attack.
- *Network Security*: The cornerstone of cybersecurity is network security. Network security measures can assist prevent an attacker from entering an organization's systems and limit the ability of an attacker who has already gained access to the network to move laterally within the business.
- *Application Security*: Among the many essential services that governments offer to their citizens are taxation and healthcare. For these applications to remain available and for the security of the data they handle and keep to remain secure, AppSec or WAF solutions are essential.

- *Endpoint Security*: Mobile devices and laptops controlled by the government are frequently the target of cyberattacks. Installing endpoint security software on a device can aid in the prevention and removal of malware infestations as well as other online dangers.
- *Mobile Security*: Cybercriminals are increasingly focusing their attacks on mobile devices as the use of these devices for business purposes has increased. Mobile security solutions can assist in controlling the danger of smishing and other attacks, as well as preventing the installation of mobile malware.
- *Consolidated Security Architecture*: A complex, unmanageable security architecture is produced when standalone solutions are used to defend against a variety of cyberthreats. Security visibility and threat detection and response capabilities are enhanced by a consolidated security architecture, which combines all necessary security features into a single solution (Norris et al., 2021).

9.4.2. Government Cybersecurity's Obstacles

The following are some of the most typical cybersecurity issues that government organizations deal with:

- *Sophisticated Adversaries*: State-sponsored hacking groups, organized crime, and hacktivists are just a few examples of the sophisticated cyber threat actors that attack government entities with the goal of stealing confidential information or impairing vital operations. Cybersecurity is more difficult than it is for smaller firms because of the necessity to defend against nation-state actors and organized crime.
- *Restricted Funds*: Government organizations frequently have restricted funds and resources available to them for cybersecurity and IT. Because of this, creating and implementing strong defenses against cutting-edge cyberattacks can be challenging.
- *Fragmented Architecture*: The majority of governments consist of separate departments and agencies with different functions, capacities, and degrees of technical know-how. This makes it more challenging to guarantee that the government is safe from cyberattacks overall (Norris et al., 2021).

9.4.3. Cybersecurity Policies and Procedures

A well-developed security plan serves as the roadmap for an efficient cybersecurity program. An unmanageable security architecture and exploitable security gaps are the outcome of trying to find, buy, and implement security solutions on the fly to handle specific threats.

Both internal and external factors should influence an organization's cybersecurity strategy. Internally, the organization's goals should be supported by the security plan, which should safeguard its data and IT resources. External influences include rules and guidelines that require specific security capabilities, like endpoint security solutions and multi-factor authentication (MFA), as well as controls that the company must implement to reach a minimally acceptable level of security (Norris et al., 2021).

9.5. MILITARY CYBER OPERATIONS

In recent years, cyber operations have showcased the alarming potential to disrupt crucial civilian infrastructure, such as power grids, hospitals, and even nuclear reactors. Historically, disruptive cyber operations have primarily occurred in non-combat situations. It is worth noting that an increasing number of States are developing military cyber capabilities, with a few even openly admitting to using cyber operations in armed conflicts (Ducheine & Pijpers, 2021).

9.5.1. Different Categories of Cyber Operations in Warfare

Cyberspace in warfare exhibits the following characteristics. During hostilities, it is not uncommon for armed groups, such as cyber commands, to engage in cyberattacks. Additionally, it is worth noting that their focus often lies on the weapon systems, headquarters, and command and control centers of their adversaries, although this is not always the case. Unlike the utilization of strategic cyberattacks during times of peace to influence the decisions of adversaries, cyberattacks during times of war often take the form of counter-force attacks (Ducheine & Pijpers, 2021).

Additionally, they have a clear military objective as they provide support to other forces during combat, as opposed to fulfilling an intelligence role. Drawing a precise line to distinguish between military and non-military cyber operations can be quite challenging. The persistence of ambiguities and the ongoing issue of attribution, along with the functional overlap with intelligence agencies' cyberespionage, contribute to the continued existence of anomalies.

As per military doctrine, conflict can be categorized into three distinct stages: tactical, operational, and strategic. Events on one level have an impact on the others due to their interdependence. Addressing the question of "how to win a war" requires a strategic approach. To achieve victory in a war, it is crucial to carefully allocate national resources and military hardware at the strategic level. In an ideal scenario, strategies would encompass the utilization of all available tools of state power, including cyber capabilities, with the ultimate goal of achieving peace. The relationship between political and strategic aspects of battle is often blurred, making it difficult to differentiate between the two. In the majority of democracies, the decision to declare war is made by elected politicians rather than generals. This highlights the significance of the political level in determining such crucial matters (Ducheine & Pijpers, 2021).

Strategic strikes, whether in the cyber or kinetic realm, are executed with the purpose of achieving specific objectives. These objectives include diminishing the willingness or capability of adversaries to engage in warfare. Strategic cyberattacks typically focus on impacting society as a whole or the power structures of a nation. Strategic cyber warfare is defined as the ability to inflict significant damage on an adversary without the need to engage in direct military confrontation, as stated in various studies. One common use for strategic cyberattacks is as an independent tool that can be deployed without the need for other, more conventional forces. According to Ducheine and Pijpers (2021), cyberattacks that focus on critical infrastructures during peaceful times are categorized as strategic.

At the operational level, the main focus is campaign management and the strategic deployment of forces across multiple theaters or geographical areas. At the operational level, the primary objective is to achieve a series of victories over the opposing forces. During military operations that take place away from civilian infrastructure, it is common for combatants to focus their efforts on engaging military targets such as enemy ships, tanks, or soldiers. Operation Overlord, the Allied invasion of Normandy, was one of several operations conducted in a specific theater of war with the strategic objective of dismantling Nazi Germany. Operational cyberattacks often serve as a complement to traditional military operations. During the initial stages of a conflict, cyber capabilities can be strategically employed to divert attention and instill fear in one area, thereby enabling other forces to make unhindered advancements in a different front (Ducheine & Pijpers, 2021).

In a combat scenario, the domain where individual warfighters and units engage in combat encounters is known as the tactical level. Here is a breakdown of how most conventional weapon systems operate. Therefore, the actions and mobility of military forces within a specific geographical area fall within the jurisdiction of the tactical level. There has been a noticeable lack of literature on the topic of tactical cyber. Tactical cyber operations are conducted within the framework of a traditional kinetic battlefield, where the specific operation's authorization, deconfliction, and control are handled at the battalion level or lower. The process of deconfliction involves reconciling areas of accountability that exist between different agencies or military command levels. This could include reconciling the responsibilities of battalion troops with those of high-level intelligence organizations (Ducheine & Pijpers, 2021). An illustrative scenario could involve a hostage rescue operation in a technologically advanced urban environment, where the surveillance cameras are manipulated to provide crucial information to the elite military forces involved. One potential application of cyber operations is the ability to disrupt soldiers' GPS devices, IT equipment, or drones. There are two ways in which cybersecurity can be approached tactically. An important aspect to consider is the integration of IT experts into small units that operate in the field. In the second scenario, soldiers have the advantage of relying on "remote cyber support" from a unit stationed at a safe distance, as mentioned by Ducheine and Pijpers (2021).

9.6. CYBER ESPIONAGE

Cyber espionage, also referred to as cyber spying, involves unauthorized individuals attempting to acquire intellectual property (IP) or sensitive/classified material for financial, political, or competitive benefits (Figure 9.2).

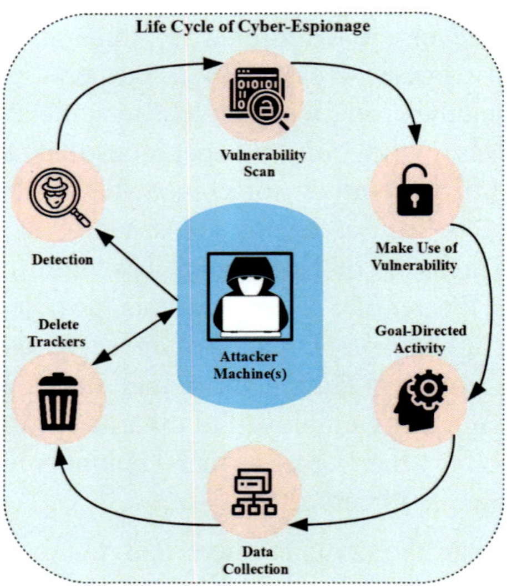

Figure 9.2. *Life cycle of cyber-espionage and intelligence activities.*

Source: Kara (2021).

Cyber espionage serves the primary objective of acquiring trade secrets, confidential or classified information, or other intellectual property that can be monetized or leveraged by the perpetrator to secure a competitive advantage. There are cases where the primary objective of a breach is to harm the victim's reputation by revealing personal information or questionable business practices (Buchan & Navarrete, 2021). Attacks conducted as a part of cyberterrorism or cyberwarfare, or in coordination with military operations, can all be driven by the pursuit of financial gain. Cyber espionage can have far-reaching consequences, causing significant damage to infrastructure, disrupting public services, and even resulting in fatalities. This is particularly true when it is employed as a component of a broader military or political strategy.

9.6.1. Targets of Cyber Espionage

Organizations such as large enterprises, governmental organizations, educational institutions, think tanks, and others that possess valuable intellectual property and technical data are often targeted by cyber espionage. This is because such information could potentially give another organization or government a competitive advantage. Targeted campaigns can be launched against various individuals, such as politicians, public servants, corporate executives, and even celebrities (Buchan & Navarrete, 2021).

There are various types of sensitive information that organizations need to protect.

- First, we have data and activities related to research and development, which are crucial for innovation and staying ahead in the market.
- Next, we have copyright-protected academic research data, including product formulations or designs. This type of information is valuable and needs to be safeguarded to prevent unauthorized use.
- Additionally, we have private data such as pay scales, bonus plans, and other confidential information about the company's internal workings. This information should only be accessible to authorized personnel.
- Another category is lists of clients or customers and payment arrangements. These details are essential for maintaining business relationships and should be kept confidential.
- Furthermore, we have strategic plans, marketing strategies, and business objectives. These documents outline the organization's direction and should not be shared with competitors.
- Also, we have political maneuvers, connections, and correspondence, which can have significant implications for an organization's reputation and success.
- Lastly, military reconnaissance is mentioned, highlighting the importance of protecting sensitive information related to national security (Buchan & Navarrete, 2021).

9.6.2. Typical Techniques Used in Cyber Espionage

Most cyber-espionage operations can be classified as advanced persistent threats (APT). An APT refers to a highly sophisticated cyberattack strategy employed by hackers. In this type of attack, the hacker strategically establishes a hidden presence within a network, aiming to surreptitiously extract confidential information over an extended duration (Buchan & Navarrete, 2021). An APT attack is a highly sophisticated and carefully planned operation that aims to infiltrate a specific enterprise and continuously evade existing security measures.

In contrast to a regular attack, an APT attack requires a greater degree of customization and expertise to carry out. Adversaries, in this context, are typically highly skilled and well-equipped groups of online fraudsters who specifically target valuable companies. The organization's weaknesses have been thoroughly investigated and analyzed, with significant investments of time and resources.

Cyberespionage attacks often involve the use of social engineering techniques to manipulate the target into taking action or revealing crucial information that can be used to advance the attack. These techniques often utilize human emotions such as fear, excitement, curiosity, or empathy to prompt impulsive or thoughtless decision-making (Buchan & Navarrete, 2021). Through these tactics, hackers manipulate unsuspecting individuals into taking actions that can have serious consequences.

9.6.3. The Global Impact of Cyber Espionage

Cyber espionage, particularly when orchestrated by nation states, has become a growing concern in the realm of security. Many criminals remain free due to the absence of extradition agreements between nations and the difficulty of enforcing international law in this regard, despite numerous indictments and legislation aimed at curbing such behavior.

The problem at hand, coupled with the growing proficiency of hackers and cybercriminals, poses a significant risk of a meticulously orchestrated and advanced attack that could disrupt various modern services, including the financial markets, the energy system, and crucial elections (Buchan & Navarrete, 2021).

9.6.4. Penalties for Cyber Espionage

In many cases, charges related to cyber espionage have been brought against individuals from foreign countries where extradition is not possible. This has been observed in several nations. Law enforcement organizations face significant challenges in pursuing cybercriminals, particularly those operating on an international scale. It is worth noting that penalties imposed on a foreign nation or business can rely on the same investigation framework that was used to support the indictments for cyber espionage. As an example, it is worth noting that the Department of the Treasury in the United States possesses the power to enforce economic sanctions on a company that has a track record of involvement in cyber espionage. This action is based on the utilization of investigative information obtained from indictments (Buchan & Navarrete, 2021).

9.7. CYBER TERRORISM

Digital terrorism, also known as cyber terrorism, involves the deliberate and disruptive attacks on computer systems by authorized terrorist groups. These attacks aim to instill fear, panic, or physically disrupt the targeted information system. It is worth noting that while cyberattacks have become a common occurrence, the concept of cyberterrorism introduces a unique and heightened level of concern (Plotnek & Slay, 2021). It is worth noting that terrorists may engage in similar activities, as computer hackers have historically been motivated by the desire to gain access to classified information for financial purposes.

The internet provides a platform for terrorists to coordinate their attacks, generate funds for their operations, and impart training to fellow terrorists. Cyberterrorism is commonly defined as the unauthorized infiltration of official or private servers with the intention of acquiring sensitive information or illicitly obtaining funds for terrorist activities.

9.7.1. Examples of Cyberterrorism

- Viruses that can infiltrate data networks that are vulnerable to their attacks.
- Server hacking which involves the deliberate act of disrupting communication and stealing confidential information.
- Vandalizing websites and rendering them unusable for the general public can have serious consequences, including disruption and monetary damages.
- Hacking communication services with the intention of using the internet to intimidate individuals with acts of terror and disrupt or obstruct communication.
- Attacks aimed at manipulating funds and instilling fear within financial institutions have been documented.

Many individuals lack awareness of the definition and potential dangers of cyber terrorism due to its non-physical nature, which distinguishes it from other forms of violence. With the ever-evolving cyberspace and the growing reliance on online services to save money and improve productivity, the number of ways IT systems can be compromised is increasing (Plotnek & Slay, 2021).

9.7.2. Strategies for Safeguarding Companies Against the Threat of Cyberterrorism

- *It is important to utilize strong passwords in order to enhance security:* A password is considered strong when it is complex, as software can rapidly attempt numerous password combinations within seconds. It is important to follow the recommended password procedures, ensuring that you change them regularly and avoid using the same password for multiple logins.
- *Stay updated on the latest news regarding cyber security:* This ensures you are well-informed about government alerts and the latest developments in the field. Understanding the latest threats is crucial in preparing for potential acts of terrorism.
- *It is crucial to foster a culture of cyber awareness within the organization:* This can be achieved by making it mandatory for all staff members to actively participate in regular training and education on cyber security. It is crucial to understand the importance of remaining vigilant and staying alert for any signs of suspicious activity.
- *It is important to thoroughly evaluate all third-party vendors:* A company's cyber security posture is heavily influenced by its third-party vendors. Businesses must prioritize requesting vendor openness regarding their cyber security policies before entering into contracts or engaging in any activity.

9.8. CYBER DEFENSE

Cyber defense and cybersecurity are often used synonymously. Despite their connection, there are notable and distinct differences between them. Cybersecurity serves as a comprehensive set of strategies and measures that organizations can employ to safeguard themselves against the myriad of online threats and dangers. A well-rounded cybersecurity strategy should encompass various aspects such as offensive measures, compliance, and defense against cyber threats. Cyber defense strategies aim to proactively thwart attacks.

Here are some common examples of cyber defense exercises:

- Setting up and maintaining the hardware and software of the security infrastructure is crucial for its smooth operation and effectiveness.
- To thoroughly analyze, identify, and address any potential weaknesses or issues within your network system.
- Implementing immediate solutions to prevent zero-day attacks.
- Initiating recovery process after experiencing partially or completely successful attack efforts.

The advent of CREEPER, the pioneering computer worm, marked the inception of cyberattacks as it spread across the ARPANET in the early 1970s. Following its initial release, the first antivirus program, REAPER, paved the way for the highly sophisticated cyber protection systems we have today (Yurekten & Demirci, 2021).

The rapid advancement of cyber defense has been necessitated by the ever-growing presence of the internet in our everyday existence. Nevertheless, the adversary managed to circumvent each and every new defense. Let's take antiviral software as an example. After the launch of CREEPER, hackers started using advanced and malicious malware such as ransomware, phishing scams, polymorphic viruses, and zero-day attacks. Firewall technology, commercial antivirus software, and, more recently, end-point detection and network detection and response have emerged as powerful cyber defenses.

9.8.1. Proactive Cyberdefense

This is a crucial aspect of safeguarding against potential threats in the digital realm. It involves taking preemptive measures to identify and mitigate vulnerabilities before they can be exploited. By staying one step ahead of potential attackers, organizations can significantly enhance their security posture and minimize the risk of cyber incidents.

Active cyber defense involves utilizing offensive tactics to hinder the advancement of attacks. Active cyber defense was initially conceptualized as a component of the Department of Defense's (DoD) cybersecurity operations strategy. The objective was to shift the balance in favor of defenders by negating attackers' advantage in an assault.

The primary goal is to effectively mitigate the threat by concealing the assailant's strategy and enhancing the level of difficulty they face in infiltrating your company's networks, systems, and applications. In addition, by improving defense tactics and strengthening incident response, active cyber defense helps organizations acquire crucial threat intelligence that helps them understand and prevent similar attacks in the future (Yurekten & Demirci, 2021).

9.8.2. The Cyber Defense Matrix

The Cyber Defense Matrix is a valuable tool for cyber defense teams as it provides a well-defined framework and a range of cybersecurity instruments to meet their security needs. By utilizing this matrix, teams can gain a comprehensive understanding of various cybersecurity practices.

In the 5-by-5 grid, the matrix's two primary components are organized both vertically and horizontally. One important aspect to consider is the five operational functions of the NIST Cybersecurity Framework: identify, protect, detect, respond, and recover (Figure 9.3).

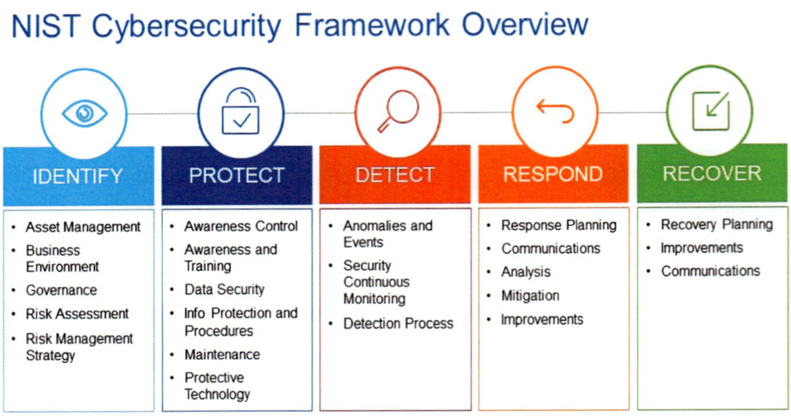

Figure 9.3. *The most common representation of the NIST Framework.*

Source: Dulavitz (2019).

9.9. CYBER RESILIENCE

Cyber resilience refers to an organization's ability to prevent, withstand, and bounce back from cybersecurity incidents. Cyber resilience encompasses the integration of business continuity, information systems security, and organizational resilience (Björck et al,. 2015). The concept revolves around the ability to achieve predetermined outcomes despite challenging cyber incidents, such as cyberattacks, natural disasters, or economic fluctuations. An organization's ability to sustain business operations without interruptions is heavily impacted by its level of information security resilience and competency.

9.9.1. Effective Cyber Resilience

For effective cyber resilience, it is crucial to adopt a collaborative approach that involves executives, all members of the company, partners, supply chain participants, and customers. A risk-based and enterprise-wide approach is essential for the plan. It is crucial to take a proactive approach in managing risks, threats, vulnerabilities, and their potential consequences on important data and auxiliary assets (Björck et al,. 2015). Effective cyber resilience encompasses several key components, including governance, risk management, data ownership awareness, and incident management. Assessing these traits necessitates the application of judgment and expertise.

When considering the potential impact of cyberattacks, an organization must carefully assess the risks in relation to its growth opportunities and competitive edge. One important consideration is the feasibility of implementing cost-effective preventive measures, along with the capability to promptly identify and resolve issues, all while ensuring a beneficial short-term effect on cyber resilience (Björck et al,. 2015). In order to achieve its goals, an organization must carefully consider and implement a combination of preventative, detective, and corrective controls. Finding the right balance between these three types of controls is crucial for success. The safety measures implemented are crucial in preventing, detecting, and resolving issues that pose a threat to the cyber resilience of a company (Björck et al,. 2015).

9.9.2. Importance of Cyber Resilience

Having a cyber resilience plan in place is crucial for the continuity of any business. Strengthening an organization's security posture and reducing the risk of exposure to its vital infrastructure can provide significant benefits. In addition, it is important to note that cyber resilience plays a crucial role in mitigating reputational damage and financial losses. In addition, it is important for a company to gain accreditation for cyber resilience in order to instill confidence in its clients and consumers. In order to enhance its competitive advantage, a cyber-resilient business can bolster its operational efficiency and effectiveness by maximizing the value it provides to its clients (Björck et al,. 2015).

Here are a few key reasons why having cyber resilience plans is crucial:

- *Reducing Monetary Loss:* Experiencing a financial setback can lead to a loss of trust from all parties associated with the company, such as consumers, employees, investors, and shareholders. According to the IBM Security 2020 Cyber Resilient Organization Report, more than 50% of enterprises experienced a cybersecurity event that resulted in disruptions to their IT and business operations. In addition, it is worth noting that according to the findings of Ponemon's 2021 Cost of a Breach Study, the average cost of a data breach stands at a staggering USD 4.24 million.

- *Gaining the Confidence and Business of Customers:* Certain businesses choose to adopt international management standards, such as ISO/IEC 27001 provided by the International Organization for Standardization, with the aim of attracting clients and securing their business (Björck et al,. 2015). The ISO/IEC 27001 standard sets out the necessary requirements for an information security management system (ISMS) to effectively safeguard valuable assets such as financial data, personnel records, intellectual property, and information entrusted to third parties. Businesses in the US have the option to apply for accreditation with the Payment Card Industry Data Security Standard (PCI-DSS) in order to process payments using credit cards.
- *Gaining a Greater Edge Over Competitors:* Having cyber resilience gives organizations a significant edge over their counterparts who lack this crucial capability. Efficient operations in businesses are established through the implementation of management systems that are built upon industry best practices. One such example is the Information Technology Infrastructure Library (ITIL). Companies enhance their operational efficiency by implementing cyber resilience management systems. Consequently, these systems offer significant benefits to their clients (Björck et al,. 2015).

CHAPTER 10

INTERNATIONAL COOPERATION IN COMBATING CYBERCRIME

Contents

Cybercrime operation is a prevalent form of crime that spans across both national and international levels. Hence, it is imperative to implement measures that are crucial for meeting national requirements and safeguarding data preservation, while also considering the importance of international cooperation. Parties have both general and specific measures in place, which require them to cooperate to the fullest extent and take immediate action to preserve data. Additionally, they are expected to implement effective mutual legal assistance, as highlighted by Bossler and Berenblum (2019).

Figure 10.1. *Pillars of the global cybersecurity index.*

Source: Katharina.kiener-Manu, n.d.

10.1. AN OVERVIEW OF THE VARIOUS INTERNATIONAL EFFORTS TO COMBAT CYBERCRIME

Internationally, numerous measures have been implemented to combat both new and existing forms of crime, while also striving to comprehend the transnational nature of these offenses. The negative impact of these crimes extends to the economic, military, and social aspects. Countries around the world, both developed and developing, have made collaborative efforts to combat these crimes through a series of treaties and agreements. One such example is the Budapest Convention, which is considered a fundamental and effective method for addressing information crime, thanks to its numerous features. Given the correlation between crime and technological progress, individuals combatting this form of crime must possess a thorough understanding of computer operations. Computers serve as crucial tools in the realm of cybercrime, enabling the identification of criminal activities and the individuals responsible for them (Bossler & Berenblum, 2019).

The rapid evolution of cybercrime has resulted in a significant lag in the development of criminal laws, best practices, and policies related to cross-border cybercrime. Collecting data and evidence across borders can present significant complexities and challenges for investigators and prosecutors. This is primarily due to the limitations imposed by territorial and jurisdictional constraints of legislation. Law enforcement officials, government attorneys, and prosecutors are faced with the ongoing challenge of adapting to the ever-evolving technologies that criminals adeptly employ. In today's world, it is becoming increasingly important to address the fact that nearly all criminal activities now have an online component. This underscores the urgent need for global cooperation and effective strategies to combat cybercrime. It is crucial for prosecutors from different nations to collaborate on an international level in order to effectively combat cybercrime and deter other criminal activities (Bossler & Berenblum, 2019).

International collaboration is crucial in the fight against cybercrime due to its global nature. Here are some essential details on how nations work together to tackle this worldwide issue:

- *Legal Frameworks*: The Convention on Cybercrime establishes a legal framework for international collaboration, which includes provisions that require nations to maintain data, engage in substantial cooperation, and offer each other legal support.
- *Federal Agency Efforts*: Federal agencies, including the Departments of State, Justice, and Homeland Security, work together with foreign countries to combat technology-driven crimes. This collaboration involves information exchange and cyber training for law enforcement personnel.
- *Resolution 65/230 of the UN General Assembly*: It highlights the importance of taking comprehensive approaches to address global issues. As part of this, the resolution emphasizes the establishment of a panel of experts to conduct research on cybercrime and explore potential avenues for enhancing legal remedies.
- *Cooperation in Cybersecurity*: It is imperative for states to come together and take immediate action to mitigate risks such as

cybercrime, attacks on critical infrastructure, espionage, data interception, and offensive cyberoperations. This collaborative effort is crucial in safeguarding our digital world.

The importance of international cooperation in effectively combating cybercrime and advancing cybersecurity worldwide is highlighted by these initiatives.

10.2. THE ROLE OF INTERPOL IN GLOBAL CYBERCRIME INVESTIGATIONS

These initiatives highlight the importance of global collaboration in effectively addressing cybercrime and promoting cybersecurity on a global scale.

INTERPOL provides crucial support to member countries in their efforts to prevent and investigate cybercrime. By leveraging their extensive resources and expertise, Interpol plays a vital role in combating this growing threat. They offer assistance in various ways, including sharing intelligence, coordinating international operations, and providing training and capacity building programs. Through these initiatives, INTERPOL helps member countries stay one step ahead in the fight against cybercriminals.

1. *Exploring Investigations and Operations*: Given the nature of cybercrime, which often involves suspects, victims, and crimes that span across different countries, it can be classified as a transnational crime. INTERPOL plays a crucial role in promoting intelligence sharing and providing guidance on effective approaches to cybercrime investigations. This enables member nations to effectively coordinate their efforts in tackling transnational cybercrime. In addition, INTERPOL has a team of cyber experts who gather and analyze all available data on illegal activities in cyberspace. This information is then shared with nations, providing law enforcement with valuable intelligence for their operations on the ground (Ayachi & Djelloul, 2023).
2. *Develop New State-of-the-Art Policing Tools*: Creativity is a vital aspect that should be nurtured and encouraged. It allows individuals to think outside the box and come up with innovative ideas and solutions. Embracing creativity can lead to breakthroughs and advancements in various fields. It is important to create an environment that fosters creativity, where individuals feel empowered to As technology advances, cybercriminals are becoming increasingly adept at their

craft, utilizing state-of-the-art tools and sophisticated strategies to evade detection by law enforcement. In collaboration with partners in the cyber industry, INTERPOL is actively working towards the development of cutting-edge policing tools at the IGCI (INTERPOL Global Complex for Innovation) in Singapore. The ultimate objective is to equip law enforcement agencies with these advanced tools for effective utilization (Ayachi & Djelloul, 2023).

3. *Digital Forensics:* Being able to extract evidence from computers, mobile phones, and other devices is crucial in conducting a successful cybercrime investigation. INTERPOL's Digital Forensics Laboratory provides global assistance with digital evidence. This includes:

- Providing comprehensive training in the latest digital forensic tools and techniques.
- Providing assistance in the examination of digital devices and analyzing malware provided by member countries.
- Deploying specialists in digital forensics to offer on-site support during investigations.

4. *Building Capacity*: INTERPOL is dedicated to ensuring that police forces worldwide are equipped with the latest technology and possess the necessary knowledge and skills to effectively combat the increasing threat of cybercrime. INTERPOL offers a wide range of training courses that cover various subjects such as investigation methods, digital forensics, and new developments in cybercrime (Ayachi & Djelloul, 2023). Obtaining professional certification is possible through various training methods, including workshops, in-person events, and online learning modules.
5. *Nationwide Cyber Assessment*: INTERPOL has the capability to assess a member nation's level of cyber-awareness, infrastructure, and expertise. One important aspect of this is that it helps nations evaluate their strengths and weaknesses in relation to cybercrime, allowing them to identify areas that require improvement (Ayachi & Djelloul, 2023).

10.3. COOPERATION BETWEEN LAW ENFORCEMENT AGENCIES ACROSS BORDERS

In the age of the internet, cybercrime has become a global issue. Given the global reach of criminals, it is imperative for law enforcement authorities to collaborate on an international scale in order to effectively combat these threats (Reitano et al., 2015)

- *Lawful Structures International Legal Accords:* It play a crucial role in facilitating cross-border collaboration in the ongoing battle against cybercrime. The Budapest Convention on Cybercrime was adopted by the Council of Europe in 2001. It serves as the main instrument for combating cybercrime and online crimes by enhancing investigation methods, harmonizing state legislation, and promoting international collaboration.
- *Information Exchange:* In order to effectively combat cyber threats, it is crucial to have a system in place for sharing information. Intelligence sharing between countries has been made more efficient and effective, thanks to the establishment of agencies such as Europol and INTERPOL. The INTERPOL Cyber Fusion Center plays a crucial role in helping member nations swiftly detect and address cybercrime incidents by providing a platform for real-time information sharing and analysis.
- *Joint Operations*: They serve as a clear demonstration of the effectiveness of cooperation. An exemplary case in point is Operation Tovar, where various multinational organizations joined forces to dismantle the GameOver Zeus botnet, which resulted in substantial financial losses worldwide. Effective operations of this nature require close collaboration and a strong sense of trust among law enforcement agencies from multiple countries.
- *Obstacles and Difficulties*: Despite these efforts, there are several challenges that hinder global cooperation. When agencies operate in different legal contexts or in the absence of extradition treaties, they may encounter jurisdictional challenges. Discrepancies in the handling of cyber events can arise due to variations in resources and technical expertise (Reitano et al., 2015).

Ultimately, it is clear that while significant strides have been made in international law enforcement cooperation against cybercrime, there remain ongoing challenges that necessitate the continuous refinement of legal frameworks, information sharing procedures, and operational coordination.

10.4. INTERNATIONAL TREATIES AND AGREEMENTS TO ADDRESS CYBERCRIME

To facilitate international cooperation (Figure 10.2), it is crucial to have comprehensive national laws that address cybercrime from both a substantive and procedural standpoint. These laws should not only prohibit cybercrime, but also establish clear standards for admissibility and criminal proceedings. Promoting international collaboration can be facilitated by harmonizing bilateral, regional, and multilateral tools on cybercrime, as suggested by Mittal and Sharma (2017). In order for regional and global cybercrime instruments to gain legal force, they need to be ratified or joined.

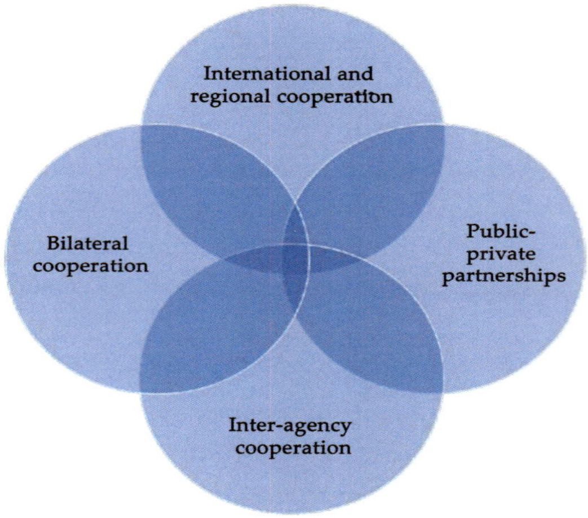

Figure 10.2. *Various types of cooperation.*

Source: Cooperation, n.d.

International cooperation in addressing cybercrime is facilitated through bilateral, regional, and multilateral agreements. These agreements are effective as long as the participating countries have laws that criminalize the activities in question. Cybercriminals often take advantage of safe havens where they can evade prosecution due to the lack of dual criminality and harmonized legislation. As we examine the well-known Love Bug virus case from 2000, we find that the individual responsible for its creation and distribution managed to evade legal consequences. Surprisingly, his actions were not considered illegal in his home country, the Philippines, at the time of the incident (Mittal & Sharma, 2017).

Nevertheless, even without a strict interpretation of the dual criminality requirement, it may still be possible to achieve international collaboration. In addition, it is important to note that when dual criminality is taken into account as a requirement, it is considered to be fulfilled regardless of whether the laws of the requested State Party classify the offense in the same category or use the same terminology as the requesting State Party. This is applicable if the conduct that forms the basis of the offense for which assistance is being sought is considered a criminal offense under the laws of both States Parties.

However, there are certain exceptions to the dual criminality requirement. As stated in the Council of Europe's 2001 Convention on Cybercrime, Article 29(3), there is no need for dual criminality when it comes to the "expedited preservation of stored computer data" for the substantive offences covered by this Convention (Articles 2 through 11). This applies to situations where the computer system is located within the territory of another Party and the requesting Party intends to seek mutual assistance for actions such as search, access, seizure, or disclosure of the data. According to Article 29(4), states have the option to reject preservation requests if they require dual criminality for providing mutual assistance in cases that are not covered by the Convention.

International collaboration requires not only dual criminality, but also a deep respect for international human rights commitments. International cooperation requests may be declined if fulfilling them would cause the responding state to violate its obligations under international law concerning human rights (Mittal & Sharma, 2017).

Formal procedures for international collaboration include bilateral, regional, and multinational cybercrime treaties. These treaties, as highlighted by Mittal and Sharma (2017), place a significant emphasis on the importance of cooperation. The Agreement on Cooperation in Combating Offenses related to Computer Information of the Commonwealth of Independent States, for instance, includes a number of articles (Articles 5-7) that focus on international cooperation. The articles in question discuss various aspects of cooperation outlined in this Agreement. These include but are not limited to:

- Information exchange
- Providing legal assistance based on international instruments
- Addressing cybercrime through prevention, detection, suppression, and investigation.

In addition, the process of requesting assistance from Member States and the corresponding guidelines that need to be followed are also discussed. Article 8 of this Agreement outlines the conditions in which a request for assistance may be denied, specifically when it goes against a state's national law. Furthermore, it is imperative for the state that refuses to provide a written notice to the requesting state, clearly elucidating the rationale behind the refusal (Mittal & Sharma, 2017).

Furthermore, it is worth noting that the Arab Convention on Combating Information Technology Offenses of 2010, established by the League of Arab States, includes provisions regarding mutual assistance, cooperation procedures, and requests for mutual aid. These aspects are specifically addressed in Articles 32 and 34 (Mittal & Sharma 2017). In addition, it is worth noting that Article

28 of the 2014 African Union Convention on Cyber Security and Personal Data Protection addresses various aspects such as information sharing, mutual legal aid in cases of cybercrime, and harmonization. States are required to establish organizations such as Computer Emergency Response Teams (CERTs) or Computer Security Incident Response Teams (CSIRTs) to facilitate the sharing of information on cybersecurity threats and vulnerabilities. According to Article 28(4), it is essential for states to utilize established methods of international cooperation, including international, intergovernmental, regional, or public-private partnerships, in their efforts to address cybercrime.

Extradition treaties and mutual legal aid serve as important mechanisms that foster international cooperation in the investigation and prosecution of cybercriminals. Mutual legal assistance treaties, also known as MLATs, are crucial international agreements that address a wide array of offenses and outline the specific types of assistance one nation will provide, such as evidence, to another nation during the course of an investigation. The list approach is no longer effective and overlooks the evolving nature of cybercrime. Under certain mutual legal assistance treaties (MLATs), countries come together to cooperate in the investigation and prosecution of various offenses that are prohibited by their own national laws, with a few exceptions. This collaboration is crucial in light of the ever-changing nature of crime, including cybercrime. When submitting a mutual assistance request, it is important to provide all the necessary details. These include the asking authority, the purpose of the request, a description of the request, and the specific investigation or court proceedings to which the request relates. It is also important to include a description of the offense or offenses and the laws that have been violated. Additionally, any requests regarding the procedures for obtaining, preserving, and transferring physical and digital evidence should be included. Deadlines for data preservation requests and carrying out these requests should also be specified. Lastly, any other information that would assist the receiving state in carrying out the request should be provided (Mittal & Sharma, 2017).

There are instances where requests for mutual aid may be declined. As an illustration, if the request were to potentially impact its security, sovereignty, and public order. As stated in Article 25(4) of the Convention on Cybercrime, mutual legal aid requests can be denied if they pertain to offenses that the requested Party deems as political or connected to political offenses. It is important to note that there are instances where requests for information may be declined. This can occur if fulfilling the request would result in the responding state violating its obligations under international human rights law (Mittal & Sharma, 2017). Some states, such as Brazil, Japan, and the Ukraine, have established reciprocal legal assistance agreements. These agreements require both the requesting state and the responding state to honor each other's requests for assistance in the future. In addition, in nations that do not have their own mechanism, the 2001 Convention on Cybercrime of the Council of Europe can be utilized as a Mutual Legal Assistance Treaty (MLAT) when a government seeks assistance (Mittal & Sharma, 2017). Assistance on cybercrime matters can also be sought through letters rogatory. These are written requests from national courts that provide detailed information about the case, the required evidence, and the reasons for needing it. In the absence of treaties and agreements, these letters also include a promise of reciprocity in future cases.

There are additional time delays, commonly known as a "timescale of months," that are connected to other official cooperation mechanisms like extradition and mutual legal assistance. The time delays become particularly problematic due to the inherent instability of digital evidence. While there are various models and rules available in different countries for letters rogatory and requests for mutual legal help, it is worth noting that this practice is not widely adopted. The Mutual Legal Assistance Request Writer Tool, developed by the United Nations Office on Drugs and Crime (UNODC), serves as a valuable resource for countries seeking assistance in drafting mutual assistance requests. The tool is designed to streamline request formats, resulting in faster processing and timely support (Mittal & Sharma, 2017).

Extradition treaties, such as the 1957 European Convention on Extradition and the 1981 OAS Inter-American Convention on Extradition, establish the procedures for apprehending and transferring individuals to the requesting country when the committed crimes meet the specified minimum sentence. Regional arrest warrants, such as the European Arrest Warrant, allow for the apprehension of individuals who have committed computer-related crimes that are punishable by a prison sentence or detention order of at least three years in the issuing Member State. The double criminality of the act does not need to be verified. For instance, the ECOWAS Convention on Extradition of 1994 sets the punishment threshold at a minimum of two years.

It is important to note that the existence of an extradition treaty does not guarantee the automatic transfer of an individual to another country. As exemplified by the case of British hacker Lauri Love, his extradition to the US was denied despite the presence of the UK-US Extradition Treaty from 2003 (Mittal & Sharma, 2017).

In addition, extradition treaties outline the specific conditions in which a request for extradition will not be granted. Requests for extradition are typically denied under the OAS Inter-American Convention on Extradition if the crime in question carries a life sentence or the death penalty (Article 9). Extradition can be refused in certain cases, such as when the person being extradited would face cruel or inhumane treatment or punishment. This is outlined in conventions like the ECOWAS Convention on Extradition and the OAS Inter-American Convention on Extradition. Extradition requests may be declined for various reasons. One such reason is the lack of sufficient evidence to support the request, as demonstrated in the Botswana Extradition Act of 1990. Another reason could be if the offense in question is not extraditable, such as a military offense, as stated in Article 7 of the ECOWAS Convention on Extradition. Additionally, if the request involves a national of the country in question, it may also be rejected, as outlined in Article 698 of the Algerian Code of Criminal Procedure and Article 5 (LI) of the Brazilian Constitution. In relation to the latter point, it is important to note that both regional and international agreements, as well as the constitution, firmly support the principle of non-extradition of nationals. According to the principles of public international law, it is legally required for states to either extradite or prosecute individuals who commit serious international crimes.

Cybercrime investigations also benefit from informal international collaboration channels, such as the sharing of information between law enforcement agencies or police-to-police cooperation. Law enforcement authorities in different states vary in the type of information they exchange through unofficial channels, as noted by Mittal and Sharma (2017). According to the UNODC, Australia's authorities have the capability to offer various forms of assistance on an agency-to-agency basis. This includes taking voluntary witness statements, conducting voluntary witness interviews, and even taking voluntary witness testimony via a video link facility. Additionally, Australia is open to hosting foreign police who are conducting inquiries within the country, sharing intelligence, conducting physical surveillance, obtaining criminal records, and obtaining publicly available material. Other nations have access to shared personal data.

10.5. SHARING BEST PRACTICES IN CYBERCRIME PREVENTION AND DETECTION

Cybercrime is an ongoing and ever-present threat. It is important to note that hackers gaining access to your financial information is not the only form of cybercrime that should be on your radar. However, it may not be as straightforward as one might think. In addition to basic financial considerations, there are numerous other factors to consider. Cybercrime threats are constantly evolving, with new ones emerging every year (Shah, Jones, & Choudrie, 2019). One might experience a sense of pressure to completely abandon the use of the internet upon discovering the multitude of cybercrimes that are prevalent.

That statement may be considered excessive. It is important to have a solid understanding of how to identify cybercrime, as this knowledge can serve as your initial defense against potential threats to your personal information. It is important to be aware of the appropriate channels for reporting illegal online activities and to take some basic safety measures (Shah, Jones, & Choudrie, 2019).

It is indeed true that preventing cybercrime is a challenging task, even if one desires to gain a deeper understanding of how to accomplish it. There are certain steps that can be taken to help protect against it:

- *Employ a Comprehensive Set of Internet Security Products:* When considering security software, it is important to choose a reliable option like Norton 360 with LifeLock Select. This software provides comprehensive protection for your devices, identity, and online privacy. It also helps to safeguard your financial and private information while using the internet (Shah, Jones, & Choudrie, 2019).
- *Make Secure Passwords:* It is crucial to refrain from using identical passwords for multiple websites and to regularly update them. Provide them with a deeper level of intricacy. In order to meet the requirements, it is necessary to utilize at least ten distinct letters, numbers, and symbols. One effective way to ensure the security of your passwords is by utilizing a password management program.
- *Update Your Software Regularly:* Understanding the importance of operating systems and internet security software is absolutely crucial. Exploits, which are known vulnerabilities in software, are frequently employed by cybercriminals as a means to gain unauthorized access to your system. Fixing those vulnerabilities and exploits can significantly decrease the chances of becoming a victim of cybercrime.
- *Adjust the Settings on Your Social Media Accounts:* It is crucial to ensure the protection of your personal and confidential data. Minimizing the amount of information you share publicly is highly recommended. Cybercriminals skilled in social engineering can easily gather your personal information using only a few data points. As an illustration, if you were to share the name of your pet or reveal your mother's maiden name, it could potentially reveal the answers to commonly asked security questions.
- *Make Your Home Network Stronger:* It is highly advisable to begin by implementing a virtual private network and employing a robust encryption password, as this demonstrates a prudent and astute

strategy. Through the use of a VPN, the traffic originating from your devices and making its way to its intended destination will be securely encrypted. Intercepting encrypted data is a challenging task that cybercriminals can only accomplish by gaining unauthorized access to your connection line. When accessing a public Wi-Fi network in various locations such as airports, hotels, cafes, or libraries, it is highly recommended to make use of a VPN.

- *Communicate with Your Kids About the Internet:* One can effectively educate their children about responsible internet usage while maintaining open lines of communication. It is crucial to emphasize to children that they have the option to reach out to you at any given moment if they find themselves subjected to cyberbullying, harassment, or stalking.
- *Keep up to Date on Major Security Breaches:* It is crucial to promptly identify the data that the hackers have accessed and take immediate action to update your password if you engage in transactions with a merchant or maintain an account on a website that has encountered a security breach.
- *Take Precautions to Guard Against Identity Theft:* Identity theft occurs when an individual cunningly obtains your personal information, typically with the motive of financial gain. Could you please explain how to do it? As an illustration, one could potentially fall victim to online scams that trick individuals into revealing personal information, or face the risk of having their mail intercepted and exploited to gain unauthorized access to account details. Protecting your personal information is of utmost importance. Virtual private networks, also known as VPNs, play a crucial role in protecting the data you transmit and receive online, especially when connecting to public Wi-Fi networks.
- *Be Aware of What to do in Case You Fall Victim:* If you have reason to believe that you have fallen victim to cybercrime, it is imperative that you promptly inform the appropriate authorities, including the Federal Trade Commission, the FBI, and your local police department. Regardless of the seemingly insignificant nature of the crime, it remains of utmost importance. This report has the potential to greatly assist law enforcement in their investigations and serve as a deterrent to prevent future victims from falling prey to the schemes of criminals (Shah, Jones, & Choudrie, 2019). If you suspect that your identity has been compromised by cybercriminals. Consider implementing these actions.

a. Establish communication with the banks and businesses that you suspect may be involved in fraudulent activities.

b. Obtain your credit reports and establish fraud alerts.

c. Report any incidents of identity theft to the Federal Trade Commission (FTC).

Addressing the issue of cybercrime is a matter that should be of interest to all individuals. It is important to recognize the responsibility we have in contributing to the ongoing effort to combat cybercrime.

10.6. COLLABORATION BETWEEN PRIVATE SECTOR AND GOVERNMENT ENTITIES

Public-private partnerships (PPPs) are a way for governments to collaborate with private sector businesses to finance and complete large-scale projects such as highways, bridges, and hospitals. These partnerships combine the incentives and innovation of the private sector with the oversight and objectives of the public sector to ensure that projects are completed on time and within budget. However, there are risks involved for both the public and private partners.

For the public partner, there is a risk that the demand for the project, such as toll roads or bridges, may not be sustained at the agreed-upon usage rates. This could result in a financial burden for the public partner. On the other hand, the private partner faces risks such as cost overruns, technological flaws, and a failure to meet quality requirements. Despite these risks, public-private partnerships offer several benefits. The private sector brings innovation and technology that can improve the operational effectiveness of delivering public services. The public sector, in turn, provides incentives to ensure that projects are completed on time and within budget. Additionally, these partnerships can diversify the economy and support infrastructure growth and related industries.

However, there are also drawbacks to public-private collaborations. The private party may face unique risks associated with building physical infrastructure, such as delays, cost overruns, or malfunctions. If the private partner fails to deliver the promised service, it also bears the availability risk. From the perspective of the general public and taxpayers, there is a concern that private operators may not be held accountable for poor quality service or violations of rights. There is also a risk of increased rates, tolls, and fees for captive customers due to legal restrictions or regional monopolies.

Public-private partnerships can also give rise to principal-agent issues and rent-seeking activities. The separation of ownership and decision-making rights can make it easier for private parties to engage in corrupt transactions or pay off political allies. This can weaken the connection between taxpayers and the private parties making decisions about the project.

Public-private partnerships are commonly used in transportation infrastructure, water and wastewater facilities, and public service accommodations such as education and correctional buildings. One example is the 407 Express Toll Route in Canada, which was a PPP between the Ontario provincial government and a private consortium. The consortium was responsible for the design, construction, financing, and upkeep of the highway, with a 99-year lease term to collect tolls from drivers.

Revenue risk is a significant concern in public-private partnerships, referring to the possibility that the private partner may not be able to recoup its initial investment or ongoing expenditures. This can be due to limitations on toll rates or lower than anticipated traffic volumes on a toll road.

Despite the advantages and disadvantages, governments continue to use public-private partnerships to finance public service projects and infrastructure. These partnerships provide a way to leverage private sector resources and expertise while ensuring that public objectives are met. However, careful consideration of the risks and benefits is necessary to ensure successful outcomes for all parties involved.

10.7. CHALLENGES IN ACHIEVING INTERNATIONAL COOPERATION IN CYBERCRIME INVESTIGATIONS

Investigating cybercrime poses several challenges, including the anonymity provided by information and communication technology. Users can participate in events while remaining anonymous, which hinders the disclosure of their identity or conduct. Cybercriminals utilize various anonymization techniques, such as proxy servers, to mask their IP addresses and conceal their identifying information (Boes & Leukfeldt, 2017).

Anonymization techniques can be used for both legitimate and illicit purposes. Privacy protection and the ability to communicate freely without consequences are some of the reasons individuals may wish to remain anonymous online. However, cybercriminals also exploit anonymity networks, such as Freenet, Tor, and the Invisible Internet Project, to encrypt traffic and hide their IP addresses (Boes & Leukfeldt, 2017).

Tor, also known as the Onion Router, was initially developed by the United States Naval Research Laboratory to safeguard intelligence. It allows for anonymous internet access, communication, and information sharing. While

Tor has been used by individuals to protect themselves from surveillance, cybercriminals have also utilized it to commit crimes and communicate tools or information necessary for internet-dependent crimes. Darknet websites, which can only be accessed through anonymity networks, host illegal activities while masking users' identities.

The internet is often compared to an iceberg, with the Surface Web representing the visible portion and the Deep Web representing the hidden portion. The Surface Web consists of publicly accessible websites indexed by search engines, while the Deep Web contains password-protected websites and forums that are not easily accessible or indexed. The Dark Web, a subset of the Deep Web, uses specialized software to enhance anonymity and obfuscate access to conceal its sites (Boes & Leukfeldt, 2017).

Attribution, the process of determining responsibility for a cybercrime, is another challenge in cybercrime investigations. Identifying the specific digital device, user, or additional parties involved in the cybercrime is crucial for attribution. Anonymity techniques make it more difficult to trace the devices and individuals behind cybercrimes. The use of malware-infected zombie computers or devices controlled by remote access tools further complicates attribution, as these devices can be used without the user's knowledge to commit cybercrimes.

10.8. THE IMPORTANCE OF INFORMATION SHARING BETWEEN COUNTRIES

In the fight against cybercrime, the exchange of information between nations is crucial. Cybercrime is a global threat that requires a global response. The annual cost of cybercrimes is estimated to be in the trillions or tens of trillions of dollars, highlighting the significant impact it has on the world economy and global security. To effectively combat cyber threats, nations must collaborate and share information (Ølnes et al., 2017).

By exchanging information, nations can pool their resources, skills, and knowledge to better fight cybercrime. Criminals often operate across multiple jurisdictions, making it difficult for law enforcement organizations to keep up. Through information sharing, nations can create a collective intelligence that is more powerful than what any one nation could achieve alone (Ølnes et al., 2017).

There are several methods and organizations that facilitate information exchange. INTERPOL's Cyber Fusion Centre and Europol's EC3 are two examples of law enforcement organizations that work together to exchange best practices and coordinate responses to cyber threats. These organizations also collaborate closely with the business sector to obtain threat intelligence

(Ølnes et al., 2017). The exchange of information has a significant impact on cybercrime investigation and prevention. It allows for more informed prevention efforts and more efficient investigation methods. By establishing cross-border connections between inconsistencies in data, it becomes easier to find and capture cybercriminals. Additionally, information sharing cultivates a cooperative culture, which is crucial for building trust and confidence between global partners (Ølnes et al., 2017).

10.9. DEVELOPING A UNIFIED STRATEGY FOR COMBATING CYBERCRIME GLOBALLY

Tropina (2020) argues that despite the existing obstacles, the cyber community can work together to ensure security, privacy, and digital rights. To take advantage of this opportunity, governments need to modify their structures, expand global collaboration, and coordinate awareness-raising efforts.

Firstly, Tropina (2020) suggests that governments should update and develop their legislative and regulatory frameworks pertaining to cyberspace, as well as their national cybersecurity strategies, with more agility. This should be done through a multi-stakeholder approach, involving the corporate sector and the technical community. Building incident response capacities across all sectors is crucial, as governments cannot act alone in ensuring effective resilience.

Another priority is harmonizing laws related to cybercrime. The Budapest Convention, which is currently the most comprehensive and worldwide pact aimed at combating cybercrime, should be considered by international organizations and nations. The Organization of American States (OAS) urges adherence to the Convention to establish quick international cooperation on information sharing and cross-border investigation (Tropina, 2020).

Secondly, Tropina (2020) emphasizes the need for global collaboration in cybersecurity. The sharing of information has increased since the COVID-19 outbreak, and this momentum should be maintained and formalized for all matters related to cyberspace. International cooperation is essential, and confidence-building measures between nations and industry should be established. Cooperation in policy, technology, and law enforcement is crucial to address future cyber threats.

Tropina (2020) highlights the example of CSIRT Americas, a regional hemispheric network of Computer Security Incident Response Teams (CSIRTs) in the Western Hemisphere. This group has successfully come together during crises like Wannacry and the COVID-19 epidemic to share real-time information and exchange knowledge, addressing regional concerns.

Lastly, Tropina (2020) emphasizes the importance of raising awareness about cybersecurity. It is crucial to educate people of all ages and levels, with a particular focus on children. Early exposure to technology and cybersecurity education can equip children with the necessary skills for the rapidly evolving technological landscape. Coordinated awareness efforts between the public and commercial sectors, such as the "Stop. Think. Connect." project, can serve as models for other initiatives.

Furthermore, consumers should not be the last line of defense in cybersecurity. They have a responsibility to inform one another and expand the impact.

10.10. FUTURE TRENDS IN INTERNATIONAL COOPERATION TO COMBAT CYBERCRIME

The international response to cybercrime is evolving alongside it, and there are several prospective developments in international collaboration that may reshape the cooperative effort to combat cyberthreats. One trend that could lead to a more uniform legal response to cybercrime is the potential ratification and implementation of the Budapest Convention by additional nations. Additionally, new treaties may be developed to address the complexity of digital evidence across national borders and new cyber risks (Sviatun et al., 2021).

Technological advancements are also expected to play a significant role in improving collaboration and information exchange in the fight against cybercrime. Blockchain, artificial intelligence (AI), and machine learning are likely to be important components of threat detection, predictive analytics, and secure data transmission (Sviatun et al., 2021). These innovations can enable a proactive approach to combating cybercrime rather than a reactive one.

Furthermore, technological advancements are expected to enhance communication and teamwork in the international effort against cybercrime. Blockchain, AI, and machine learning can be crucial elements in identifying threats, conducting predictive analytics, and ensuring secure data transmission. By adopting a proactive approach, law enforcement agencies and cybersecurity professionals can stay ahead of cybercriminals.

However, there are obstacles that need to be managed as collaboration grows. Conflicting national.

INDEX

FSC
www.fsc.org
MIX
Papier | Fördert gute Waldnutzung
FSC® C083411

Kolibri 360 GmbH
Ferdinand-Jühlke-Straße 7
99095 Erfurt, Deutschland
produktsicherheit@kolibri360.de